T0135072

Retrogame Archeology

John Aycock

Retrogame Archeology

Exploring Old Computer Games

 Springer

John Aycock
Department of Computer Science
University of Calgary
Calgary, Alberta, Canada

ISBN 978-3-319-80703-4   ISBN 978-3-319-30004-7   (eBook)
DOI 10.1007/978-3-319-30004-7

Printed on acid-free paper

This Springer imprint is published by Springer Nature
The registered company is Springer International Publishing AG Switzerland

For my mother,
who gave me computers and games
that are now retro

Preface

I'm not very good at playing computer games. However, through sheer luck I happened to be alive, using computers and playing games, at more or less the right time to have experienced the retrogame era. I also happened to learn programming and study computer science at a time when there was a strong emphasis on low-level work, when getting a program working sometimes meant being clever enough to sidestep all kinds of limitations.

Now, fast-forward several decades. After reading two compelling books – Montfort and Bogost's *Racing the Beam* and Maher's *The Future Was Here*[1] – it finally dawned on me that I could use my training and good fortune to dig into the guts of old games, to seek and showcase game authors' implementation marvels that lurked under the hood. In Ian Bogost's book *How to Do Things with Videogames*, he wrote[2] 'We need more media entomologists and media archeologists overturning rocks and logs to find and explain the tiny treasures that would otherwise go unseen.' I wanted to become a retrogame archeologist.

What I found surprising in my research was that many retrogame implementation techniques had modern applications, and not only in games. I won't go so far as to say that retrogames were the first to use these techniques or that modern uses are directly inspired by retrogames, but I *will* claim that retrogames are an interesting way to learn about them. Furthermore, having taught computer science students in university for many years, I think it's fair to say that modern programmers aren't always exposed to these techniques nor to the constraints that precipitated their use. This book is an attempt to fix that.

The material in these pages tends to be fairly low-level and technical by its nature, so a full understanding of the content will undoubtedly require at least some proficiency in programming. However, my hope is that I've made the explanations clear enough to be appreciated at some level by nonprogrammers, retrogame enthusiasts, historians, and researchers in game studies.

I should also say something about the retrogame screenshots: a few years ago I read a book about modern art and was disappointed that more images weren't

---

[1] MIT Press, 2009 and 2012, respectively.
[2] University of Minnesota Press, 2011, p. 148

included. I understand now. The time and effort for me to get copyright permission to use the images that appear here has literally ranged from minutes to months, and that's only for the cases where an identifiable copyright holder still exists. In other cases, companies have gone defunct or been absorbed through a long chain of acquisitions, or unfortunately, people who would have held the copyrights have passed away. Static images also don't really capture all nuances of an interactive medium like computer games; I encourage you to watch retrogame walkthrough videos on the Internet to complement your reading.

Thank you to all the people who were kind enough to take the time to respond to my random emailed questions, namely Scott Adams, Shahid Ahmad, Mike Austin, Bill Budge, Melanie Bunten, David Crane, Don Daglow, John Darragh, Andrew Davie, Dale Dobson, Jim Dramis, Randy Farmer, Ira Goldklang, Roland Gustafsson, Paul Hagstrom, Alex Handy, Wendell Hicken, Paul Hughes, Mike Lake, Peter Langston, Al Lowe, Kirk McKusick, Kem McNair, Alan McNeil, Steve Meretzky, Jeff Minter, Chip Morningstar, Dan Oliver, Dave Platt, Eric S. Raymond, Jon Ritman, John Romero, Roger Schrag, Manuel Schulz, Michael Schwartz, Stefan Serbicki, Paul Urbanus, Bruce Webster, Ken Wellsch, Wayne Westmoreland, Robert Woodhead, and Don Worth. Parts of the copy protection and code obfuscation chapters have benefited greatly, directly and indirectly, from people whom I know only via Twitter: @a2_4am, @antoine_vignau, @D5AA96, @dosnostalgic, and @yesterbits. I apologize if I accidentally omitted anyone!

This work would not have been possible without the multitude of emulators and tools that are freely available. I would especially like to thank all the contributors to ADTPro, B-em, Catakig, DASMx, DCC6502, defedd, DOSBox, FreeDOS' DEBUG, Frotz, Fuse, GMQCC, LensKey, the Level 9 interpreter, MAME, MESS, NAGI, OpenEmulator, qcc, ScottFree, ScummVM, SIMH, Stella, VICE, xtrs, ZILF, and Ztools, as well as the authors of some online emulators in JavaScript: Jan Bobrowski's Qaop/JS, Matt Dawson's VIC-20 emulator, and Will Scullin's Apple II emulator. The efforts of people and organizations like the Internet Archive to preserve material and make it widely available have been invaluable too.

Closer to home, I'd like to thank John Brosz for helping with the visualization studio I used for some analyses, Rob Furr for letting me sit in on his game history class, Darcy Grant for loaning the camera equipment, Ben Stephenson for soldering up a data transfer cable for the Apple IIc, and Dean Yergens for giving me access to a working Commodore 64 system. Jeff Boyd and Tyson Kendon provided me with dual-tape cassette decks for experiments. The students in my inaugural CPSC 599.82 class on retrogames were both eager and patient with me as we went through this material on its maiden voyage, for which I am eternally grateful. I am also hugely indebted to the people who took time to help proofread this book: Jörg Denzinger, Peter Ferrie, Paul Hagstrom, Nigel Horspool, and Jim Uhl.

Finally, a special thank you to both Darcy Grant, who suffered through lengthy detailed descriptions of my game analysis *du jour*, and Kathryn Kawalec for her loving, unwavering support throughout the long research and writing process.

Calgary, Canada   John Aycock

Contents

List of Figures

List of Tables

Chapter 1
Introduction

What is a retrogame? It seems like a simple question, but it turns out to be surprisingly difficult to answer. It is an important question to answer, though, because it's hard to study something that can't be clearly identified.

One approach would be to say that a retrogame is a game from someone's childhood, one that evokes a sense of nostalgia. This may work perfectly for any one person, but it's a very subjective definition and doesn't scale: no two people will share the same childhood, or the same nostalgic yearnings.[1] Ideally what we want is an objective test. In other words, given an arbitrary game, which of its characteristics could we use to unambiguously decide whether it's a retrogame or not?

As a starting point, we could define "retrogame" to simply mean an old game. In fact, a number of writers do just that. One author talks about 'computer games from the 80s (so-called retrogaming)' [50]; another puts 'games from the 1980s, and even early 1990s' into the 'retro' camp [39, p. 29]. We already have a problem, in that there is no clear year that divides retro and non-retro. Or perhaps it's a relative measure, and after a certain number of years have passed by, a game magically transforms into a retrogame like a butterfly emerging from a cocoon. But how many years? Will *Halo* (2001) eventually be a retrogame, or maybe it is already? What about a game produced in 2015, or 2050?

If *when* doesn't conclusively make a game a retrogame, we could look at *what* instead. One tangible characteristic that games have even prior to startup is their computing platform. This would certainly include hardware; software, such as an operating system or even something as rudimentary as code in a system ROM, was not always present in old games. This avenue seems more promising, because there would probably be general agreement that games running on systems with 8-bit CPUs would be retrogames: this would include the Atari 2600, the Apple II, the Commodore 64, and many others. Then we would also have to include as retrogames anything running on a 16-bit CPU, since 8- and 16-bit CPUs overlapped in time early on, with the 16-bit Intellivision and TI-99/4 both released in 1979.

---

[1] Although we do not pursue nostalgia further, it has been explored in relation to games, e.g., [23, 50].

© Springer International Publishing Switzerland 2016
J. Aycock, *Retrogame Archeology*, DOI 10.1007/978-3-319-30004-7_1

We would also start needing to consider 32-bit processors, because companies like
Apple, Atari, and Commodore began releasing computers in the mid-1980s based
on the (arguably) 32-bit Motorola 68000 CPU, while the 8-bit machines were still
in production. 32-bit CPUs still were going strong many decades later, meaning that
this hardware-based characterization also becomes fuzzy for classifying retrogames.

Further adding to the confusion with hardware are two tricky cases. First, a philo-
sophical case: if running on 8-bit hardware (for example) makes a retrogame, then
is an 8-bit game for the Atari 2600 still a retrogame if it is played via emulation on
modern hardware? Second, less common but more practical, is where a new, modern
game is created that runs on old hardware. This includes new original games, and
also remakes of new games for old platforms, called demakes. For instance, a version of *Halo* was created for the Atari 2600, *Halo 2600* (2010),[2] and *Doom* (1993)
has been recreated for a number of old platforms, including *vicdoom* (2013) for the
Commodore Vic-20.

Maybe the key to retrogame classification is not the hardware the game runs
on, but something else the player can touch, the interface. Many early games had
simple gameplay controls – the one-button Atari 2600 joystick is practically iconic.
However, the contemporary Intellivision controller had a disk to press for direction
in place of a joystick, along with a keypad and multiple buttons.[3] The arcade version
of *Defender* (1981) had controls that were notoriously complex for the time [4, 16,
30], and text adventure games aspired to use the most challenging gameplay controls
of all, human language. Figure 1.1 shows the beginning of a text adventure game and
how the user interacted with it.[4] Clearly the simplicity of a game's interface isn't the
deciding retrogame factor.

Or, is the telling part of the interface not what the player touches, but what
the player sees, namely the graphics. Blocky graphics are surely the hallmark of
a bygone era. This definition falls apart quickly, even ignoring the fact that not all
retrogames had graphics to begin with, like text-only adventure games. A graphics-
based definition would see *Doom* be a retrogame with its chunky stylings, but
Myst (1993) was released the same year with much better graphics. Both *Doom* and
Myst are 3D, and even the extra dimension doesn't separate old from new: prominent arcade games like *Night Driver* (1976), *Battlezone* (1980), *Q*bert* (1982), and
Zaxxon (1982) were all dabbling in the third dimension early on [20, 55]. Insisting
on 2D *and* blocky graphics is no help, either. The game shown in Fig. 1.2 would
then be retro at a casual glance, were it not for the fact that the image belongs to
VVVVVV (2010).

Having now gone to the trouble of pointing out the many flawed ways to define
retrogames, this book uses one of the first and easiest that was mentioned – age. The
game examples used here span the range 1973–1993, with one outlier in 1996 and
a suspiciously large concentration of examples from the 1980s. This is not a book

---

[2] The game's author, Ed Fries, posted a fascinating account of its development [24].

[3] I can attest that it was, and is, ghastly to use.

[4] As nearly as I was able to determine, this text is from Dave Platt's 1979 version of *Adventure*,
based on source code comparison and [43, 52]. Apart from involving lowercase characters, the text
here is almost identical to that in the source for Crowther's original version in 1976.

```
You are standing at the end of a road before a small brick
building.  Around you is a forest.  A small stream flows out of
the building and down a gully.
? enter building
You are inside a building, a well house for a large spring.

There are some keys on the ground here.
There is a shiny brass lamp nearby.
There is food here.
There is a bottle of water here.
? take keys
Ok.
? west
You're at end of road again.
? south
You are in a valley in the forest beside a stream tumbling
along a rocky bed.
? south
At your feet all the water of the stream splashes into a 2-inch
slit in the rock.  Downstream the streambed is bare rock.
? south
You are in a 20-foot depression floored with bare dirt. Set into
the dirt is a strong steel grate mounted in concrete.  A dry
streambed leads into the depression.

The grate is locked.
? open grate with keys
The grate is now unlocked.
? enter
You are in a small chamber beneath a 3x3 steel grate to the
surface. A low crawl over cobbles leads inward to the west.

The grate is open.
?
```

Fig. 1.1 Playing a text adventure game; user input is in bold

on game history, and the game examples are not necessarily the first, or the best, or the most influential. A few games mentioned here are downright obscure. However, they have been chosen because some aspect of their implementation is notable.

1.1 Constraints

One theme that runs throughout this book is the idea of constraints. Retrogame programmers were limited in ways that would be nearly incomprehensible to a modern programmer. And yet, these same limitations can drive creativity – necessity is the mother of invention. David Braben, co-author of *Elite* (1984), had this to say when

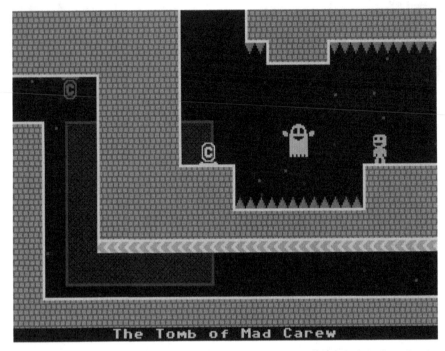

Fig. 1.2 Retro, or not retro? (Image by Terry Cavanagh – http://thelettervsixtim.es/, used under CC BY-SA 3.0 license [11])

asked about a particular limitation in an interview [17]: 'I think that what it has done is very much focus us. In a sense, any limitations, and there are always limitations, do help. It's just part of the creative process.'

The same idea is echoed by other game authors and designers. 1980s game developer Tom Griner remarked on the Commodore VIC-20 [28] 'The limitations all seemed like a fun challenge.' More recently, *Halo 2600* author Ed Fries argued for using constraints to spur creativity [22, 41, 42], and problems were observed in the *lack* of constraints on the Sony Playstation 2 [30, p. 568–569].

Interestingly, this constraint-creativity sentiment is shared by people in other creative fields. The composer Igor Stravinsky, for example, said [49, p. 87] 'my freedom will be so much the greater and more meaningful the more narrowly I limit my field of action and the more I surround myself with obstacles. Whatever diminishes constraint, diminishes strength.'

But what were the constraints in retrogames? That there were technical constraints probably comes as no surprise, but before turning to those, we look at retrogame constraints in two other areas: constraints on the player, and constraints on the developer.

1.1.1 Player Constraints

Retrogames on larger computing systems would impose constraints on the players at times, particularly with respect to running games. Big computers would have been enormously expensive, and funded by institutions or research grants; it's easy to see why a dim view was taken of gaming.

Adventure (1977)[5] imposed limits in the form of 'prime time' hours when the game's setting, Colossal Cave, was closed. Running the game during those times would present the player with

```
I'M TERRIBLY SORRY, BUT COLOSSAL CAVE IS CLOSED.
```

along with a display of the "hours of business" that were internally represented with integers. Weekday hours, for instance, had the octal value 00777400, and the cave was closed if the bit corresponding to the hour of the day was set; here, the cave was closed for ten hours during the weekday, from 8am–6pm. The cave hours were followed by the message

```
ONLY WIZARDS ARE PERMITTED WITHIN THE CAVE RIGHT NOW.
```

Undoubtedly with a nod to *Adventure*, *Rogue* (1980)[6] checked the system to see if there were too many users, or if the system was too busy (i.e., the load average). If a hardcoded threshold was exceeded, a hapless player running the game might see

```
Sorry, aycock, but the system is too loaded now.
Try again later.  Meanwhile, why not enjoy a
slime-mold?
```

followed by an unceremonious exit from the game... unless the player happened to be the game author. Later versions added a special message for the latter case:

```
However, since you're a good guy, it's up to you
```

1.1.2 Developer Constraints

Early developers had a bewildering assortment of platforms to choose from. By way of illustration, consider the January 1980 issue of *Byte* magazine [9], which had been publishing for over four years by that time. Its editorial headline assures readers that 'The Era of Off-the-Shelf Personal Computers Has Arrived,' and the advertisements in that issue give a sense of the landscape:

> Cromemco Z-2H ('11 megabytes of hard disk and 64 kilobytes of fast RAM in a Z80A computer for under $10K'); TI 99/4; North Star Horizon; Ohio Scientific's Challenger III

---

[5] This is from the source code for the Crowther and Woods version of the game; the code for Crowther's original version didn't have this feature. It is also backed up by the analysis in [29].

[6] Based on *Rogue* source code (version 3.6), and also code for the 4.2 and 4.3 BSD versions.

series; Intertec Data Systems' SuperBrain; Heathkit ('The easy way to learn about computers: BUILD ONE'); Atari 400 and 800; Smoke Signal Broadcasting's Chieftain (!); Apple, featuring the old rainbow logo; Compucolor Corporation's Compucolor II; Radio Shack's TRS-80 Model II; Commodore's PET 2001 ('FREE SOFTWARE & PET DUST COVER').

This is only a glimpse of the computing market, and doesn't take into account game consoles. The first issue of *Electronic Games* magazine in 1981 mentions the Atari 2600, Intellivision, Odyssey^2, and Channel F;[7] more would join them soon. Even this view ignores the computer systems embedded in arcade machines of the time.

This embarrassment of riches may seem like the opposite of a constraint, with so much choice. In fact, most of these systems would have been mutually incompatible. Even systems with the same CPU gave no assurances that code for one would work in any meaningful way on another, given that games required programming many things that were system-specific, like video, audio, and I/O. For example, the Atari 2600, Commodore 64, Apple II, and Nintendo NES all used (some variant of) the 6502 CPU, but they were very different creatures to program.

Furthermore, the programming tools that developers had at their disposal were rudimentary if not nonexistent. Beginning with editors for writing code, some early game programmers coded using line editors. For example, Bill Budge used a line editor to write *Pinball Construction Set* (1983) [8]; David Crane (e.g., *Pitfall!*, 1982) used a line editor [13][8]; Carol Shaw used one to write games at Atari (e.g., *3D Tic-Tac-Toe*, 1979) [19].

To illustrate what this means, consider a programmer wanting to write a short program in C:

```
int main()
{
    printf("Hello, world!\n");
}
```

Using a typical programming environment circa 2015, a programmer would have multiple large color screens, and a graphical development environment that would show the program in its entirety, along with a window showing the structure of the files in the programming project the code belongs to, another window showing warning and error messages from the compiler, and yet another displaying the output from running the program. There would easily be enough screen real estate remaining to have a web browser showing documentation or vital social media updates. Any edits to the program would be shown immediately on screen and, in fact, not all of it would need to be typed in: the editor, upon seeing the opening "{" brace entered, would automatically insert the closing "}" and position the cursor between them, indented perfectly to receive the `printf`.

---

[2] This is not a footnote. The console happened to have the superscripted "2" as part of its name.

[7] This issue also featured a question-and-answer section that led off with 'Do videogames damage television sets?' [21, p. 24].

[8] The use of line editors at Activision was also mentioned by Carol Shaw [19].

```
 1   $ ed
 2   i
 3   main()
 4   {
 5   }
 6   .
 7   2a
 8       printf("Hello, world!\n");
 9   .
10   1s/^/int /
11   1,$p
12   int main()
13   {
14       printf("Hello, world!\n");
15   }
16   w foo.c
17   46
18   q
```

Fig. 1.3 Line editor usage example

By contrast, a retrogame programmer in line-editor days would likely have a monochrome text-only display, able to show a modest amount of text – the display used for writing *Pitfall!* could show at most 24 lines of 80-column text [13, 31]. Entering the short example program with a line editor is shown in Fig. 1.3, using the ed line editor; this editor was developed prior to the first release of Unix in 1971 [47] and, for better or worse, is still present in largely unchanged form on Unix-derived systems. Similar line editors, like EDLIN for MS-DOS [18], existed for other systems.

Upon starting ed at the $ prompt (line 1), what is immediately striking is the lack of feedback. There is not even a user prompt. Line 2 is the i command to insert text into the currently-empty file, and after typing a skeletal program (lines 3–5), line 6's period is the command to exit text entry mode. The printf is missing, and the 2a at line 7 says to append after the second line in the file. It's reasonable to ask how the programmer would know what line number to specify, and the answer is simply "by counting manually." After the printf is added (line 8, with the end of text entry at line 9), line 10 prepends int before main. At no point does the programmer see the up-to-date edited code. Line 11 is a command to print the entire file, finally, followed by writing the file to foo.c (line 16, with the number of bytes written printed by ed at line 17), and a quit command to exit the editor.

Obviously, the retrogame development environment demanded a radically different working style, and an excellent mental model of the code. David Crane elaborates [13]:

> It was not unusual to make dozens of changes before looking back at what was done. And the printers of the day were so slow that we would only print every second or third day. In that case we printed the entire program and kept the one copy for all editing going forward. Only when the printout was covered with deletions and change notations, or when the printout no longer represented the actual program would we bother to make a new listing.

Placing code into a file presupposes that there were appropriate tools to compile or, more likely, assemble the code into binary form. At times, tools would be constructed by the game programmers themselves, like debuggers [26] and cross-assemblers [3, p. 143].[9] Infocom built an entire compiler, assembler, and interpreter toolchain for their text adventure games [32, 24:18]. A few programmers would shun assemblers altogether, astoundingly, using limited "mini-assemblers" or translating their assembly instructions into binary form manually.[10]

```
* STORE KEYBOARD INPUT INTO
* BUFFER UNTIL "X" PRESSED


GETKEY    EQU      $FD35
BUFFER    EQU      $900                  800: LDX #0
                                              JSR FD35
          ORG      $800                        STA 900,X
          LDX      #0                          INX
LOOP      JSR      GETKEY                       CMP #D8
          STA      BUFFER,X                     BNE 802
          INX                                   RTS
          CMP      #"X"
          BNE      LOOP
          RTS
```

Fig. 1.4a Assembly code   **Fig. 1.4b** Mini-assembler code

A2 00 20 35 FD 9D 00 09 E8 C9 D8 D0 F5 60

Fig. 1.4c Binary (hexadecimal) code

As a comparison of the different ways of writing code, the same program is shown expressed three different ways: in assembly code for an assembler (Fig. 1.4a), using a mini-assembler on the Apple II (Fig. 1.4b), and in a binary form that hand assembly would have to produce (Fig. 1.4c). All of these programs are equivalent, at least in terms of their operation, but there are obvious differences even without understanding the code. All of the helpful semantic information in the assembly code – comments, meaningful label names and expression values – is lost immediately when writing in the mini-assembler; moving to a binary representation, all mnemonic information is gone completely. Working at these lower levels for any program of nontrivial size would definitely be an impressive feat.

Not only would retrogames have to run on technically-constrained machines, but it was not unusual for computer game developers (as opposed to console game

---

[9] Bill Budge, reflecting back, laments *not* having written his own assembler [7, 46:43].

[10] John Romero tells how Nasir Gebelli used the mini-assembler in the Apple II [3, p. 11], which is confirmed by Gebelli in an interview [46, 1:12]; several other game programmers used VIC-MON [5, 6] that was substantively similar [1, 12]. Sandy White hand-assembled his Z80 code for *Ant Attack* (1983) [44, 53, 54]. The Apple mini-assembler was also used for creating some games' copy protection [25], a topic I return to in Chap. 7.

developers) to be doing their programming on the same constrained machines they were developing for. John Harris wrote the Atari version of *Frogger* (1982), whose development was immortalized in the book *Hackers* [34], on an Atari 800 [26]. Apple II games developed on the Apple II included *Pinball Construction Set* [8], *The Bilestoad* (1982) [27], and both of *Karateka* (1984) and *Prince of Persia* (1989) [36].

1.1.3 Technical Constraints

Throughout this book we'll see ways that retrogame programmers managed the technical constraints of machines; those constraints are outlined here to give an initial high-level view. Not all of them would apply to any one game, barring incredible misfortune, but handling any of these constraints well could be challenging.

Beginning outside the machine, input and output (I/O) could involve slow displays, with potentially huge variation in how a program needed to command them. Secondary storage, for its part, could be slow and small. For example, some retrogames were loaded from cassette tape, whose players did not read programs any faster than they played Top 40 music. The Apple II's $5\frac{1}{4}''$ floppy disks held a whopping 140 K of content.[11]

Costs for integrated circuit (IC) chips were at a premium. This played itself out three main ways. First, there was a push to build computers (which includes game consoles and arcade games) with fewer chips in general: in an economy of scale, one less chip on a shipping system could save a company \$100 K [30, p. 71], also keeping in mind that fewer chips represent fewer components to wire in and fewer components to fail. Second, expensive hardware would result in design decisions that shifted work into cheaper software, meaning extra effort for a programmer. Third, even where chips were necessary, such as for memory, smaller and less expensive memories would be attractive.

To give a rough idea of cost,[12] the Atari 2600 was released in September 1977. An advertisement in the September 1977 issue of *Byte* magazine [10] touts the 'World's Lowest IC Prices' and lists the price of a '74S200' as \$2.95. (Apparently there was some truth to their claim, as a later ad in the same issue had the same part listed at \$6.95.) The 74S200 was a RAM chip offering 256 bits of memory [48]. An engineer aspiring to the wanton luxury of having 256 *bytes* would require eight of those, and the total price of almost \$24 would be a sizeable chunk of the already-high \$199 debut price of the Atari 2600 [38]. Fortunately the 2600 could get by with less memory than that.

---

[11] Using DOS 3.3 [56].

[12] This is only a first-order approximation, of course. A company like Atari would have gotten a volume discount on parts.

The CPUs for retrogames could be highly constrained too. A slow clock rate and limited instruction set – such as not being able to multiply or divide – would naturally influence programming decisions. Along with this, some common retrogame CPUs had few registers, 8 bits wide, with at most 16 address lines giving $2^{16} = 65536$ bytes of addressable memory space.

Example 1.1 (Atari 2600). The Atari 2600 has been politely described as having 'humble capabilities' [35, p. 186]. It has also been described as 'a wood-paneled console that had more joystick ports than onscreen pixel capacity and sounded like a vuvuzela attached to an elephant dying of flatulence'[13] which is less polite but not entirely inaccurate.

The 2600 contained only three chips of note:[14] a combination RAM-timer-I/O chip, a custom chip for video and sound, and a 6507 CPU.

Of the three, the CPU had the least number of pins. The 6507 is a cut-down version of the 6502 CPU that has only 13 address lines, making it able to only address 8 K of space. There was little to address, anyway. The 2600 had a meager 128 bytes of RAM, which had to suffice for all of a game's temporary storage including any stack requirements. There was no ROM in the system, until a game cartridge was plugged in, because the ROM chips were located inside the cartridges.

The lack of RAM meant that there was no memory for a video framebuffer. On most systems, then and now, there is memory called a framebuffer devoted to holding the contents of what is shown onscreen.[15] The 2600 didn't provide a framebuffer, essentially leaving the programmer responsible for drawing each individual line displayed on the screen. This task had to be performed in addition to managing sound, player input, and updating the positions of all game elements. And it had to be done using a relatively slow CPU before the display's electron beam swept across the screen to render a line's contents – programming the Atari 2600 was thus referred to as "racing the beam" [37]; effectively, the 2600's design imposed a soft real-time constraint on its programmers. Getting the timing correct entailed counting the number of clock cycles each CPU instruction in the critical screen update code would take. Those instructions needed to be carefully chosen, because each scan line equated to 76 of the 6507's clock cycles, and the fastest 6507 instruction occupied 2 cycles, with the majority taking three cycles or more. The reference manual for the 2600's graphics chip helpfully observes that the number of usable cycles is 'actually less becuase [sic] the microprocessor must be <u>ahead</u> of the raster' [57].

Technical constraints indeed.

---

[13] From [14, 1:10]. Copyright Defy Media, LLC, used with permission.

[14] Information for this section is from [2, 45, 57].

[15] In fact, this was done long prior to the 2600. A 1971 research article describing a video system with a framebuffer (although it was not called that at the time) cavalierly talks about the memory requirements [40, p. 148]: 'allocation of 5080 words, or some similar order of magnitude of the computer's core storage, does not seem unreasonable in terms of foreseeable technological advances.'

1.1.4 Meet the 6502

This brings us to the 6502 CPU, which was widely used in many retrogame systems. Other CPUs will show up later in the book, that can be seen in terms of how they differ from the baseline 6502.[16]

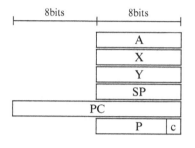

Fig. 1.5 Registers in the 6502 CPU

As shown in Fig. 1.5, the 6502 has six registers. The accumulator (A) is the one used for most arithmetic and logical operations. There are two index registers (X, Y) that are often used as counters and offsets, and a stack pointer (SP); the stack is hardwired to the memory locations $100...$1ff.[17] (The "$" is used to denote a hexadecimal, or base 16, number.) A program counter (PC) keeps track of the location of the instruction currently being executed, and there is also a status register (P) that contains bits indicating various conditions, like whether or not the last instruction resulted in a value of 0. Most of these bits won't be referred to directly except for the carry bit, denoted c. All registers except the program counter are 8-bit registers.

The 6502 has a few relevant characteristics of note:

- It is a little-endian CPU, meaning that it expects to find 16-bit values like addresses stored with their bytes reversed. For example, the address $1234 would be stored in two consecutive bytes as $34 $12. A big-endian CPU, by contrast, would store it as $12 $34.
- The addressable space of the CPU is 64 K. The address range from $00...$ff is called "zero page," and is prime memory real estate, because instructions accessing it are both shorter in terms of bytes, and take fewer cycles to execute. Having the low part of memory spoken for by zero page and the stack, 6502 systems usually locate any ROM in high memory.
- For anyone familiar with more recent CPUs, the 6502 has no restrictions on data or instruction alignment. Code and data may be mixed freely, and self-modifying code is possible.

---

[16] 6502 information in this section is drawn mostly from memory, as well as [33, 51].

[17] The Atari 2600 quietly maps this into $00...$ff, a fact that will prove useful later.

Assembly code shown here for the 6502, as well as for later CPUs, will be written in an abstracted pseudo-assembly code notation for consistency and clarity. There is significant variation in assembly languages between processors, and even between different assemblers for the same processor. Furthermore, some assembly instructions have operands that are implied and not explicitly stated, not to mention having to divine whether "add R1, R2" means R1 = R1 + R2, R2 = R1 + R2, or something else entirely.

The basic pseudo-assembly syntax is inspired by C/C++/Java, and one line of pseudo-assembly corresponds to one line of assembly code. Memory accesses are represented like accesses to an array M, which is written M_w when a word is fetched (as opposed to a byte). Some instructions operate on values that are effectively concatenated together, which is denoted with a $\|$ symbol. For example, the 6502's rotate left instruction rotates nine bits rather than eight bits, by rotating through the carry bit. Rotating the accumulator left one bit would therefore be written as

```
c||A = rotateleft(c||A)
```

Figure 1.6 shows how the assembly code in Fig. 1.4a would be represented using pseudo-assembly code. The $800: is a label indicating the address where the instruction is located, and loop: is another label used for control flow whose precise address is not important to show. More operations will be gradually introduced as we proceed through different code examples.

```
$800:    X = 0
loop:    call $fd35
         M[$900+X] = A
         X = X + 1
         compare A with "X"
         if A != "X" goto loop
         return
```

Fig. 1.6 Pseudo-assembly code example

Programmers reading this may wonder why code is expressed one way when there is a seemingly obvious, shorter alternative. For instance, why would a programmer not have written X = X + 2 instead of one of

```
A = X            X = X + 1
A = A + 2        X = X + 1
X = A
```

Many of the CPUs discussed here were far from being orthogonal, meaning that it was not generally possible to perform all operations using all registers. Additionally, there may be programming considerations involving the instruction's size, or how long it takes to perform. Having analyzed great quantities of assembly code, it was rare to find obvious inefficiencies; retrogame programmers were masters of their craft.

1.2 Present Day

Another theme in this book is that the techniques used in the implementation of retrogames have modern applications. Many if not most of the techniques described here have echoes in present-day games, but there is a danger when choosing modern games as examples, because it may appear that these are only game techniques. In actuality, these are general techniques useful in non-game areas and, to emphasize this, I have deliberately chosen application examples outside games. These examples are set apart from the retrogame material by being enclosed in boxes,

like this.

1.3 Boring Academic Stuff

In one of his books, famed computer scientist Edsger Dijkstra wrote [15, p. xvii] 'For the absence of a bibliography I offer neither explanation nor apology.' I mention this because this book has no ludography, or game bibliography; I'll follow Dijkstra's lead insofar as I won't apologize, but I will offer an explanation. Even for early games, identifying authorship could be difficult, and the actual date a game was produced could vary from the release date, which itself could vary depending on geographic location. Rather than offer information which would be both incorrect and incomplete, the first mention of a game in a chapter gives its year as nearly as I could determine, for use as a rough reference point. The specific platform of the game is given either explicitly in the text or implicitly by its context, when relevant.

The references I used are cited, of course, being a good academic. The nature of some retrogame information is such that it is duplicated and scattered widely on the Internet. For materials like this without an obvious One True Location, I have supplied enough reference information to locate at least one copy with a search engine. There was also a lot of original research that went into this book, and I have made every effort to verify technical claims. I think this latter point is especially important, because people's memories can fade or play tricks over time, and an offhand comment made in an interview may not accurately reflect the reality of code written long ago. Footnotes throughout the book document how I have verified material, which will hopefully be useful information for future researchers.

As final pedantic notes, I've used *computer* game in preference to *video* game, because some games are text-based and could even be played on teletypes [34]. Atari's popular console is referred to as the Atari 2600 consistently throughout to avoid confusion, even though it was originally called the Atari VCS. Units are denoted using the symbols prevalent at the time, e.g., 'K' for kilobyte, rather than the newer standardized binary prefixes for consistency with the original source material.

References

1. Apple Computer, Inc.: Apple II Reference Manual. Apple Computer, Cupertino (1978)
2. Atari: Atari Video Computer System field service manual, model 2600/2600A domestic (M/N) (c. 1983)
3. Barton, M.: Honoring the Code: Conversations with Great Game Designers. CRC Press, Boca Raton (2013)
4. Barton, M., Loguidice, B.: The history of *Defender*: The joys of difficult games. Gamasutra (2009). http://www.gamasutra.com/view/feature/132467/the_history_of_defender_the_joys_.php
5. Blackford, J.: Jeff Minter: The programmer behind *Gridrunner* and *Attack of the Mutant Camels*. Compute!'s Gazette **1**(2), 52–53 (1983)
6. Blackford, J.: Jimmy Huey: The programmer behind *Galactic Blitz, Sidewinder*, and *Swarm!* Compute!'s Gazette **1**(1), 49–50 (1983)
7. Budge, B.: Classic game postmortem: Pinball Construction Set. Game Developer's Conference 2013 (2013). http://www.gdcvault.com/play/1018258/Classic-Game-Postmortem-Pinball-Construction
8. Budge, B.: Email Communication (28 July 2013)
9. Byte: The Small Systems Journal, vol. 5 (1). McGraw-Hill, Peterborough (Jan 1980)
10. Byte: The Small Systems Journal, vol. 2 (9). BYTE Publications, Peterborough (Sept 1977)
11. Cavanagh, T.: VVVVVV – The Tomb of Mad Carew. http://commons.wikimedia.org/w/index.php?title=File:VVVVVV_-_The_Tomb_of_Mad_Carew.png&oldid=115713263 (2010). CC BY-SA 3.0 license (http://creativecommons.org/licenses/by-sa/3.0/deed.en), no changes made
12. Commodore Home Computer Division: Machine Code Monitor (VICMON) User Manual (1982)
13. Crane, D.: Email Communication (25 June 2014)
14. Croshaw, B.: *E.T.* – "the worst game ever". The Escapist. http://www.escapistmagazine.com/videos/view/zero-punctuation/9625-E-T-The-Worst-Game-Ever (6 Aug 2014)
15. Dijkstra, E.W.: A Discipline of Programming. Prentice Hall, Englewood Cliffs (1976)
16. Donovan, T.: Replay: The History of Video Games. Yellow Ant, East Sussex (2010)
17. Edge staff: WiiWare: Developer impressions. Edge Online. http://www.edge-online.com/features/wiiware-developer-impressions/
18. EDLIN. In: R. Duncan (ed.) The MS-DOS Encyclopedia. Microsoft Press, Redmond (1988)
19. Edwards, B.: VC&G interview: Carol Shaw, the first female video game developer. Vintage Computing and Gaming. http://www.vintagecomputing.com/index.php/archives/800 (12 Oct 2011)
20. Egenfeldt-Nielsen, S., Smith, J.H., Tosca, S.P.: Video game aesthetics. In: Understanding Video Games: The Essential Introduction, chap. 5, 2nd edn., pp. 117–155. Routledge, New York (2013)
21. Electronic Games. Reese Publishing Company, New York (Winter 1981)
22. Fawcett, K.: Demaking Halo, remaking art: 'Halo 2600' developer discusses the promise of video games. Smithsonian Magazine (2014). http://www.smithsonianmag.com/smithsonian-institution/de-making-halo-remaking-art-180949802/
23. Fenty, S.: Why old school is "cool:" a brief analysis of classic video game nostalgia. In: A. Whalen, L.N. Taylor (eds.) Playing the Past: History and Nostalgia in Video Games, chap. 2, pp. 19–31. Vanderbilt University Press (2008)
24. Fries, E.: Reply to "Halo for the 2600 released at CGE! download the game here!". AtariAge Forums. http://atariage.com/forums/topic/166916-halo-for-the-2600-released-at-cge-download-the-game-here/?p=2062848
25. Gustafsson, R.: Email Communication (13 Jan 2015)
26. Hague, J.: John Harris. In: Halcyon Days: Interviews with Classic Computer and Video Game Programmers. http://www.dadgum.com/halcyon/ (2002)

27. Hague, J.: Marc Goodman. In: Halcyon Days: Interviews with Classic Computer and Video Game Programmers. http://www.dadgum.com/halcyon/ (2002)
28. Hague, J.: Tom Griner. In: Halcyon Days: Interviews with Classic Computer and Video Game Programmers. http://www.dadgum.com/halcyon/ (2002)
29. Jerz, D.G.: Somewhere nearby is Colossal Cave: Examining Will Crowther's original "Adventure" in code and in Kentucky. Digital Humanities Quarterly 1(2) (2007). http://www.digitalhumanities.org/dhq/vol/1/2/000009/000009.html
30. Kent, S.L.: The Ultimate History of Video Games. Three Rivers Press, New York (2001)
31. Lear Siegler, Inc.: ADM-3A Interactive Display Terminal Operators Manual (1979)
32. Lebling, D.: Classic game postmortem: Zork. Game Developer's Conference 2014 (2014). http://www.gdcvault.com/play/1020612/Classic-Game-Postmortem
33. Leventhal, L.A.: 6502 Assembly Language Programming, 2nd edn. Osborne McGraw-Hill, Berkeley (1986)
34. Levy, S.: Hackers: Heroes of the Computer Revolution. Dell, New York (1984)
35. Loguidice, B., Barton, M.: Vintage Games: An Insider Look at the History of *Grand Theft Auto*, *Super Mario*, and the Most Influential Games of All Time. Focal Press (Elsevier), Burlington (2009)
36. Mechner, J.: The making of Prince of Persia: Journals 1985–1993. http://www.jordanmechner.com/backstage/journals/
37. Montfort, N., Bogost, I.: Racing the Beam: The Atari video computer system. MIT Press, Cambridge (2009)
38. Moriarty, C.: The real cost of gaming: Inflation, time, and purchasing power. IGN. http://ca.ign.com/articles/2013/10/15/the-real-cost-of-gaming-inflation-time-and-purchasing-power (15 Oct 2013)
39. Newman, J.: Videogames, 2nd edn. Routledge, New York (2012)
40. Noll, A.M.: Scanned-display computer graphics. Commun. ACM 14(3), 143–150 (1971)
41. Nutt, C.: MIGS 2010: Ed Fries argues for the artistic necessity of constraint. Gamasutra. http://www.gamasutra.com/view/news/122057/MIGS_2010_Ed_Fries_Argues_For_The_Artistic_Necessity_Of_Constraint.php (8 Nov 2010)
42. Pearson, D.: Ed Fries: Creativity and constraint, Halo 2600 and a Donkey Kong haiku. GamesIndustry.biz. http://www.gamesindustry.biz/articles/2011-05-12-ed-fries-creativity-and-constraint-halo-2600-and-a-donkey-kong- haiku-blog-entry (12 May 2011)
43. Platt, D.: Email Communication (29 Oct 2013)
44. Retro Gamer staff: Ant Attack! Retro Gamer (55), 26–31 (2008)
45. Rockwell: R6532 RAM-I/O-Timer (RIOT). Data sheet (1987)
46. Romero, J.: Nasir Gebelli at Apple II reunion. https://www.youtube.com/watch?v=4Me1ycLxDlw (8 Aug 1998)
47. Salus, P.H.: A Quarter Century of UNIX. Addison-Wesley, Reading (1994)
48. Signetics: N74S200/201, N74S301 – 256 bit TTL Ram. Signetics Memories – Bipolar Ram data sheet (undated)
49. Stravinsky, I.: Poetics of music in the form of six lessons. Harvard University Press (1970). Trans. A. Knodel and I. Dahl
50. Suominen, J.: The past as the future? nostalgia and retrogaming in digital culture. Fibreculture Journal 11 (2008). http://eleven.fibreculturejournal.org/fcj-075-the-past-as-the-future-nostalgia-and-retrogaming-in-digital-culture/
51. Synertek Incorporated: SY6500/MCS6500 microcomputer family programming manual (1976)
52. Wellsch, K.: Email Communication (30 Oct 2013)
53. White, S.: Sandy White – an Ant Attack homepage. http://sandywhite.co.uk/fun/ants/
54. White, S.: Untitled. http://sandywhite.co.uk/fun/ants/AAsource.htm
55. Wolf, M.J.P.: Z-axis development in the video game. In: Perron, B., Wolf, M.J.P. (eds.) The Video Game Theory Reader 2, chap. 8, pp. 151–168. Routledge, New York (2009)
56. Worth, D., Lechner, P.: Beneath Apple DOS. Quality Software, Reseda (1981)
57. Wright, S.: 2600 (STELLA) Programmer's Guide (3 Dec 1979). Updated by D. May, 1988

Chapter 2
Memory Management

Not only do the memory management techniques used in retrogames underlie those seen in modern operating systems, but memory and its management continues to be an issue, like fitting data into caches for efficiency, and trading space for time in programs. The techniques used in retrogames can be grouped into three categories: handling too much memory, handling not enough memory, and (ab)using memory for keeping track of a program's state.

2.1 Too Much Memory

It may seem paradoxical that retrogames needed to handle the situation of having too much memory. Given the comparatively small memory sizes and sky-high memory costs back then, this would appear to be the last thing programmers would need to concern themselves with. However, as time went on, memory grew larger and its price fell. The problem became one of addressability: it's not possible to directly refer to 128 K of memory, for instance, with a CPU that is not physically capable of specifying more than 64 K unique addresses.

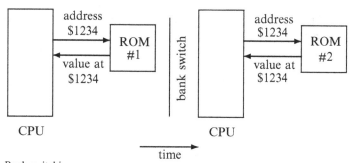

Fig. 2.1 Bank switching

© Springer International Publishing Switzerland 2016
J. Aycock, *Retrogame Archeology*, DOI 10.1007/978-3-319-30004-7_2

Enter bank switching. The basic idea is to have more than one "bank" of RAM or ROM responding to the exact same memory address. Hardware addressing circuitry is used to ensure that only one of the banks, the currently-selected one, responds to any requests from the CPU. Figure 2.1 illustrates the process. The CPU requests the value at memory address $1234, when ROM #1 is initially selected and responds with the appropriate value. Then a bank switch occurs, which is typically performed by the programmer coding an instruction to access a special "soft switch." The value written to or read from the soft switch is irrelevant; it is the reference to the switch's address that changes its state. Once the bank switch is done – here, resulting in ROM #2 being selected instead of ROM #1 – the CPU can request the exact same address, but this time sees a value from ROM #2, which can be completely different from the value in the other ROM. The CPU is oblivious to one bank of memory being exchanged for another.

Bank switching is still seen on smaller systems, such as embedded systems and microcontrollers [24, 30]. Banked memory has the additional benefit that unused memory banks may be placed into a low-power mode to conserve electricity and prolong battery life [31].

We will explore how bank switching was handled in increasingly elaborate ways by looking at examples from the Atari 2600 and various home computers from the retrogame era.

Example 2.1 (Atari 2600). The Atari 2600 had a wide range of bank switching schemes in use. More precisely, the *cartridges* for the 2600 did, because these mechanisms were not part of the 2600 console's hardware proper. Any bank switching hardware needed to be located inside a game cartridge. We will focus primarily on the "F8" bank switching scheme that allowed a cartridge to have 8 K of ROM, i.e., two banks of 4 K apiece.[1] F8 soft switches were located at $1ff8 to switch to Bank 0, and $1ff9 to switch to Bank 1.

It is necessary to fully embrace the concept of mirroring in order to understand code in the Atari 2600. Mirroring is when some component like RAM or ROM appears to be in many different memory locations simultaneously, and it is caused by incomplete hardware decoding of address information. With the 6507 processor neglecting to run three address lines outside the CPU, there was no opportunity to distinguish between many 16-bit memory addresses used inside the CPU; the 2600 had more mirroring than a carnival fun house. In other words, the ROM and soft switches were nominally located between $1000...$1fff, but in fact would appear to be at any address whose most significant bits were xxx1 (where "x" means "don't care"). The ROM and F8 soft switches thus appeared at $1000...$1fff, as well as $3000...$3fff and so on, all the way to $d000...$dfff and $f000...$ffff.

---

[1] Information for this section is from [20] unless otherwise noted.

	Bank 0		Bank 1
$dff0:	M[$fff9] = A	$dff0:	M[$fff8] = A
	goto M_w[$f7]		goto M_w[$f7]

Fig. 2.2 Bank switching in *Asteroids*

With that in mind, Fig. 2.2 shows the bank switching code for *Asteroids* (1981).[2] To call code in a different bank, the programmer would load the destination address in $f7...$f8, then go to $dff0. The first instruction there toggles the appropriate soft switch to change ROM banks, and as a result the CPU actually fetches the goto instruction from the *other* bank. The M_w[$f7] means that the CPU fetches the 16-bit address (word) placed in $f7 and $f8 and uses that as the destination address to jump to.

A more unusual method of bank switching in the Atari 2600 involves dynamic code generation. In modern systems, dynamic code generation would be used by just-in-time compilers to provide a speed advantage. However, some games for the 2600 dynamically generated code into RAM to perform bank switching – an unexpected find, given how scarce a resource RAM was on that platform.[3]

```
1    A = $48
2    M[$87] = A
3    A = $f5
4    M[$88] = A
5    A = $ad
6    M[$83] = A
7    A = $f9
8    M[$84] = A
9    A = $ff
10   M[$85] = A
11   A = $4c
12   M[$86] = A
13   goto $83
```

Fig. 2.3 Bank switching with dynamic code generation in *E.T.*

Figure 2.3 shows what the code for this looked like in the infamous game *E.T.* (1982).[4] Lines 1–4 are storing the destination address in RAM, lines 5–10 create an instruction in RAM to toggle a soft switch, and lines 11–12 place the opcode for a goto instruction. Line 13 jumps to the code that was just generated in RAM at location $83, which looks like:

```
$83:   A = M[$fff9]
       goto $f548
```

---

[2] Verified in-emulator.

[3] Thanks to David Crane for the tip-off [15, 42:12].

[4] These dynamic code generation examples were verified in-emulator, and all are F8 cartridges.

This code also appears in *Raiders of the Lost Ark* (1982), and both it and *E.T.* were programmed by Howard Scott Warshaw, so this commonality is perhaps not surprising.[5] Substantially similar code from different programmers is in *Congo Bongo* (1983). Structurally, arranging the code so that the address was put into memory first allowed the tail of this code (lines 5–13) to be reused with different addresses.

While not bank switching per se, one last method of handling too much memory on the Atari 2600 was to cram it into cartridges. The memory in question was not ROM, though, but RAM. The problem is not straightforward, because the 2600's cartridges were not supplied with a read/write signal that would normally be necessary for RAM chips. There was no need, given the assumption that cartridges would only consist of ROM. The Atari 'Super Chip' (a.k.a. Sara) solved the problem by dedicating separate address ranges for reading and writing [20, 34]. A write to the extra 128 bytes of on-cartridge RAM the Super Chip provided would be at $f000, but the address $f080 would be used to read that same location. Effectively, one of the address lines was used as a read/write signal.

The Apple II series used a full-fledged 6502 processor as opposed to its more limited 6507 cousin in the Atari 2600, but its ability to access a full 64 K didn't absolve it of the need for bank switching.

Example 2.2 (Apple II). The Apple II had an optional 16 K RAM card whose functionality came standard by the time of the Apple IIe.[6] With 12 K of ROM abutted by space for memory-mapped I/O, there was no clean way to bank 16 K into high memory. Instead, the 12 K ROM was banked with 12 K of RAM, and 4 K of *it* could be bank switched with another 4 K RAM bank. Figure 2.4 illustrates.

Soft switches located at $c080...$c08f allowed selection of a veritable potpourri of memory bank configurations, including arrangements where reads were from ROM, but writes went to RAM. A programming note in the Apple reference manual dramatically cautions that 'Careless switching between RAM and ROM is almost certain to have catastrophic effects' [4, p. 69].

Commodore computers, meanwhile, moved from basic bank switching hardware to something more complex.

Example 2.3 (Commodore 64 and 128). Like the Apple II, the Commodore 64 also had a variety of ways to slice and dice memory banks. One interesting configuration mapped all 64 K as RAM, using four 16 K banks. A programmer doing this might seem to have painted themselves into a corner, as it were, because soft switches located in some memory-mapped I/O space would be inaccessible. There would be no way to switch to any other memory configuration. The solution is based on the

---

[5] In fact, after finding this code in *E.T.*, a hunch led me to check Warshaw's other games. The code is also present in a 1984 prototype on which Warshaw was a co-author.

[6] Information for this section is from [4, 28, 29].

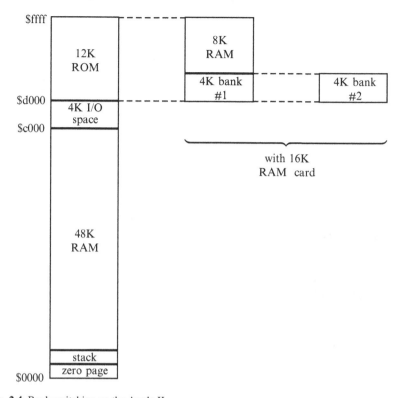

Fig. 2.4 Bank switching on the Apple II

particular variant of the 6502 CPU that the Commodore 64 used, the 6510. This CPU had an I/O port hardwired to address $0001 that was used to control (among other things) bank switching [14].

The Commodore 128 upped the ante by incorporating a memory management unit (MMU) that gave more sophisticated options to the programmer. The MMU still allowed memory configurations to be set directly, and up to four memory arrangements could be pre-configured and flipped to by toggling soft switches. In addition, the stack and zero page could be re-mapped to other locations [1, 13].

Finally, the Tandy Color Computer 3 had a 6809 CPU. The architectural differences between it and the 6502 are not as relevant here as one similarity: the 6809 could also only address 64 K of memory directly.

Example 2.4 (Color Computer 3). A relative latecomer with a 1986 release, the Color Computer 3 had an MMU with a well-structured method to select between 8 K banks of RAM [27, 33]. As illustrated in Fig. 2.5, the upper three bits of the 6809's 16-bit address (A_{15}, A_{14}, and A_{13}) were fed into the MMU, which would replace them with three bits stored in the MMU's configuration registers, *and* add

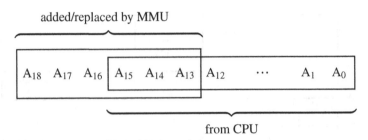

added/replaced by MMU

from CPU

Fig. 2.5 Memory mapping in the Color Computer 3

three more bits on to the address, extending it into a 19-bit address that could reference 512 K locations. The six bits from the MMU, in essence, acted as a bank select for 8 K RAM banks.

> Memory management units are now commonplace on commodity processors, and are used by operating systems to provide virtual memory support as well as memory protection. In other words, programs can address much more memory than is physically present in the system, and one (accidentally or maliciously) misbehaving program can't affect other programs or crash the entire system. Normally.

2.2 Not Enough Memory

The case of retrogames not having enough memory seems more intuitive. Programmers in early games bumping into a memory limit would need to design their programs such that not all the code was needed in memory at any one time, and swap one large hunk of game code for another. Each hunk was referred to as an overlay.

The management of overlays was initially manual and left to the programmer. Between having to manage the overlays and having slow I/O devices to read overlays into memory from, it is not surprising that manual overlays tended to be fairly coarse-grained. For example, *Trek73* (1973) was a text-based *Star Trek* game, programmed in BASIC. The game code was divided into six parts, which were explicitly loaded as necessary by the programmer using BASIC's "CHAIN" command, e.g.,[7]

```
CHAIN "TREK0"
```

---

[7] Verified in source code, using [19] to interpret the BASIC of the time.

would overlay the BASIC code currently in memory with the BASIC code in the "TREK0" file. Variables in the program declared as "common" would be preserved across the chain loading, allowing game state to persist between different program files. *Elite* (1984) brought in an overlay for trading and generating textual location descriptions when the player's spaceship was docked; when undocked, that overlay was exchanged for an overlay that produced the graphics for flying [10, 39:12].

```
swapedit:      X = 0
               call swapsectors
               goto $9500
swapwire:      X = 1
               call swapsectors
               goto $9513
swapdisk:      X = 2
               call swapsectors
               goto $9510
swapuser:      X = 3
               goto swapsectors
   .
   .
   .
swapsectors:   A = count[X]
               M[sectorcount] = A
               A = sector[X]
               M[temp] = A
               A = track[X]
               X = M[temp]
               goto readsectors

count:         byte $39,$0a,$08,$0a
track:         byte $0b,$0c,$0d,$0e
sector:        byte $08,$09,$07,$09
```

Fig. 2.6 Simplified overlay code for *Pinball Construction Set*

A game's code didn't need to be overlaid in its entirety. A clear example of this is in *Pinball Construction Set* (1983), where core game code would always be memory-resident (including the code to load overlays), but other pieces would be loaded into a memory area for overlays as need be [12, 33:41]. The simplified code for this is shown in Fig. 2.6.[8] Each overlay has a corresponding code stub that loads a different value into X and calls the code that reads in the overlay from disk. Once loaded, the stub jumps to the entry point for the overlay's code. The disk parameters are found by indexing into `byte` arrays using the value of X. For instance, the "wire" overlay would be 10 sectors located on disk starting at track 12, sector 9 ($0a, $0c, and $09 respectively).

---

[8] Based on the real source code.

2.2.1 Fine-Grained Memory Overlays

The programmer obviously needed to do a fair bit of work to manage overlays manually. This did not remain the case, however. The game *Beyond the Titanic* (1986) is interesting in this regard because it's written using Turbo Pascal, and has a number of procedures in the code declared using the "overlay" keyword, such as[9]

```
overlay procedure Initialize;
```

What this represents is a shift in labor: instead of the programmer having to manage overlays, the compiler and run-time system do the work.

Early versions of Turbo Pascal had a comparatively limited overlay mechanism. Keep in mind that there was no hardware assistance, and the overlays had to be implemented in software only.[10] Figure 2.7 illustrates how overlays worked in Turbo Pascal 3, released roughly the same time as *Beyond the Titanic*. Space to load the code for overlays was reserved in the program's memory, sized to contain the code of the largest overlay procedure or function. The bottom of the figure shows what happens when overlay code is loaded: overlay *B* is the largest overlay, and occupies the entire overlay area. Overlay *D*, when loaded, leaves lots of extra space free in the overlay area, but it goes to waste. This early overlay support loaded only one overlay at a time, and came with a litany of restrictions the programmer had to observe – for example, one overlay routine could not call another one, because they couldn't both occupy the same overlay space.

The overlay support for later versions of Turbo Pascal was considerably more advanced, but yet still condemned to provide support only through software. As Fig. 2.8 shows, the overlay area was relocated to reside between the program's stack and heap memory areas, whose direction of growth is indicated in the figure. An overlay file itself could still be separate from the executable file, but there was the option to append it onto the executable, no doubt to simplify software distribution for the programmer.

The overlay area could now be quite a lot larger than the code for any one overlay, and for good reason. The overlay area has become a ring buffer that can hold multiple overlays' code at once; as overlays are required, they are loaded at the head of the buffer, with code at the tail of the ring buffer being ejected from memory to make room.[11]

Figure 2.9 shows how overlay buffer management works conceptually. The arrow beside each buffer diagram represents the order of overlays in the ring buffer. Initially, the buffer is empty, and as overlays *A*, *E*, and *D* are called, they are loaded in at the head of the buffer. Overlay *B* being called presents a problem, because the buffer does not have enough free space left to hold it. Overlays *A* and *E*, the "oldest"

---

[9] Verified in the source code.

[10] Details in this section regarding version 3 are from [7], and later versions' behavior is from [8, 9, 11]. In particular, Figs. 2.7 and 2.9 are based on examples in [7, 9]... but really, how many distinct ways can you show a ring buffer in action?

[11] This is a simplified explanation. The full buffer management algorithm is FIFO with second-chance, to avoid removing old but frequently-used overlays [32].

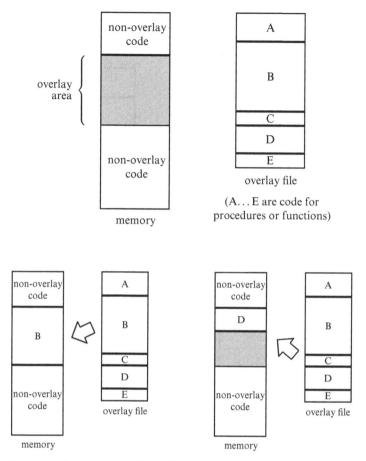

Fig. 2.7 Overlay mechanism in Turbo Pascal 3.0

ones at the tail of the ring buffer, are discarded and overlay *D* – the new buffer tail – is shifted in the buffer to make room. Another call to *A* requires it to be reloaded at the head of the buffer, in a different location than it previously occupied.

The overlay management code thus needs to be able to perform three tasks reliably. First, all calls to overlay code must be intercepted to allow the overlay manager to load the overlay if it is not already in memory. Second, overlay code may need to be removed from memory. Third, overlay code may be shifted to a different location in memory. What makes the second and third tasks nontrivial is that the code subjected to this cup-and-ball trick may be in the midst of use, with return addresses on the stack pointing to the code. Moving or removing the code carelessly could result in the 'catastrophic effects' formerly reserved for bank switching.

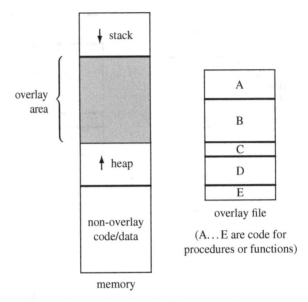

Fig. 2.8 Overlay mechanism in Turbo Pascal 6 and 7

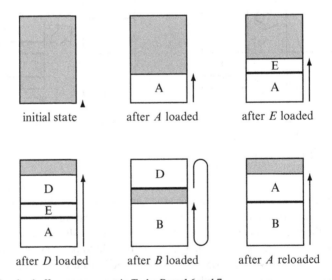

Fig. 2.9 Overlay buffer management in Turbo Pascal 6 and 7

The solution is a familiar one for programmers. Or, to put it another way, 'Any problem in computer science can be solved with another level of indirection.'[12] Calls to overlay code pass through an indirection layer as shown in Fig. 2.10. All calls to overlay *B*, for instance, go instead to a stub that initially calls the overlay manager.

---

[12] Attributed to David Wheeler [22].

| | *Initial state* | | *After B loaded* |
			at address $1234
A:	call overlaymanager	A:	call overlaymanager
B:	call overlaymanager	B:	goto $1234
C:	call overlaymanager	C:	call overlaymanager
⋮		⋮	

Fig. 2.10 Loading overlay code on demand

Once *B* is loaded, the stub's instruction is replaced with a direct jump to *B*'s code. The initial use of the call is important, because it results in the return address being pushed on the stack; the overlay manager uses that stack information to find out which stub entry to patch.

Unloading and relocating overlay code is a bit messier. The overlay manager needs to walk through the stack and find all the return addresses that refer to the overlay code in question, rewriting each to point to the manager for appropriate repair later.

2.2.2 Paging and Virtual Memory

The overlays discussed so far have mapped well into a logical view of a game's code. Procedures and functions in higher-level languages; manually-selected, functionally cohesive code in lower-level languages. An alternative is to blindly slice code into uniformly-sized pages.

Infocom created the "Z-machine," a virtual machine underlying their text adventure games like *Zork I* (1980), with the goal of shoehorning an extensive game into a small amount of memory.[13] We will return to it in more detail in Chap. 4, but for now the Z-machine can be thought of as providing a layer of abstraction on top of the CPU, giving an instruction set defined and implemented completely in software.

Z-machine games divided the computer's memory into three parts:

1. Mutable memory represented the current state of the game that would change as the game was played. Saving a game or restoring a saved game only involved this area.
2. Immutable resident memory contained code and data that always remained in memory, but was never altered. A frequently-used game element like the dictionary would be an obvious choice to place in this memory area.
3. Immutable nonresident memory could also not be changed, and all of it was not present in the computer's physical memory at once. Pages of this memory were read in from disk as required; in operating system parlance, this is called demand paging [32].

---

[13] This section is mostly based on [6] with details of the 'segment table' from [26].

It is this last memory area that is of interest here. The Z-machine's layer of abstraction from the real CPU meant that it could effectively monitor every memory access made by the game. A request that mapped to an already-loaded page could proceed; otherwise, the Z-machine would load the appropriate page from disk, creating room if necessary by overwriting another page of immutable nonresident memory. Taken together, the Z-machine was transparently providing the game with virtual memory, a memory address space larger than the physical memory the machine possessed. It may seem that the combination of virtual machine and reading from disk would present a substantial performance impediment, but text adventure games were not fast-paced to begin with. Infocom's own internal documentation says [26, p. 5] 'The design goal also requires no more than a few seconds response time for a typical move.'

As the games got larger over time and pictures joined the text, one game no longer equaled one disk, and the disks needed to be managed in addition to the memory. The Z-machine kept track of page-to-disk mappings using what Infocom called a 'segment table,' shown in Fig. 2.11. The final layer of swapping sometimes fell to the human, however, because discovering the disk number and location on disk was irrelevant if there was only one disk drive, and the wrong disk was in it.

Paging and virtual memory, with hardware support, are mainstays of modern commodity operating systems. Overlays were an evolutionary predecessor of virtual memory, and still have niche applications [18, 23].

2.3 Memory for State Information

Finally, we look at something contained in memory that is very important for games: state information. This is not the game code, but the game data that describes, for instance, where the player is located, what objects they're carrying, what the score is, where enemies are currently located, and so on. Obviously this will differ considerably depending on the game, and the ability to save and restore in-progress games must capture all or part of the state information.

From the programmer's point of view, game state is either statically or dynamically allocated. Static game state variables and structures are declared in the code and are assigned locations by the compiler, assembler, or linker. This is easy to program, albeit inflexible. Dynamic allocation defers allocation of space until the game is running, which gives more flexibility at the cost of more code to perform allocation and deallocation, and more space for allocation's bookkeeping overhead.

Approaches vary. It would be very surprising to find an Atari 2600 game that could afford the extra code or space to dynamically allocate its pittance of RAM. Even Infocom text adventures, for their seeming complexity, did not perform

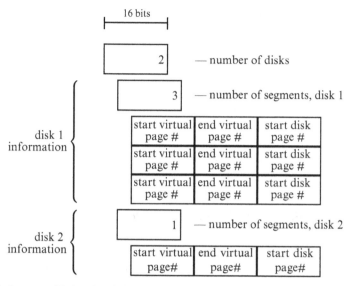

Fig. 2.11 Segment table in Infocom's Z-machine

dynamic allocation [6]. The Commodore 64 client for *Habitat* (1986), by contrast, had a best-fit dynamic memory allocator complete with garbage collection, all implemented in assembly language.[14]

If game state had to be saved on one platform and restored on a different platform, then the state information would have to convey the same meaning on both, regardless of how it was allocated. This is hampered by the fact that platforms may not share the same data representations; for example, the 6502 CPU stores 16-bit values in little-endian format with the low byte first, whereas the 6800 CPU is big-endian and would expect the same value with the high byte first. Pointers in data structures also present a problem, even on the same platform, because the pointers' memory addresses may no longer be valid when data is reloaded. The usual solution is to save data in a canonical form that is platform-neutral, a process called serialization.[15]

```
<tuple>
    <string>abc</string>
    <integer>42</integer>
    <float>123.45</float>
    <boolean>False</boolean>
</tuple>
```

Fig. 2.12 XML data representation

---

[14] Mentioned in [25, p. 76], and verified in the source code.

[15] Discussion of game data formats, including serialization and XML, may be found in [17].

As an example, consider the Python data

```
('abc', 42, 123.45, False)
```

This is a 4-tuple containing a string, an integer, a floating-point number, and a Boolean value, in that order. Figure 2.12 shows how this might be represented in XML format, textual and verbose. Figure 2.13 illustrates a more concise format that Python uses,[16] taking 27 bytes instead of the 123 bytes the XML occupies; each box in the figure shows the contents of one byte, where typewriter font indicates an ASCII character value used. Most lengths are converted into four-byte long little-endian values, even on machines where this is not the native representation.

2.3.1 Static Allocation: Saving and Restoring

Platform-agnostic game state representations were not the norm except as an occasional side effect. A virtual machine like Infocom's, abstracted from the real hardware, could impose a common representation across platforms.[17] The Z-machine design decision to corral dynamic game state into the one mutable memory area certainly made game saving and restoration easier, a fact they were well aware of: 'To "save" the game situation just requires writing this part of storage onto a disk or tape, and to "restore" is the opposite' [6, p. 87].

If the game state consists of statically-allocated structures and variables (without pointers), an alternative approach can be seen used by retrogames in BSD Unix distributions. An abstracted view of the key data structure behind this approach is in Fig. 2.14. This C code defines an array of structures, each with the address and the size of a piece of game state to save (and later, restore), that is initialized with a pointer to each structure and variable worth saving. It is a simple matter to write code that traverses each entry of this array in order and writes the indicated state to a file. This technique was used in 1983 for *Trek*, and by the last release of BSD Unix in 1993, others like *Adventure* had been rewritten to use this method as well.[18] The underlying assumption is that the saved game will be restored on exactly the same platform as the one on which it was saved, therefore blasting the data out in native binary form doesn't present any cross-platform compatibility issues.

---

[16] Python 2.6.6, using the `marshal` module, format version 0. Python is used here for expository reasons, but in fact the language dates back to 1991.

[17] An early paper claims that the Z-machine's integers are 16 bits, with 'the normal bit-level representation used by the hardware' [6, p. 83], but a much later reference with the advantage of hindsight notes that integers are in fact big-endian [36], which I verified on a *Zork I* game file.

[18] Confirmed in source. *Adventure* changed to this method between 4.3 BSD-Reno (1990) and 4.4 BSD (1993). *Rogue* in 4.3 BSD-Reno is conceptually similar, but hardcoded a sequence of writes for saving rather than using the more elegant array-based approach here.

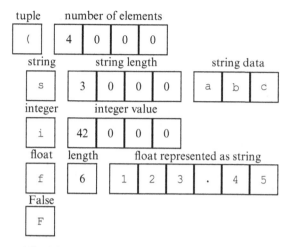

Fig. 2.13 Python serialized data representation

```
struct {
        void *address;
        unsigned int size;
} saveme[] = {
        &structure1,    sizeof(structure1),
        &structure2,    sizeof(structure2),
        ⋮
        &variable1,     sizeof(variable1),
        &variable2,     sizeof(variable2),
        ⋮
        NULL,           0
};
```

Fig. 2.14 An agenda for saving static state

2.3.2 Dynamic Allocation: Saving and Restoring

Dynamically-allocated game state presents a few more complications. Now, dynamic memory allocation is presented as an abstraction to the programmer: ask for memory, and ye shall receive. Memory allocation and deallocation (possibly via automatic garbage collection) is a "black box" whose details are hidden away. This was not always the case, though, and to understand how some retrogames saved and restored their state, we need to look more closely at dynamic memory allocation.

With dynamic allocation, the programmer requests memory of size N, and the allocator finds and reserves space of at least size N. The allocated memory resides in the heap,[19] an area of memory usually situated after the program and growing towards high memory. This arrangement is hinted at in Fig. 2.8.

Example 2.5 (Apple Pascal). For the Apple II, the first instalments of *Wizardry* (1981) were written in Apple Pascal,[20] as was *Sundog: Frozen Legacy* (1984).[21] They all made use of Apple Pascal's dynamic allocation facilities.

Apple Pascal's dynamic allocation support [2] had a NEW procedure for the programmer to request memory, but had no corresponding procedure to free memory later. The ability to explicitly allocate but not deallocate might imply that the language performed garbage collection; Apple Pascal did not. What it did provide were procedures called MARK and RELEASE. Before allocating memory, the programmer would call MARK to bookmark the current top of the heap. Allocation could then be done repeatedly using NEW, and to deallocate dynamically-allocated memory, the programmer would call RELEASE with the previously-obtained "bookmark" from MARK. Apple Pascal's RELEASE simply assigned that value to the top-of-heap pointer, deallocating *en masse* all the memory obtained from NEW.

This dynamic allocation scheme may seem crude, but does have advantages. Allocation is cheap, merely a matter of moving the top-of-heap pointer, and mass deallocation is a simple assignment to the top-of-heap pointer. Admittedly deallocation has coarse granularity, and a stack discipline is imposed on allocation and deallocation, but this is still useful in some applications. For instance, the data for a game level follows this pattern – allocate then deallocate at the end of the level – and is amenable to using this kind of "stack allocator" [17].

Arguably MARK and RELEASE forced a programmer to consider the heap directly and violate the abstraction layer built atop it by dynamic memory allocation. Now consider the approach to saving and restoring used in a 1987 version of *Trek73*; the same technique was employed as early as 1981 by *Rogue*.[22] This approach treated abstraction layers with all the subtlety of high explosives.

Figure 2.15 illustrates how it worked. The programmer declared a global variable with version information, knowing that the compiler and linker would allocate it statically in the game's data section, a part of the executable and memory used to store preinitialized data. More importantly, because of where they declared it in the code, the programmer expected it to be situated at the *beginning* of the data section. Gameplay would proceed normally, complete with any dynamic memory allocation. Later, to save the game state, the programmer would request the current top-of-heap

---

[19] This is not to be confused with heap data structures. The use of "heap" here only refers to a general memory area and doesn't imply anything about its structure or organization.

[20] Mentioned in [5, p. 72] for *Wizardry*, and verified in-emulator for *Wizardry*, *Wizardry II* (1982), and *Wizardry III* (1983). Later releases may use Apple Pascal too, but *Wizardry III* was so annoying to run that I'm finding it hard to care.

[21] Verified in-emulator. Use of Apple Pascal's dynamic allocation facilities by the games' P-code was checked with guidance from [3, 21] and a *Wizardry III* decompilation [16].

[22] Verified in source: the version of *Trek73* posted to the Usenet newsgroup comp.sources.games in 1987 (whose comments suggest the code in question was acquired from Berkeley in 1982) and *Rogue* 3.6.

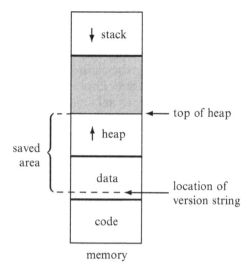

Fig. 2.15 Saving statically
and dynamically allocated
data

address and write out *all* memory contents from the version variable's location in
the data section to the top of the heap. This captured contents of both statically and
dynamically allocated memory, including anything the C language libraries might
have placed there. Restoring a game was the reverse: setting the top-of-heap pointer,
then reading saved data over top of everything from the version variable to the top
of the heap.[23] The number of assumptions that had to pan out in order for this to
work is breathtaking.

Why stop at the data and heap sections? Crowther & Woods' 1977 version of
Adventure for the PDP-10 reminded an exiting player to 'SAVE YOUR CORE-
IMAGE' which, in other words, means saving the entire address space of the game
including the code, that could be resumed later. This was carried through into
later implementations. The *Adventure* in 4.2 BSD Unix retained much of the structure of the original Fortran code, despite being rewritten in C.[24] Its manual page
remarks [35] 'Saving a game creates a large executable file instead of just the information needed to resume the game.' In this latter version's game code, a new executable was constructed for the player from four pieces: the original executable's
file header, with some low-level modifications; the original executable's code; the
current in-memory contents of the data section and heap; the message data for the
game, appended onto the end of the executable. Retrogame programmers clearly
needed to be conversant with more than just blocky pixels.

---

[23] In Unix, sbrk(0) gets the current top-of-heap location (cf. MARK) and brk() sets the top-of-
heap location (cf. RELEASE).

[24] Make of that statement what you will. Claims about both *Adventures*' properties in this regard
were verified in source, and the core image saving on the PDP-10 was tried in-emulator.

The Emacs text editor still uses this dump-and-restore technique,[25] although the details of modern virtual address spaces and executable file formats like ELF are insanely complicated. However, this allows Emacs Lisp code (an extension language in Emacs), that might otherwise be slow to load, to be preloaded and captured for quick startup later [37]. In a very real way, users of Emacs are running a core dump.

References

1. Andrews, M.: Commodore 128 Assembly Language Programming. Howard W. Sams & Co., Indianapolis (1986)
2. Apple Computer, Inc.: Apple Pascal Language Reference Manual. Apple Computer, Cupertino (1980)
3. Apple Computer, Inc.: Apple Pascal Operating System Reference Manual. Apple Computer, Cupertino (1980)
4. Apple Computer, Inc.: Apple II Reference Manual (for IIe only). Apple Computer, Cupertino (1982)
5. Barton, M.: Dungeons & Desktops: The History of Computer Role-Playing Games. A K Peters, Wellesley (2008)
6. Blank, M.S., Galley, S.W.: How to fit a large program into a small machine, or how to fit the Great Underground Empire on your desk-top. Creat. Comput. 6(7), 80–87 (1980)
7. Borland International: Turbo Pascal Version 3.0 Reference Manual. Borland International, Scotts Valley (1985)
8. Borland International: Turbo Pascal 6.0 Programmer's Guide. Borland International, Scotts Valley (1990)
9. Borland International: Turbo Pascal 7.0 Language Guide. Borland International, Scotts Valley (1992)
10. Braben, D.: Classic game postmortem: Elite. Game Developer's Conference. http://www.gdcvault.com/play/1014628/Classic-Game-Postmortem (2011)
11. Bucknall, J.: Gyre and gimble. .EXE Magazine 6(8), 68–76 (1992)
12. Budge, B.: Classic game postmortem: Pinball Construction Set. Game Developer's Conference. http://www.gdcvault.com/play/1018258/Classic-Game-Postmortem-Pinball-Construction (2013)
13. Commodore Business Machines, Inc.: Commodore 128 Programmer's Reference Guide. Bantam, Toronto (1986)
14. Commodore Computer: Commodore 64 Programmer's Reference Guide. Commodore Business Machines and Howard W. Sams & Co., Wayne/Indianapolis (1982)
15. Crane, D.: Classic game postmortem: Pitfall! Game Developer's Conference. http://www.gdcvault.com/play/1014632/Classic-Game-Postmortem-PITFALL (2011)
16. Ewers, T.W.: Wizardry_iii_SourceCode (27 Mar 2012)
17. Gregory, J.: Game Engine Architecture. A K Peters, Natick (2009)
18. He, H., Debray, S., Andrews, G.: The revenge of the overlay: Automatic compaction of OS kernel code via on-demand code loading. In: 7th ACM & IEEE International Conference on Embedded Software, Salzburg, pp. 75–83 (2007)

---

[25] Verified in the Emacs 24.3 source code.

19. Hewlett-Packard: 2000C: A Guide to Time-Shared BASIC (1971)
20. Horton, K.: Info About Cart Sizes and Bankswitching Methods (1997). V6.00
21. Kusche, W.: Apple II Pascal 1.1 P-code interpreter 6502 disassembly (c. 1990s)
22. Lampson, B.: Principles for Computer System Design. ACM Turing Award Lecture (1992). doi:10.1145/1283920.2159562
23. Levine, J.R.: Linkers & Loaders. Morgan Kaufmann, San Francisco (2000)
24. Liu, T., Xue, C.J., Li, M.: Joint variable partitioning and bank selection instruction optimization for partitioned memory architectures. ACM Trans. Embedded Comput. Syst. **12**(3), Article 76 (2013)
25. Lucasfilm: Habitat technology transfer seminar, Lucasfilm → Fujitsu (1988). Presentation slides
26. PKWARE, Inc.: APPNOTE.TXT – .ZIP file format specification. https://pkware.cachefly.net/webdocs/casestudies/APPNOTE.TXT (2014). Version 6.3.4
27. Radio Shack: Tandy Service Manual: Color Computer 3 NTSC/PAL Version with 512K Expansion RAM Card. Radio Shack (undated). Catalog number 26-3334
28. Sather, J.: Understanding the Apple II. Quality Software, Chatsworth (1983)
29. Sather, J.: Understanding the Apple IIe. Quality Software, Chatsworth (1985)
30. Scholz, B., Burgstaller, B., Xue, J.: Minimal placement of bank selection instructions for partitioned memory architectures. ACM Trans. Embedded Comput. Syst. **7**(2), Article 12 (2008)
31. Steinfeld, L., Ritt, M., Silveira, F., Carro, L.: Optimum design of a banked memory with power management for wireless sensor networks. Wireless Netw. **21**, 81–94 (2015)
32. Tanenbaum, A.S.: Modern Operating Systems, 2nd edn. Prentice Hall, Englewood Cliffs (2001)
33. Tepolt, L.A.: Assembly Language Programming For The COCO 3. TEPCO, Portsmouth (1987)
34. Unknown: TIA 1A television interface adaptor (model 1A) (undated). Labelled "Confidential," probably an internal Atari document
35. Various contributors: Adventure(6) Manual Page. 4.2 BSD Unix (1983)
36. Various contributors: The Z-Machine Standards Document (1997)
37. Various contributors: GNU Emacs internals. Version 24.3 source code, `internals.texi` (2013)

Chapter 3
Slow, Wildly Incompatible I/O

Retrogames that ran on home computers and game consoles gave the computer running the game code a direct, fast connection to user input devices (keyboard, joystick) and output display devices (monitor or television). This was not the case for all retrogames. Some ran on much larger computers, and the player played the game using a "dumb terminal," a text-based device with a monitor and keyboard whose sole purpose was this communication. The dumb terminal ran no game code; every player keystroke had to be transmitted from the terminal to the remote computer for processing by the game, and every character of the game shown on the dumb terminal's screen had to make the reverse journey.

There was a vast range of data transfer speeds to and from dumb terminals that somehow needed to be supported. It is a difficult notion to convey properly in the static text of a book, except through reader participation. With a stopwatch or countdown timer running, read every part of the passage below, quoted from [8]:

> Quo usque tandem abutere, Catilina, patientia nostra? Quam diu etiam furor iste tuus eludet? Quem ad finem sese effrenata jactabit audacia? Nihilne te nocturnum praesidium Palatii, nihil urbis vigiliae, nihil timor populi, nihil concursus bonorum omnium, nihil hic munitissimus habendi senatus locus, nihil horum ora vultusque moverunt. Patere tua consilia non sentis? Constrictam omnium horum scientia teneri conjurationem tuam non vides? Quid proxima, quid superiore nocte egeris, ubi fueris, quos convocaveris, quid consilii ceperis, quem nostrum ignorare arbitraris? O tempora, O mores! senatus haec intellegit, consul videt; hic tamen vivit. Vivit? immo vero etiam in senatum venit, fit publici consilii particeps, notat et designat oculis ad caedem unum quemque nostrum. Nos autem, viri fortes, satis facere rei publicae videmur, si istius furorem ac tela vitemus. Ad mortem te, Catilina, duci jussu consulis jam pridem oportebat, in te conferri pestem istam.

Reading the passage in 26 s corresponds to a data transfer rate of 300 baud, 6 s corresponds to 1200 baud, and less than a second is 9600 baud or higher. This particular text is almost exactly the same number of characters as half of an 80×24 screen. In other words, to redraw the full screen contents for a commonly-sized dumb terminal at a given baud rate would take *twice* as long as it did to read the quote. Updating the display of a game by completely redrawing the screen contents was clearly out of the question.

© Springer International Publishing Switzerland 2016
J. Aycock, *Retrogame Archeology*, DOI 10.1007/978-3-319-30004-7_3

Fortunately dumb terminals were not quite *that* dumb. Many had the capability to clear the screen, or position the cursor at a particular location, or clear to the end of a line, for example. The problems were threefold. First, the terminals didn't always have the same capabilities. Second, the terminals' features were triggered by the computer sending special codes, but they weren't the same codes for each terminal type. Third, there were a lot of different types of terminals.

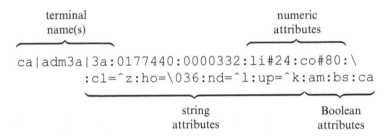

Fig. 3.1 `ttycap` entry for ADM-3A terminal, c. 1977, from 1 BSD Unix

But before games come tools to make games, which is where the story starts. Around 1977 at Berkeley, a person named Bill Joy was building a full-screen editor called `vi` for dumb terminals, a descendant of which I am using to write this text. Faced with the dumb terminal problems above, one programming solution would be to hardcode support for each and every terminal into the editor. Joy took a different path. He extracted the information about these terminals into a separate system database of sorts, and programmed a library to access and use this information,[1] a library that could be used by `vi` and any other program that might need to perform elaborate feats with dumb terminals. The resulting database was called `ttycap`, an example entry of which is shown in Fig. 3.1 for the ADM-3A terminal. The terminal name and any aliases it went by came first. Numeric attributes, here the number of `lines` and `columns`, could be specified. String-valued attributes were commands that, if sent to the terminal, would cause it to perform a specific function such as `clear` the screen or move the cursor to the home position. The string attributes could be written for greater readability, like "`^z`" for Control-Z and "`\036`" for the character having octal value 36. Finally, Boolean attributes could be present that acted as flags; "ca," for example, means that the terminal's cursor can be moved, but doesn't give any information as to how that might be accomplished.

By 1979, `ttycap` had become `termcap`,[2] a database that is still present on some modern Unix systems. Figure 3.2 shows `termcap` entries for the ADM-3A (for comparison) and the much more elaborate DEC VT100 (still a widely-emulated terminal type). More features could be specified in `termcap`: for the ADM-3A

---

[1] Verified in 1 BSD source. Historical aspects are from [23, 26], although they omit mention of the `ttycap` evolutionary step. The actual `ttycap` entry for the ADM-3A was a single line, but Joy's library code supported the line continuations shown in the figure.

[2] Verified in 2 BSD source.

```
adm3a|3a|lsi adm3a:\
        :am:do=^J:le=^H:bs:cm=\E=%+ %+ :cl=1^Z:co#80:ho=^^:\
        :li#24:ma=^K^P:nd=^L:up=^K:

vt100|dec-vt100|vt100-am|vt100am|dec vt100:\
        :do=^J:co#80:li#24:cl=50\E[;H\E[2J:sf=2*\ED:\
        :le=^H:bs:am:cm=5\E[%i%d;%dH:nd=2\E[C:up=2\E[A:\
        :ce=3\E[K:cd=50\E[J:so=2\E[7m:se=2\E[m:us=2\E[4m:\
        :ue=2\E[m:md=2\E[1m:mr=2\E[7m:mb=2\E[5m:me=2\E[m:\
        :is=\E[1;24r\E[24;1H:if=/usr/share/tabset/vt100:\
        :rs=\E>\E[?3l\E[?4l\E[?5l\E[?7h\E[?8h:ks=\E[?1h\E=:\
        :ke=\E[?1l\E>:ku=\EOA:kd=\EOB:kr=\EOC:kl=\EOD:kb=^H:\
        :ho=\E[H:k1=\EOP:k2=\EOQ:k3=\EOR:k4=\EOS:pt:sr=2*\EM:\
        :vt#3:xn:sc=\E7:rc=\E8:cs=\E[%i%d;%dr:
```

Fig. 3.2 `termcap` entries for ADM-3A and VT100 terminals, from 4.4 BSD Unix; see Appendix A for legal information

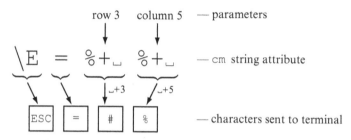

Fig. 3.3 Parameter usage in `termcap` entries; ⌴ indicates a space character

entry, the clear screen command has become "1^Z" where the "1" adds a 1 ms delay when issuing that command. Cursor motion commands could now be specified, albeit in a curious fashion. The "cm" entry for cursor motion allowed parameters to be given for the row and column, and the "%+" incorporated each parameter value by adding it to the character value after the "%+", namely the space (Fig. 3.3).

The vt100 entry, besides showcasing how elaborate termcap descriptions can get, has even more involved string attributes. On the last line, the "cs" attribute uses the command "%i" that adds one to a parameter's value, and "%d" formats a parameter as C's printf would. Terminal descriptions are essentially expressed using a small, terse, domain-specific programming language, and any program wanting to employ them needed code to appropriately select and use terminal attributes from the database.

The accompanying termcap manual page confesses that its use at the time was for editors and support programs [30]: '*Termcap* is a data base describing terminals used primarily by *ex* (UCB) and *vi* (UCB), and also by *tset* (UCB).' This was about to change.

3.1 Curses

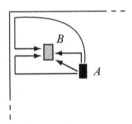

Fig. 3.4 Moving the cursor
from point *A* to point *B*

A library called "curses" was created by Ken Arnold that leveraged the `termcap` database along with, quite literally, some of Bill Joy's editor code for efficient cursor motion [4]. Cursor motion was 'The most difficult thing to do properly' [4, p. 5] and, to understand why, consider the diagram in Fig. 3.4. Say the cursor is at point *A* and it needs to be moved to point *B*. What is the optimal way to do this in terms of time and the number of characters sent to the terminal?

- Move the cursor up, then left.
- Move the cursor to the top of the screen, then down.
- Move the cursor to the leftmost column of the line, up one line, then tab in.
- Issue a direct cursor movement command.

Now, recall that all terminals won't have all the above capabilities, and some may have delays required for certain commands, and the complexity of this seemingly simple problem becomes apparent. A dumb terminal only places characters where its cursor is, making the cursor's location of paramount interest. Less than optimal cursor motion would be painfully obvious to a user watching the cursor plod along their terminal screen at a low baud rate.

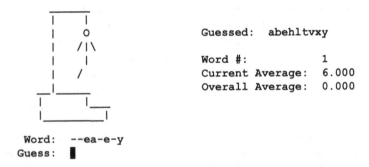

Fig. 3.5 *Hangman* on BSD Unix, emboldened for legibility, with cursor shown at bottom; see Appendix A for legal information

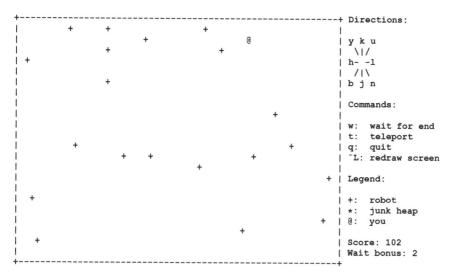

```
+--------------------------------------------------------+ Directions:
|        +      +         +                         |
|                  +              @                 | y k u
|                  +                  +             |  \|/
| +                                                 | h- -l
|                                                   |  /|\
|                  +                                | b j n
|                                                   |
|                                          +        | Commands:
|                                                   |
|                                                   | w:  wait for end
|        +                                  +       | t:  teleport
|            +   +                 +                | q:  quit
|                         +                         | ^L: redraw screen
|                                                   |
|                                             +     | Legend:
|                                                   |
| +                                                 | +:  robot
|                                                   | *:  junk heap
|                                      +            | @:  you
|                                                   |
| +                              +                  | Score: 102
|                                                   | Wait bonus: 2
+--------------------------------------------------------+
```

Fig. 3.6 *Robots* on BSD Unix, emboldened for legibility; see Appendix A for legal information

What the curses library did for the programmer was to hide all this detail and more. The result was a high-level interface to command different terminals that was, and is, very easy to use from a programming standpoint.[3] Now full-screen games could be written for dumb terminals. Figure 3.5 shows *Hangman* (1983), which has cursor motion between the input prompt, the word, the letters guessed, and parts of the ill-fated stickman on the gallows. *Robots* (1980) has more cursor activity, with the player (@) and all the robots (+) moving each turn; see Fig. 3.6. *Rogue* (1980) was another game that reaped the benefits of curses.

Figure 3.7 gives an example curses program. Line 4 tells curses to initialize itself. Line 5 clears the screen, and text is placed at specific rows and columns by the two pairs of lines at 7–8 and 9–10. For reasons explained below, no screen updates happen until the call to `refresh` at line 11. In fact, if that line is missing, this program will run and have no visible output at all. Finally, line 13 tells curses to shut down and restore the screen to a sensible state if necessary. Notice that there is no code that deals with specific terminals, or even the name of the terminal type – curses handles it all.

To make screen updating better overall, screen update commands issued to curses are not reflected on the terminal immediately. This allows curses freedom to perform more global optimization of cursor movement and updates. In *Robots*, for instance, a naive approach to moving all the robots is to send the terminal's cursor to each one and update them individually. However, there will be a number of consecutive + characters once the robots cluster together, and a global view of the screen data can spot that and move the cursor only once to update many robots.

---

[3] A visualization I wrote to help analyze a retrogame for this book used curses on a visualization wall that provided 1580 columns and 356 rows of text.

```
1   #include <curses.h>
2
3   int main() {
4           initscr();
5           clear();
6
7           move(10, 7);
8           addstr("Hello");
9           move(13, 15);
10          addstr("world!");
11          refresh();
12
13          endwin();
14          return 0;
15  }
```

Fig. 3.7 A sample curses program and its output

Curses thus keeps two in-memory representations of the screen. One is curscr, an internal representation of what the terminal screen's contents *should* be. This may or may not be accurate, but a program has no way to know the actual state of a dumb terminal's screen; there may be transmission errors, or output from other running programs may have been blasted on the terminal's screen. Many full-screen programs for dumb terminals include an option so the user can request a screen redraw for this reason (see ˆL in Fig. 3.6). Besides curscr, curses has stdscr, its internal representation of what the screen should be changed to upon the next call to refresh. These two screen representations are used by curses to compute the differences, i.e., the smallest set of screen updates it can find to change stdscr into curscr. The goal is to minimize cursor motion and characters output to the terminal.

Abstracting away details, pseudocode for the screen refresh algorithm used by early versions of curses is given in Fig. 3.8.[4] Differences were looked for only between corresponding lines, a search optimized by keeping track of the first and last characters on a line that had changed. The nested loop in updateline may seem redundant, but there could be multiple sequences of changed *and* unchanged characters within a single line. The algorithm also watches for opportunities to take shortcuts, such as clearing to the end of the line rather than outputting numerous spaces.

As an example, say that a line in curscr contains (showing spaces explicitly):

HELLO␣WORLD␣␣␣

and the same line in stdscr is updated to instead read

HELP!␣␣␣␣␣␣␣␣␣␣

---

[4] Based on 4.2 BSD Unix source; the update algorithm was fairly similar between 4 BSD and 4.3 BSD.

```
foreach line j in stdscr:
    if stdscr[j] changed:
        updateline(stdscr[j], curscr[j])
        mark stdscr[j] unchanged

def updateline(stdline, curline):
    i = first changed character in stdline
    last = last changed character in stdline
    while i ≤ last:
        if curline[i] ≠ stdline[i]:
            move cursor to that spot on the line
            while curline[i] ≠ stdline[i] and i ≤ last:
                if rest of stdline is blank:
                    output clear-to-end-of-line code
                    change rest of curline to blank
                    return
                else:
                    output stdline[i]
                    curline[i] = stdline[i]
                    i = i + 1
        else:
            i = i + 1
```

Fig. 3.8 Pseudocode for curses' screen update algorithm

A refresh would leave the HEL alone, move the terminal's cursor right after it to write P !, followed by the terminal's code to clear to the end of the line.

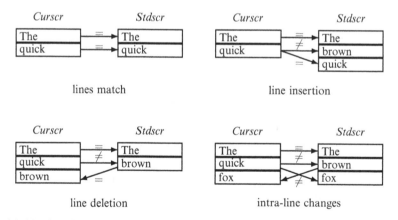

Fig. 3.9 Line insertion and deletion cases

This algorithm's view is limited to changes within individual lines, and does nothing to capture entire lines moving around. While this is probably sufficient for

Rogue and *Robots*, it can be improved.[5] Many dumb terminals are able to insert and delete whole lines, and to take advantage of that the refresh algorithm would need to spot whole-line differences. As Fig. 3.9 shows, there are four cases to consider, assessing each line from top to bottom of the screen. The first case is where the lines match. (In practice, each line would have a hash value or other unique identifier for efficient comparison, rather than comparing lines character by character.) Second comes insertion: when corresponding lines don't match, stdscr's later lines can be searched for the line in question, which also reveals how many lines need to be inserted. Third, if the insertion check fails, there may have been one or more lines deleted. The mismatching line from stdscr is searched for in curscr to discover if this is the case. Fourth, if neither insertion nor deletion is detected, then the algorithm reverts to making intra-line updates as before.

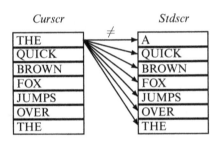

Curscr   *Stdscr*

Fig. 3.10 Insertion troubles

Formally, transforming one screen into another can be seen as a variant of the string-to-string correction problem [11], the success of which can be measured in terms of the "edit distance," roughly the number of editing steps it takes to change one string into another [31]. Besides screen updates, this same formal problem crops up in areas like file comparison and spelling correction [18], in addition to areas as seemingly far-flung as computational biology [12]. Any algorithm can potentially have worst-case behaviors, however, and the line insertion and deletion algorithm just described has some bad failure cases. Figure 3.10 gives one: the algorithm would find a mismatch on the first line, then search for an insertion point to resynchronize, to locate one at the very bottom of stdscr. The net result is a six-line insertion and needless redrawing of five lines, all for what is actually a one-line change. Newer versions of curses address this by keeping track of lines in stdscr as they are moved, rather than trying to guess how lines have moved after the fact.[6]

Efficient screen updates might seem like a historical curiosity, but as a general principle, it can often be much less work or consume much less bandwidth to perform updates with differences rather than using a new, updated version in its entirety. This idea was applied beyond dumb terminals within the retrogame era.

Example 3.1 (Keen Dreams, 1992). Kushner's story of Id Software, the people that eventually produced *Doom* (1993), recounts a watershed moment in their game tech-

---

[5] This discussion is based on the cases from [9, pp. 102–104].

[6] For example, ncurses 5.9.

nology [19, p. 49]: 'What if, Carmack thought, instead of redrawing everything, I could figure out a way to redraw only the things that actually change?' Exploiting differences found its way into Id's pre-*Doom* offering, the *Commander Keen* series on MS-DOS. By keeping an array of flags tracking bitmap tiles that required updating, their graphics code could limit copying 'from the master screen to the current screen' to only those tiles. The array also gave an easy way to separate single-tile copying from multi-tile copying by peeking ahead to the next flag, allowing different optimized code to be invoked for each case.[7]

Depending on the computing capability of the device on the receiving end of differences – dumb terminals had none, of course – differences can be combined with compression for even more gains.

Compressed differences, or "deltas," are used for updates by operating systems [10] and anti-virus software [5, 17], for example. In the case of binary executables, computing the differences between two binaries and then compressing the difference information can be many orders of magnitude smaller than compression alone [25, 27].

3.2 Flexibility via External Data

Ttycap and termcap are examples of another general principle, that of gaining flexibility by using external data. "External data" could, in this case, be thought of as the programmer externalizing or factoring out data from a game that would normally be hardcoded or built in. This gives us a design spectrum for game code, one that is not linked to age or game evolution, but is indicative of different program design choices. Four models, points along the design spectrum, are illustrated in Fig. 3.11.

3.2.1 Model A: Monolithic

Not much needs to be said about Model A, as it is in some ways the "natural" way to consider implementing a game. This first model is where the game code and its data are a monolithic, inseparable entity. The perfect embodiment of this in retrogames, both physically and conceptually, is the game cartridge that contains code and data as a single discrete unit.

---

[7] As seen in *Keen Dreams* source code, quote from comments in both id_rf_a.asm and id_vw_ae.asm.

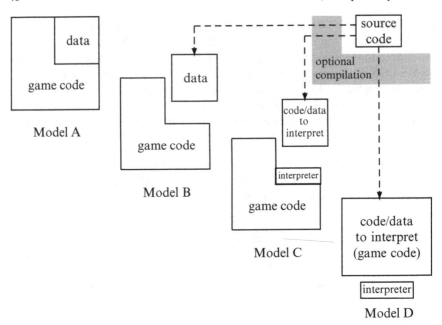

Fig. 3.11 A game code design spectrum

3.2.2 Model B: Interchangeable Data

Model B moves away from being strictly monolithic, with at least part of a game's data being factored out. One hunk of game data becomes interchangeable with another hunk of game data; the game code uses the data but does little if anything in terms of interpreting the data, compared to later models. Changing data around can be done without recompiling or reassembling game code, underscoring the independence of the two.

Example 3.2 (Ttycap). The `ttycap` database factored information about dumb terminals out from code into a single system-wide repository, but there was no meaningful interpretation of the collected information beyond that.[8] Numeric and Boolean attributes held information for the program; string attributes were commands the program would send to the terminal verbatim to perform specific functions. The big implementation advantage was that a single program could work with many different terminals, including terminals that did not exist when the program was written and compiled, without having to hardcode special cases for each one into the program.

A program working with externalized data must have some way to select it, a database key. For `ttycap`, there were two: the terminal name to choose a `ttycap`

---

[8] Verified in `ttycap` library manual page and source code.

entry, and then the two-character names of individual attributes within the entry. *Doom* generalized this notion, making its database akin to a simple read-only filesystem.

Example 3.3 (Doom). Game data in *Doom* was stored in external "WAD" files, e.g., DOOM1.WAD. It has been suggested that WAD stands for "Where's All the Data?" [13, 19] but this is a backronym – it was simply an off-the-cuff answer to the question 'what's a bunch of lumps?' [14, 4:56] where a lump was the name used for a hunk of game data in their previous games.[9]

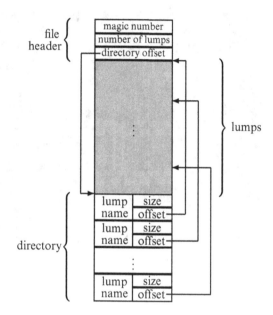

Fig. 3.12 WAD file structure in *Doom*

The structure of a WAD file is shown in Fig. 3.12. A file header contained three parts: a "magic number" identifying the file type, in this case one of the four-byte ASCII sequences IWAD or PWAD; the number of total lumps (pieces) of data in the WAD file; the file offset to the WAD's directory information. The directory was an array of structures, one structure per lump, each containing an eight-byte lump name, the lump's size, and the lump's offset within the WAD file. This suggests that *Doom* used the lump names as keys, but this was only partially true – level data, for example, was expected to have lumps in a certain order, and as a result some lump names were effectively ignored and were not unique. In these cases, a zero-length "pseudo-lump" name acted as a marker to locate the start of a level's lumps in the directory, e.g., E1M1 to locate episode 1, map 1.[10]

---

[9] Confirmed in *Keen Dreams* source code.

[10] From *Doom* source code analysis and construction of a WAD dumping tool.

Separating game data from the game code makes the game code transition into more of a generic game "engine" and facilitates game modification, or modding, where players can alter aspects of a game. The *Doom* developers encouraged this through their design [19], and there are *Doom* game level editors galore, but they were certainly not the first to provide level-editing functionality.

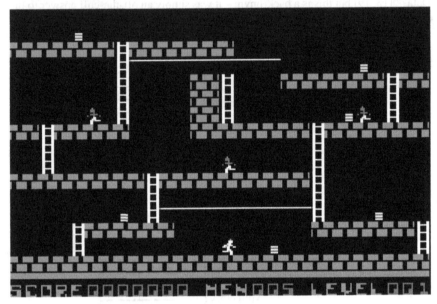

Fig. 3.13 *Lode Runner* on the Apple II (Image ©Tozai, Inc., used with permission; see Appendix A for additional legal information)

Example 3.4 (Lode Runner, 1983). *Lode Runner* was an early retrogame that came with a level editor. On the Apple II disk, each level's data was padded out to be 256 bytes, the size of one disk sector, making individual levels easy to access using the level number as the key.

Figure 3.13 is a screenshot of the first level of *Lode Runner*. The objective is for the player (the figure at center bottom) to collect the gold (squares) and avoid being captured by the non-player characters, or NPCs (the three figures higher up on the screen). The grid for each level is 28 columns by 16 rows, and each grid cell can contain one of ten items; that means that each cell's contents can be encoded in a nibble,[11] and two cells' contents can be stored in one byte. In total, one level's data fits in 224 bytes.

The data representing this first level is given in Fig. 3.14. When represented in hexadecimal, the two digits of each byte's value shows its two nibbles, making the encoding fairly straightforward to see – the player and NPCs are highlighted in the

---

[11] One nibble, also written nybble, consists of four bits. It can hold $2^4 = 16$ different values.

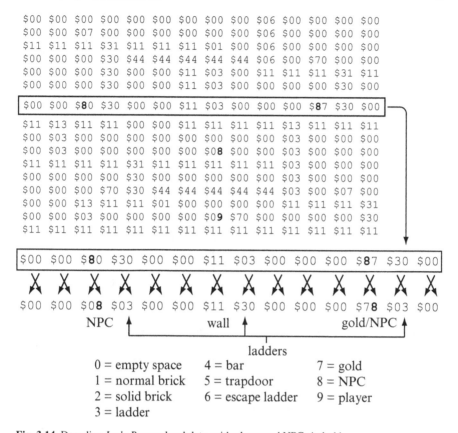

Fig. 3.14 Decoding *Lode Runner* level data, with player and NPCs in bold

data as reference points. The seventh row, the row on the screen with two NPCs, has the encoding broken down. Each byte's nibbles are actually swapped to arrive at the cell order onscreen, and then each nibble's value can be mapped to the cell contents with the values shown at the bottom of the figure.[12]

3.2.3 Model C: Partial Interpretation

With Model C, we see some of the code morph into data. The majority of the game code stays intact and implemented in a traditional manner, such as in assembly code or C. However, some of the responsibilities that would have formerly been hard-coded the same way are factored out from the game code proper in this model. The factored code is expressed in a new language that is interpreted and, for this reason,

---

[12] I used an analysis of Commodore 64 *Lode Runner* level data as a guide [6], and verified it on the Apple II version with a program I wrote that extracted and reconstructed the levels.

the game code must be enhanced with an interpreter that can make sense of the new language. This model is not frequently seen in most retrogame genres; interpretation adds overhead that would be intolerable for game code already struggling to keep up.

Example 3.5 (Termcap). Termcap expands on ttycap by performing rudimentary interpretation of the string attributes in dumb terminals' termcap entries [30]. The interpreter itself was not directly part of any termcap-based retrogames; it was located in the termcap library routines.[13] Besides implementing padding delays specified in string attributes, parameters (e.g., row and column numbers) could be substituted into strings, have limited arithmetic operations applied to them, or be part of simple conditional expressions.

One game genre that does see partial interpretation is the niche of programming games, where the player plays the game vicariously by writing programs to act on their behalf. This genre has a long history even by retrogame standards. The programming game *Darwin* was played in 1961 on an IBM 7090 mainframe, for example [3, 22]. (Game history aficionados will note that that places it earlier than *Spacewar* (1962), an example invariably raised when discussing early games.)

Example 3.6 (RobotWar, 1981). Set in the 'future' of 2002 [24], the programming game *RobotWar* for the Apple II had the player write programs to control robots that battled one another for supremacy in a game arena the game simulated. A robot program's source code was assembled into 'object code' that was interpreted. Figure 3.15 gives an example of robot source code for a robot that employs a "run-and-gun" strategy, randomly and continuously moving while it scans for other robots, firing at any it finds.[14] The minutia of controlling robots is less of interest than the language design, which owes a lot to BASIC. In particular, the GOTO and GOSUB are drawn directly from it, with ENDSUB acting as a RETURN statement. The TO is an assignment of a value *to* a variable, and also hints at a possible COBOL influence. There is a fairly direct mapping of program statements into object code; this example assembles into 30 low-level object code instructions.

Of course, as computers became faster, this allowed on-the-fly partial interpretation to be added to faster-paced games.

Example 3.7 (Quake, 1996). *Quake* admittedly pushes the envelope of the span of years we're claiming for retrogames. However, it is instructive to see what such a language would look like. Figure 3.16 gives an example of *Quake*'s language,[15] called QuakeC, which was compiled to instructions that were then interpreted. At first glance, a lot of the syntax is drawn directly from C: the comments, the use of braces, and various statement types. Lines 5–8, however, are actually directives that

---

[13] Confirmed in 2 BSD termlib source code.

[14] Placing 4–5 of these in the arena has the visual effect of a drunken, heavily-armed ballet troupe.

[15] Created based on QuakeC language documentation [29], and run through two different QuakeC compilers to check for errors.

```
]    200 TO RANDOM
] LOOP
]    GOSUB MOVE
]    GOSUB SCANFIRE
]    GOTO LOOP
] MOVE
]    RANDOM - 100 TO SPEEDX
]    RANDOM - 100 TO SPEEDY
]    ENDSUB
] SCANFIRE
]    0 TO AIM
] SCANLOOP
]    AIM TO RADAR
]    IF RADAR < 0 GOTO FIRE
]    AIM + 90 TO AIM
]    IF AIM = 0 ENDSUB
]    GOTO SCANLOOP
] FIRE
]    0 - RADAR TO SHOT
]    ENDSUB
```

Fig. 3.15 Robot source code for *RobotWar*

could be embedded into QuakeC source files for a *Quake* utility program, making this an embedded language inside an embedded language. Lines 10–19 show some syntactic sugar in QuakeC, a shorthand way to express transitions between frames (here, a three-frame cycle) and associated per-frame code to execute. A more traditional computation is illustrated in lines 26–30, to demonstrate the slightly unusual function declaration syntax. The integer Fibonacci function uses floating point numbers here because QuakeC had a selection of data types specialized for the game, and floats were used in place of integers and Boolean values.

3.2.4 Model D: Full Interpretation

The final step along the design spectrum is Model D, where the entire game is implemented in an interpreted language. All that remains in native code is an interpreter and, compared to Model C, the native code base shrinks substantially. Previously the focus has been on being able to swap data for other data, and certainly that is still the case – one native interpreter engine can be re-used for different games' interpreted code. A notable difference is that the *interpreter* can be changed for another one too, yielding a very flexible design.

Example 3.8 (Infocom). Infocom's Z-machine games are an excellent example of Model D and its advantages. Many different games (all expressed as interpreted Z-machine code) could run on the same Z-machine interpreter for a platform, and

```
1    /*
2     *   Commands for model definitions
3     */
4
5    $cd /quake/models/super
6    $origin 0 42 0
7    $scale 2
8    $frame frm_super1 frm_super2 frm_super3
9
10   void() super1 = [ $frm_super1, super2 ] {
11           if (random() < 0.1) {
12                   // whistle annoyingly at max volume
13                   sound(self, CHAN_VOICE,
14                           "sounds/whistle.wav",
15                           1.0, ATTN_NORM);
16           }
17   };
18   void() super2 = [ $frm_super2, super3 ] { };
19   void() super3 = [ $frm_super3, super1 ] { };
20
21   /*
22    *   Everyone needs to compute Fibonacci numbers
23    *   during a deathmatch, obviously
24    */
25
26   float(float n) fib = {
27           if (n == 0) return 0;
28           if (n == 1) return 1;
29           return fib(n - 1) + fib(n - 2);
30   };
```

Fig. 3.16 QuakeC source code example

creating a Z-machine interpreter for a new platform allowed Infocom's library of games to run on it. This gave their games a high degree of portability,[16] which was especially important given the diversity of platforms in the early retrogame era. For Infocom games and others that took a similar approach, time has shown this to be a future-proof strategy too, as decades-old game data files can be resurrected to run using modern interpreters.

As we started seeing with Model C, once interpretation is added, there is a shift in focus to the interpreted language as more of the game code moves into this form. How would game programmers express themselves in the interpreted game language? It is rare to see this view, because these languages tended to be internal and proprietary. There are numerous cases where it's widely known that an interpreted

---

[16] They mentioned this early on with respect to *Zork* [7, 20].

language was used, and there are modern tools to run the games' interpreted code (i.e., the compiled version of it that was distributed with the game), but no one knows what the code looked like to the programmers.

Example 3.9 (Platt's Adventure, 1979). Dave Platt's re-implementation of *Adventure* introduced a domain-specific language that was compiled into an interpreted 'A-code.' Figure 3.17 contains the source code in this language for a very simple game that will be used as a running example. The game consists of one location (a phone booth), one object (a phone), and one verb (look); its stimulating gameplay is shown in Fig. 3.18.

The source may appear lengthy for such a limited game, but a lot of this is infrastructure that, once in place, can be easily added to with richer game content.[17] Lines 1–3 are declarations, followed by the location and its textual description (lines 5–6), the messages the game outputs (lines 8–11), and the object and its description (lines 13–14). Lines 16–18 define how to respond to the player looking at the phone, which can be expressed more generally for more complex games with many objects. Looking about the current location is handled by lines 19–26: HERE is a reference to the current place, so "SAY HERE" prints out the current place's description. The ITOBJ is the start of a loop that iterates over game objects, and the IFNEAR conditional filters out only those objects that are near to the player (i.e., in the current location). Using NAME as opposed to SAY for output allows parameter substitution – the object's name is filled in at the string's "#" placeholder.

The entry point for the game's code is INITIAL at line 28. Line 29 moves the phone object into its starting location, and line 30 moves the player into their location. Finally, lines 32–38 are repeated indefinitely to get the input (which is parsed to identify nouns and verbs) and dispatch to an appropriate handler (line 34).

Example 3.10 (Infocom's ZIL). It may seem odd that Infocom appears a second time as a Model D example, but their language warrants its own separate look. Infocom games were implemented in an in-house language known as ZIL, for Zork Implementation Language, that was derived from a more elaborate language named MDL [7]. Figure 3.19 shows what the phone booth game would look like in ZIL. The language's Lisp heritage [7, 21] is plainly apparent with the abundance of parentheses and angle brackets, especially on line 16. GO is the entry point for the code, and this routine establishes the current location and the whereabouts of the player (lines 18–19), does the initial LOOK on line 20, then goes to the main game loop. This loop (lines 14–16) repeatedly calls the parser and, if there are no errors, invokes code to perform the player's command. The phone booth "room" (lines 1–4) has a description to print and various other attributes, like the fact that the room is lit. Lines 6–11 define the phone: it has both short and long descriptions (the latter is

---

[17] More elaborate games' source unfortunately doesn't easily fit into a smallish figure. I developed and ran them all through a modern A-code interpreter for verification.

```
1    VARIABLE  I
2    SYNON     14,VERB
3    VERB      LOOK
4
5    PLACE     BOOTH
6              You are in a telephone booth.
7
8    TEXT      WHAT?
9              Huh?
10   TEXT      THEREISA
11             There is a # here.
12
13   OBJECT    PHONE
14             The phone is a robust contraption with a rotary dial.
15
16   ACTION    LOOK PHONE
17             SAY PHONE
18             QUIT
19   ACTION    LOOK
20             SAY HERE
21             ITOBJ I
22                 IFNEAR I
23                     NAME THEREISA,I
24                 FIN
25             EOI
26             QUIT
27
28   INITIAL
29             APPORT PHONE,BOOTH
30             GOTO BOOTH
31   REPEAT
32             INPUT
33             BIT ARG1,VERB
34                 CALL ARG1
35             ELSE
36                 SAY WHAT?
37             FIN
38             QUIT
```

Fig. 3.17 Phone booth game code

printed when the player looks directly at the phone), and the synonym and adjective attributes permit more freedom in expression. A player can "look at the phone" as well as "look at the rotary telephone," for instance.[18]

---

[18] Constructing accurate ZIL examples is tricky because no full game source has ever been released, only an internal ZIL training manual [16]. I have written this example as faithfully as possible to that specification, and checked it using a modern ZIL compiler and Z-code interpreter. LIGHTBIT should actually be ONBIT, but the modern ZIL system uses LIGHTBIT and it makes more sense semantically, so I have retained that one incompatibility.

```
? xyzzy
Huh?
? look
You are in a telephone booth.

There is a phone here.
? look phone
The phone is a robust contraption with a rotary dial.
?
```

Fig. 3.18 Playing the phone booth game; user input is in bold

```
1    <ROOM PHONE-BOOTH
2          (LOC ROOMS)
3          (DESC "You are in a telephone booth.")
4          (FLAGS LIGHTBIT)>
5
6    <OBJECT PHONE
7          (LOC PHONE-BOOTH)
8          (DESC "phone")
9          (SYNONYM PHONE TELEPHONE)
10         (ADJECTIVE ROTARY)
11         (LDESC "The phone is a ... with a rotary dial.")>
12
13   <ROUTINE MAIN-LOOP ()
14         <REPEAT ()
15               <COND (<PARSER>
16                     <PERFORM ,PRSA ,PRSO ,PRSI>)>>>
17   <ROUTINE GO ()
18         <SETG HERE ,PHONE-BOOTH>
19         <MOVE ,PLAYER ,HERE>
20         <V-LOOK>
21         <MAIN-LOOP>>
```

Fig. 3.19 Phone booth game code in ZIL

Finally, we discover more Model D examples if we extend the notion of programming language into a more generalized idea, that of a system for game development.

Example 3.11 (Scott Adams). Scott Adams' text adventure games interpreted data files that were akin to other Model D games' interpreted object code. Figure 3.20 gives an excerpt of the data file for the phone booth game.[19] (Suggestions of movement commands in the data file might seem odd for a game that has no movement, but certain elements were mandatory in Adams' data files.) This would be a daunting

---

[19] I wrote infrastructure code allowing me to produce this and other games whose operation was verified on a modern interpreter. Decoding of the data file format was guided by [1, 2, 28].

```
0  0  0  19  1  1  1  0  3  0  1  1

2857
   0  0  0  0  0
   150  0

"AUT"
"ANY"
"G"
"NOR"
"*GO"
"SOU"
"*WAL"
"EAS"
"*RUN"
"WES"
   .
   .
   .
"LOO"
"  "

0  0  0  0  0  0  "holding room for objects"
0  0  0  0  0  0  "telephone booth."

"  "

"The phone is a robust contraption with a rotary dial."

"phone/PHONE/"  1

"  "

0  0  0
```

Fig. 3.20 Sample data file for a Scott Adams game

task to produce manually. Adams used a menu-driven program written in BASIC to produce these data files, and the programmer's view of game creation is shown in Fig. 3.21.[20]

---

[20] The code for this was kindly supplied by Scott Adams.

```
MENU:
1-EDIT ITEMS 2-BUILD ITEMS. MAX 60
3-EDIT COMMANDS 4-BUILD COMMANDS. MAX 151
5-EDIT ROOMS 6-BUILD ROOMS. MAX 33
7 EDIT VOCAB 8-BUILD VOCAB. MAX 59
9-EDIT MESSAGES 10-BUILD MESAGES.  MAX 71
11 SAVE FILE 12-VERIF Y FILE 13-STRING SPACE USED/LEFT
14 LIST ADVENTURE 15 CHANGE ADVENTURE NUMBER NOW 2
16-EXIT
17-XREF
18-CHANGE TABLE SIZES / VERSION:  0
19-RUN ADVENTURE.
?
```

Fig. 3.21 Programmer view of a Scott Adams game

All of these design models see use by modern programs in general, not just games. Model B is used by internationalized programs that have their strings extracted out to allow one language to be exchanged for another. A program refers to output strings using unique database keys like numbers (e.g., POSIX NLS) or strings (e.g., GNU gettext); translation data is specified in separate files that are "compiled" into binary format data files that the program uses. This separation of program resources for localization can be seen as far back as Apple Macintosh development in 1981 [15]. Model C manifests itself frequently in game and non-game programs as embedded languages, from extension languages in office application suites to general-purpose languages like Lua, Python, and Tcl embedded in programs. Arguably the most successful language embedding of all time is HTML and JavaScript in modern web browsers. As for Model D, many widely used (scripting) programming languages are implemented using interpreters, the topic of the next chapter.

References

1. Adams, S.: An adventure in small computer game simulation. Creative Comput. **5**(8), 90–97 (1979)
2. Adams, S.: Pirate's adventure. Byte **5**(12), 192–212 (1980)
3. $\aleph_0$: Darwin. Softw. – Pract. Exp. **2**, 93–96 (1972)
4. Arnold, K.C.R.C.: Screen updating and cursor motion optimization: a library package. 4.2 BSD documentation (1980). 4.2 BSD had a 1983 release, but the cited parts are located in files dated 1980
5. Aycock, J.: Computer Viruses and Malware. Springer, New York/London (2006)
6. Bätzler, T.: Lode Runner decoded. http://baetzler.de/c64/games/loderunner/
7. Blank, M.S., Galley, S.W.: How to fit a large program into a small machine, or how to fit the Great Underground Empire on your desk-top. Creative Comput. **6**(7), 80–87 (1980)

8. Cicero, M.T.: First Oration of Cicero Against Catiline. Copp Clark (1886). Annotated by J. Henderson, Project Gutenberg #24967
9. Finseth, C.: The Craft of Text Editing: Emacs for the Modern World. Springer, New York (1991)
10. Gkantsidis, C., Karagiannis, T., Rodriguez, P., Vojnović, M.: Planet scale software updates. In: ACM SIGCOMM 2006, Pisa, pp. 423–434 (2006)
11. Gosling, J.: A redisplay algorithm. In: ACM SIGPLAN SIGOA Symposium on Text Manipulation, pp. 123–129 (1981)
12. Gusfield, D.: Algorithms on Strings, Trees, and Sequences: Computer Science and Computational Biology. Cambridge University Press, Cambridge (1997)
13. Hall, T.: *DOOM* Bible (1992). Revision .02
14. Hall, T., Romero, J.: Classic game postmortem: DOOM. Game Developer's Conference. http://www.gdcvault.com/play/1014627/Classic-Game-Postmortem (2011)
15. Horn, B.: The Grand Unified Model (1) – resources. http://www.folklore.org/StoryView.py?project=Macintosh&story=The_Grand_Unified_Model.txt
16. Infocom: Learning ZIL, or everything you always wanted to know about writing interactive fiction but couldn't find anyone still working here to ask. Infocom internal document (1989)
17. Kouznetsov, V., Ushakov, A.: System and method for distributing portable computer virus definition records with binary file conversion. United States Patent #7,231,440 (12 June 2007)
18. Kukich, K.: Techniques for automatically correcting words in text. ACM Comput. Surv. **24**(4), 377–439 (1992)
19. Kushner, D.: Masters of Doom: How Two Guys Created an Empire and Transformed Pop Culture. Random House, New York (2003)
20. Lebling, P.D.: Zork and the future of computerized fantasy simulations. Byte **5**(12), 172–182 (1980)
21. Lebling, P.D., Blank, M.S., Anderson, T.A.: Zork: A computerized fantasy simulation game. IEEE Computer **12**(4), 51–59 (1979)
22. McIlroy, M.D., Morris, R., Vyssotsky, V.A.: Letter to $\aleph_0$, c/o C. A. Lang, editor, *Software – Practice and Experience* (29 June 1971). http://www.cs.dartmouth.edu/~doug/darwin.pdf
23. McKusick, M.K.: Twenty years of Berkeley Unix: From AT&T-owned to freely redistributable. In: DiBona, C., Ockman, S. (eds.) Open Sources: Voices from the Open Source Revolution. O'Reilly (1999)
24. Muse Software: RobotWar manual (1981)
25. Percival, C.: Naïve differences of executable code (2003). http://www.daemonology.net/papers/bsdiff.pdf
26. Salus, P.H.: A Quarter Century of UNIX. Addison-Wesley, Reading (1994)
27. The Chromium Projects: Software updates: Courgette (c. 2009). http://dev.chromium.org/developers/design-documents/software-updates-courgette
28. Various contributors: Definition. Included file in ScottFree v. 1.14
29. Various contributors: QuakeC specs v1.0. http://www.inside3d.com/qcspecs/qc-menu.htm
30. Various contributors: Termcap manual page. 2BSD Unix (1979)
31. Wagner, R.A., Fischer, M.J.: The string-to-string correction problem. J. ACM **21**(1), 168–173 (1974)

Chapter 4
Interpreters

What is an interpreter? An interpreter takes the place of a CPU, in some sense; it executes a program that is written in a language. This sounds vague, but the concept of interpretation is very general and widely applicable, and as a result "program" and "language" are used broadly here on purpose. For example, an interpreter could directly interpret a program expressed in a human-readable programming language. Or, that same program could be interpreted, but in a "tokenized" representation where each formerly human-readable statement is abbreviated into a more compact format.

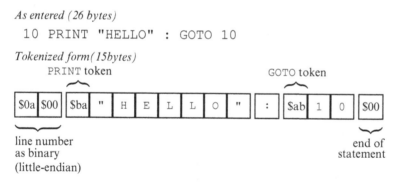

As entered (26 bytes)
```
10 PRINT "HELLO" : GOTO 10
```
Tokenized form (15 bytes)

Fig. 4.1 BASIC program and its tokenized representation

Example 4.1 (Applesoft BASIC). Richard Garriott's *Akalabeth* (1980) was implemented using the Applesoft BASIC that came standard on the Apple II. Figure 4.1 shows how this BASIC stored a human-readable program the programmer entered in tokenized form.[1] Each box shows the value of one byte, and a typewriter font indicates an ASCII character value. This particular program, when run, prints HELLO

---

[1] Verified in-emulator, cross-checked using [6, 24].

© Springer International Publishing Switzerland 2016
J. Aycock, *Retrogame Archeology*, DOI 10.1007/978-3-319-30004-7_4

in an infinite loop. The reserved words PRINT and GOTO are each reduced to a single byte, the line number 10 is converted into binary form (but not the line number used by the GOTO statement, interestingly), and all spaces have vanished. Listing the program reconstitutes it from this tokenized representation and gives the programmer back their program in a canonicalized form in terms of layout and spacing, regardless of whether the programmer had written the statement as in the figure, or as 10 PRINT "HELLO" : GOTO 10.

Tokenization is a fairly lightweight transformation of the programmer's code. In other cases, the human-readable language might be compiled or assembled into a lower-level virtual machine language, and this new program in the virtual machine language would be interpreted. This was the approach used by Infocom, compiling human-readable ZIL code into low-level Z-machine instructions for their interpreter. Whatever the language being interpreted, it is typically comprised of instructions that the CPU cannot execute directly.[2] This could be extended in the retrogame context to say "instructions that a CPU cannot execute directly anymore," as running old games on modern machines requires emulators to interpret once-native game code.

The reasons to use an interpreter are compelling. We have seen many of these in passing already, and portability to different platforms is high on the list. This platform-independence abstracts away from the native CPU, enabling the interpreter to perform memory management tricks such as paging and virtual memory with software alone. A game-specific or game-genre-specific interpreted language is really a domain-specific language, and expressing a game's functionality in this way can yield code that is much more concise (read: fewer bytes, an important retrogame consideration) than the equivalent in native code. The darker side to interpretation is that a substantial speed impact is incurred, making interpreters unusable for fast-paced retrogames or retrogames with real-time constraints such as those imposed by the Atari 2600. Also, not all platform-specific details can be abstracted away. For example, different platforms may have different graphics resolutions, and while the lowest common denominator can be targeted, the visual results would likely be suboptimal on the better platform.

Many interpreters encountered in the wild are ones that interpret an assembly-like virtual machine code, and express code in an imperative style, as a sequence of instructions to be performed in order. We will be focusing on those shortly, but it is also interesting to consider more diverse examples and whether or not they might fit a broad definition of an interpreter.

Example 4.2 (Lode Runner, 1983). In the last chapter, *Lode Runner* was categorized as Model B, which allowed exchanging one hunk of data for another – level data, in *Lode Runner*'s case – but deferred more involved interpretation to Model C. Perhaps another look is warranted, though: James Bratsanos, an early contributor to the game that would become *Lode Runner*, was quoted as saying 'I felt it was logical at the

---

[2] There are applications where it's necessary to interpret CPU X's instructions on CPU X itself, however [8].

time to build an engine that could interpret a game level' [27, p. 21]. The game data included a level's composition and the initial position of gold, NPCs, and the player, but no explicit instructions as to how the game was played. It could not therefore be considered imperative. An argument could be made that the level data provided a declarative description, expressing *what* the level consisted of but not *how* the level was played. Other declarative languages like HTML or Prolog have the same property; for example, a web page's HTML description can label text according to its logical structure, but gives no guidance as to exactly how the page will be laid out.[3] In a declarative way, *Lode Runner* could indeed be seen as an interpreter.

The argument that the game code is an interpreter of a level's data can be extended to other retrogames as well.

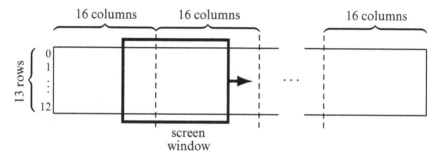

Fig. 4.2 Level data in *Super Mario*

Example 4.3 (Super Mario Bros., 1985). Super Mario on the Nintendo Entertainment System (NES) was a side-scrolling game with what amounted to 32 levels (eight 'worlds' with four levels each). The level specification is an interesting counterpoint to *Lode Runner*, where a level was small and placed on screen in its entirety.

Levels in *Super Mario* are fixed in height with 13 rows of graphical tiles, but the horizontal width of a level is bounded only by how far Mario can travel before the level's timer elapses. It would be prohibitive to specify an absolute horizontal position for elements in a level, because of the large number of bits that would be required for wide levels. Furthermore, the level data needs to be arranged for efficient access as Mario moves to the right (a level never scrolls back to the left).

This is solved by dividing the level data into pieces, each 16 columns of tiles wide.[4] The screen the player sees can be thought of as a moving window on this level data, one that is 13 rows high and 16 columns wide, although it will not always be precisely aligned to the level data's columns because the window moves with a

---

[3] Expressing aesthetically offensive, ill-sized page layouts is a task left to CSS.

[4] Level data information from static and dynamic game analysis, with help from [17]; analysis confirmed by experimentation, using a program I wrote to inject new level data into *Super Mario*. When finalizing the files for this book, I discovered that the recently-published [5] discusses the level data too; while it was not one of my sources, I point it out here an alternative viewpoint.

finer granularity. This arrangement is illustrated in Fig. 4.2. Onscreen elements are each described in two bytes, and they are arranged in order of appearance, making it relatively easy and efficient for the game engine to determine which elements can and can't be displayed. Certain level attributes are set globally in a two-byte level header, like the level's timer value and the background type, avoiding the need to continuously specify them throughout the level.[5]

Looking closer at the two bytes describing a game level element, the first byte contains the row and column coordinates of the element. With only 13 rows, the row number can easily fit into a four-bit nibble, and the extra values left over are used to signal special element types. Dividing the level into 16-column pieces means that the column number fits into four bits as well. The high bit of the second byte is set if the column number should be interpreted as part of the next 16-column piece; this clever encoding scheme allows the column coordinate to grow arbitrarily large while consuming only five bits. The remaining seven bits in the second byte specify the element type along with any necessary parameter.

A complete example is given in Fig. 4.3. The two level header bytes specify, among other things, no background and the two-tile high ground throughout the level. All other game elements are described by two-byte pairs. For elements A–E, the starting column and row numbers can be seen in the first byte's nibbles; element D's high bit is set, making it and future elements' column numbers to be taken relative to the second 16-column piece of the level data. Notice that A and E are specified with exactly the same byte values, but end up in different places because of D's high bit. Element F's row is the invalid row number $f, which is used to select special element types, the stairs in this case, that are anchored to the ground making the vertical position implied. All the elements' length and height arguments are decreased by one, because zero-length elements make no sense, and this allows the arguments' range to extend by one extra value. Finally, the value $fd acts as a sentinel to mark the end of the level data.

Although the level data is stored differently than *Lode Runner*, the idea is the same: the level data declaratively describes the level, and the game engine interprets the data according to the game rules. *Super Mario* can thus also be seen as using an interpreter.

The last stop before plunging into more traditional imperative interpreters is a system where the interpreted specification is neither declarative nor imperative by itself, but its data plugs in to a decidedly imperative framework.

Example 4.4 (Scott Adams). Scott Adams' series of games, such as *Adventure-land* (1978), were text adventure games with a relatively simple input structure that ran on multiple platforms. The interpreter would read a line of input from the user, e.g., TAKE AXE, and split it into a verb and noun. The interpreter would then run through a set of guarded statements – in other words, statements executed only if a set of conditions are true. The "program" that Adams' interpreter executed spec-ified the conditions and actions, and by doing so provided the overall structure of

---

[5] Although most global attributes can be changed on the fly via special types of elements in the level data.

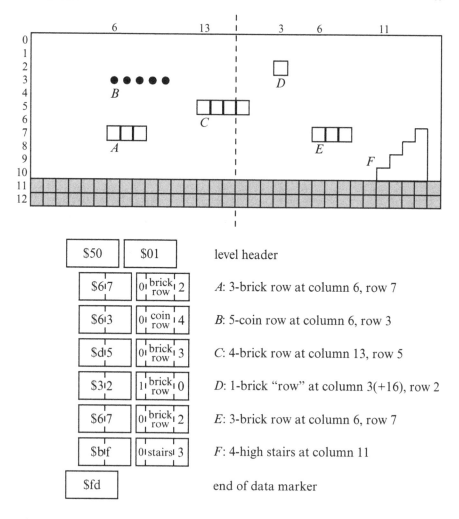

Fig. 4.3 *Super Mario* level data example

the game.[6] Figure 4.4 shows the conceptual structure of one of Adams' guarded statements, along with what portions were drawn from the interpreter's program (in italic). Up to five Boolean conditions and four actions could be given, the nature of which was not free-form but selected from the palette of conditions and actions that the interpreter supported. Some conditions were, for instance, "item #*k* carried," "not in room #*k*," and "flag #*k* set," where the exact value for each *k* was given by the programmer as an argument in the data file. Actions were similarly limited, and had

---

[6] As before, this is based on my interpreter-tested code, with information from [1, 2, 33].

```
if verb = "verb" and noun = "noun" and
   condition1 = True and
   condition2 = True and
   condition3 = True and
   condition4 = True and
   condition5 = True:
        action1
        action2
        action3
        action4
```

Fig. 4.4 Guarded statement structure of Scott Adams games

side effects: an action could print out a message, where each message corresponded to a different action number; two other example actions were "set flag #k to True" and "exit game."

4.1 Interpreter Design

Looking at interpreters for low-level, assembly-like imperative code, there are a number of designs and variants thereof that have been used over the years. Not all of them use consistent terminology, to make matters even more confusing. In this section we examine three of these designs to show their range and some key differences between them.

4.1.1 Classical Interpreters

The first interpreter design's origins are lost in the mists of time, and even a 1981 paper called this method 'so old and so ubiquitous' [21, p. 967].[7] A classical interpreter mirrors a real CPU's operation, mimicking the steps the CPU performs.

1. Opcode fetch from memory. "Opcode" refers to the type of the instruction.
2. Instruction decode. Once fetched, a determination is made as to what type of instruction it is, typically resulting in the interpreter transferring control to code that implements that operation.
3. Operand fetch. An "operand" is a parameter required for the instruction. Some instructions won't require any operands, whereas others will require one or

---

[7] Specifically, Klint was referring to the variant of this interpretation method using the opcode as an index into a table of addresses. We follow him in calling a non-threaded interpreter design a 'classical' interpreter.

more operands. Depending on the instruction encoding, information about the operands – or even the operand values themselves – may be encoded in the same byte(s) as the opcode.

4. Execution. Once the operands are available, the operation can be performed.
5. Result storage. Operations that compute results will need to write them to the appropriate location.

```
1   pc = 0
2   while (True) {
3       opcode = program[pc]        program:    instr_2
4       pc = pc + 1                              instr_1
5       switch (opcode) {                        instr_1
6           case instr_1:
7               ...                                 ⋮
8           case instr_2:
9               ...
10      }
11  }
```

Fig. 4.5 Pseudocode for a classical interpreter and its interpreted program

This is very easy to implement, even in a high-level language. Figure 4.5 shows how this would look in C-like pseudocode. The interpreter's "program counter," or pc, is first initialized to the index of the first instruction in the program being interpreted. This program is stored as an array in memory, and because opcodes' encoding can often fit into a byte, interpreted code is generically referred to as byte-code. Line 2 starts the program interpretation loop. The opcode fetch is performed at line 3, the instruction decoding is done by the switch at line 5, and execution would occur at lines 7 and 9 (that code would fetch operands and store results as needed).

A good compiler will translate the switch into an efficient jump table *if* it can detect that the cases' values are densely clustered together [10, 29]. The opcode value then becomes an index into an array of addresses, each entry pointing to the code to implement an operation. The low-level implementation, whether output from a compiler or written by hand, would resemble the pseudo-assembly in Fig. 4.6. Here, the opcodes for instr_1 and instr_2 need to be 0 and 1, respectively, to select the correct addresses from the jump table.

Example 4.5 (Meteor, 1979). Meteor was a (physical) pinball game that used a Motorola 6800 CPU. Internally, the software used a system called PIGS, the 'Pinball Interpretive Game System' [23] which had the structure of a classical interpreter.[8]

---

[8] PIGS' author called this a 'token threaded interpreter' [23], and it corresponds to a 'tokenized encoding' in [15].

```
                        pc = 0
        loop:           opcode = program[pc]
                        pc = pc + 1
                        address = jumptable[opcode]
                        goto address

        instr_1:  ...
                        goto loop
        instr_2:  ...
                        goto loop

        jumptable:
                        word &instr_1
                        word &instr_2
```

Fig. 4.6 Pseudo-assembly code for a classical interpreter

The design allowed assembly code to be freely mixed with interpreted code.[9] A programmer used the 6800's software interrupt (SWI) instruction in their assembly code to start the interpreter. The interpreter loop read byte-sized opcodes from memory immediately following the SWI instruction, using the opcode as an index into a jump table to locate the address of the opcode's handling routine. Opcode handlers were invoked with a subroutine call, meaning that they could simply end with a one-byte return instruction rather than a three-byte goto. Once the interpreter loop finished (it watched for a flag byte to be zero), execution of assembly code would resume following the end of the interpreted instructions.

One last design question is where operands are placed relative to the instruction opcodes. Most interpreters, including PIGS, simply placed operands inline following the opcode. The code implementing an operand is then responsible for advancing pc accordingly so that it indexes the next instruction to be interpreted by the time control returns to the interpreter loop.

4.1.2 Direct Threaded Interpreters

An alternative to a classical interpreter is a direct threaded interpreter, often simply called a threaded interpreter, and the code that it interprets is referred to as threaded code.[10] Threaded code is a sequence of addresses. A threaded code address acts as an opcode; each one is a pointer to the code that implements the operation. In its purest form there is no interpreter loop, and every operation's code is responsible

---

[9] Based on static analysis of *Meteor* disassembly, with 6800 information from [22].

[10] This section on threaded code is based on [9, 21] unless stated otherwise. Threaded code is equivalent to Debaere and Van Campenhout's 'pointer based encoding' [15], although the implementation they suggest is the one with centralized dispatch at the end of this section.

for advancing the program counter and dispatching the next interpreted instruction. This creates 'interpretive code which needs no interpreter' [9, p. 371], that by all accounts was the fastest type of interpreter [9, 21, 28].

```
1   start:
2       pc = 0
3       address = program[pc]
4       pc = pc + 1
5       goto address
6                                   program:  | &instr_2 |
7   instr_1:                                  | &instr_1 |
8       ...                                    | &instr_1 |
9       address = program[pc]
10      pc = pc + 1
11      goto address                                    :
12
13  instr_2:
14      ...
15      address = program[pc]
16      pc = pc + 1
17      goto address
```

Fig. 4.7 Pseudo-assembly code for a threaded interpreter and its interpreted program

A threaded code interpreter is hard to express using high-level languages, even in standard C unless extensions are used [19]. Figure 4.7 gives a pseudo-assembly implementation, however. There is no longer a loop, and the interpreter's starting code just dispatches the first interpreted instruction (line 5). The interpreted instruction implementations each have their own dispatch code (lines 9–11 and 15–17), and the interpreted program's representation is now an array of addresses.

```
            pc = 0
    loop:   address = program[pc]
            pc = pc + 1
            goto address

    instr_1: ...
            goto loop
    instr_2: ...
            goto loop
```

Fig. 4.8 Pseudo-assembly code for a threaded interpreter with central dispatch

The code duplication at the end of each routine to perform the next instruction dispatch is apparent. For some architectures the dispatch could be implemented with a single instruction, like the PDP-11 [9] or the Motorola 6809 [28]. Where that was not possible, it made more sense to instead jump to one central dispatch routine – as Fig. 4.8 shows, this edges the design back towards the classical model but without the compact opcode representation.

Example 4.6 (Sea Wolf II, 1978). The arcade game *Sea Wolf II* used a Z80 CPU and had a threaded code interpreter [23]. To fully understand everything happening in the interpreter, we need to step back and examine the Z80 along with a specific programming language, Forth.

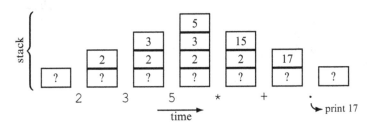

Fig. 4.9 Forth example

Forth [11] is a stack-based language whose programs are written in postfix, or reverse Polish, notation. For example, a statement like "print 2 + 3" would be written in Forth as

    2 3 + .

which means, in this order: push 2 on the stack; push 3 on the stack; pop the top two numbers off the stack, add them together, and push the result back on the stack; pop the topmost item off the stack and print it (.). Similarly, "print 2 + (3 * 5)" becomes

    2 3 5 * + .

with the order of arithmetic operations controlled by the programmer. Here, 3 and 5 are at the top of the stack when the multiplication is performed; this leaves 2 and 15 at the top of the stack when the addition operator is encountered (Fig. 4.9). This stack-based language design lives on in the PostScript page description language [3] and 'superficially' in the omnipresent PDF file format [4]. In fact, Forth has a dual-stack computation model. There is a "data" stack for arguments, computation, and return values; a "return" stack is used for return addresses.

Sea Wolf II did not just have a threaded code interpreter. It had a threaded *Forth* interpreter, implying that there was a way to implement one on the Z80 CPU that was efficient enough for use in an arcade game. Like the 6502, the Z80 was a little-endian, 8-bit CPU with a 16-bit address space (i.e., it could address a maximum of 64 K).[11] The Z80 had a *lot* more registers, though: Fig. 4.10 contains only a subset

---

[11] Z80 information in this section is from [36], and game details are from static and dynamic analysis.

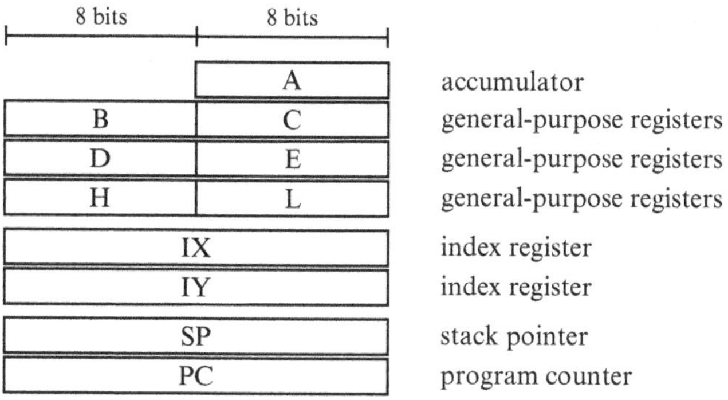

Fig. 4.10 (Partial) registers in the Z80 CPU

of the available registers. Certain 8-bit register pairs could be used separately or taken together to form 16-bit registers, e.g., registers *B* and *C* could become *BC*, or B∥C in pseudo-assembly notation.

The register assignments that *Sea Wolf II* used to implement Forth dedicated register pairs to specific tasks. *BC* pointed to the threaded code addresses, *IX* was the return stack pointer, and *SP* was the data stack pointer. Using the native CPU's stack for the data stack allowed use of native push and pop instructions for Forth's stack-heavy processing. *IY*, the other index register, always held the value $0043. While the Z80 had more registers than the 6502, they were still high-demand resources, and it may seem extremely odd to devote a register to a single constant value. However, $0043 was the address of the interpreter's central dispatch routine, and consequently threaded code routines could end with the two-byte instruction goto IY instead of goto $0043, saving one byte per threaded code routine.

```
$0043:   A = M[B∥C]
         B∥C = B∥C + 1
         L = A
         A = M[B∥C]
         B∥C = B∥C + 1
         H = A
         goto H∥L
```

Fig. 4.11 Threaded code dispatch in *Sea Wolf II*

The central dispatch loop's pseudo-assembly code is shown in Fig. 4.11. It loads the two-byte code address pointed to by *BC* into *HL*, one byte at a time. *BC* is incremented along the way to point to the next code address, and finally the dispatch routine jumps to the address now stored in *HL*. As *Sea Wolf II*'s code shows, threaded code dispatch on the Z80 was far from a one-instruction affair.

A disadvantage of threaded code is size, in general. On retrogame machines, an address was at least two bytes, and on modern machines it is substantially more. Not only is this representation larger than that of a classical interpreter, but requiring an address precludes cramming additional information (about operands, for instance) into spare opcode bits.

4.1.3 Indirect Threaded Interpreters

One last interpreter design is the indirect threaded interpreter, that 'requires less space' [16, p. 330] with the addition of an extra layer of indirection.[12] It is probably obvious that this design tradeoff comes with a performance cost from the extra memory reference required.

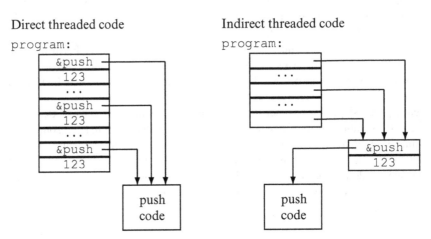

Fig. 4.12 Direct versus indirect threaded code

Figure 4.12 compares direct threaded code with indirect threaded code. Whereas a direct threaded program might repeat code/value pairs (assuming inline operands) multiple times throughout the code, an indirect threaded representation factors the repeated values into a common place.

Example 4.7 (Hat Trick, 1987). The hockey game *Hat Trick* on the Atari 7800 was implemented in Forth and used indirect threaded code.[13] The instruction set of the Atari 7800's 6502 CPU was not terribly well suited to double indirection, and pseudo-assembly for the central dispatch code is shown in Fig. 4.13.

---

[12] This section is based on [16, 21], but their space-saving argument for indirect threaded code – that every variable needs its own specialized compiler-generated code to access it – is rather specious given direct threaded code using inline operands.

[13] Confirmed with source code; other information from static and dynamic analysis.

```
 1      Y = 1
 2      A = M[Mw[$f8] + Y]
 3      M[$fc] = A
 4      Y = Y - 1
 5      A = M[Mw[$f8] + Y]
 6      M[$fb] = A
 7      c = 0
 8      A = M[$f8]
 9      c||A = A + 2 + c
10      M[$f8] = A
11      if c = 0 goto L
12      M[$f9] = M[$f9] + 1
13  L:  goto $fa
```

Fig. 4.13 *Hat Trick*'s indirect
threaded code dispatch

Lines 1–6 are copying the two-byte address pointed to by $f8...$f9 (the indirect
threaded code's pc) to $fb...$fc. Then, lines 7–12 are incrementing the program
counter by two, leaving pc pointing to the next instruction's address. Line 13 performs the dispatch at last, or so it would seem. In fact, it is jumping to an indirect
jump instruction located in the 6502's zero page – lines 1–6 were actually filling in
the address into the indirect jump. The net result of the dispatch code in Fig. 4.13
plus the indirect jump is the indirect threaded interpreter's instruction dispatch.

4.2 Instruction Set Design

Intertwined with interpreter design is the design of the instruction set being
interpreted. In some cases, such as interpreting/emulating a pre-existing CPU's instructions, there is no flexibility in the instruction set design. In other cases, and in
particular for retrogames, the instruction set for interpretation could start from a
blank slate. A primary consideration for retrogames would have been balancing the
design to yield both a small program size and also ease of expressing the program.
The latter has ripple effects on the complexity of generating the interpreted code
in the first place, as well as the complexity (and size) of the interpreter itself. In
general, any of these decisions will have tradeoffs.

4.2.1 Alignment

Normally within the purview of hardware-based instruction sets, requiring data or
interpreted code to be aligned at a specific boundary has uses for software-defined
interpreted instruction sets too. The number of bits within an instruction that are
devoted to describing a data or code address will be finite and fixed, meaning that
only a finite, fixed range of addresses can be specified. Alignment restrictions extend

the range of addresses that can be specified with the same number of bits, at the cost of occasionally wasting a few bytes to pad out data and code to the correct boundary.

For example, an instruction set that reserves 8 bits for a function address – say, the target of a `call` instruction – will only be able to call $2^8 = 256$ different code addresses. If the functions being called must start at a four-byte boundary, then the same eight bits (*bbbbbbbb*) can now effectively call $2^{10} = 1024$ addresses, because every aligned code address has its lower two bits implied: *bbbbbbbb*00.

Example 4.8 (Infocom). Infocom's Z-machine required strings and functions to be aligned.[14] The exact alignment restrictions increased over time as Infocom's games and the machines they ran on grew in size. Early versions of the Z-machine demanded two-byte alignment; late versions increased this to four-byte alignment, plus adjustment by an offset given in the game's data file header. This header offset was itself a reference to an eight-byte boundary, thus two separate alignment restrictions were used simultaneously. For example, given a header function offset[15] of $1000 and an instruction containing a function address of $42, the function's actual memory address would be

$$\$42 \times 4 + \$1000 \times 8$$
$$= \$108 + \$8000$$
$$= \$8108$$

extending the range of an in-instruction address considerably.

4.2.2 Operand Type

A discussion of operand type might be better thought of as describing the number of operands that interpreted instructions usually have. At the coarsest granularity, the design choice is binary: a stack-based instruction set versus a register-based instruction set. A pure stack-based computation would need no operands, because the location of operands is implied, i.e., on the top of the stack like Forth. A register model would instead allow operands to explicitly refer to specific "registers" or, as would be more apropos for retrogame interpreters, specific variables. Stack-based instruction sets tend to give smaller code [31], and would therefore seem to be a natural fit for size-conscious retrogames; register-based ones are arguably more flexible in terms of expressing code, however. In practice, as we'll see, the distinctions retrogames made were not always so clear-cut.

---

[14] From [26], which gives an internal view of a late Z-machine version, and the more longitudinal information in [34, section 1.2.3].

[15] This field was called FOFF internally.

Diving deeper into the register-based instruction sets, the following examples illustrate how the number of operands could vary.

Example 4.9 (Quake, 1996). QuakeC is an extreme example, both in its release date and also the number of operands, but again it provides a useful reference point as computers' resources became less constrained. QuakeC's instructions are three-operand, where the instruction's opcode plus all three operands occupied "short" integers – in other words, every instruction was a fixed-size eight bytes in length.[16] The advantage to three-operand instruction sets is the ability to issue instructions like c = a + b where a, b, and c are all distinct. Any judgment on this design should be tempered by John Carmack's comments accompanying the compiler's source code characterizing it as [sic] 'basically rather embarassing crap' and the generated code as [sic] 'horribly nieve and space ineficient' [13].

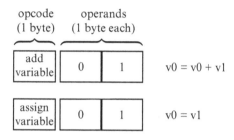

Fig. 4.14 Example AGI instructions

Example 4.10 (AGI engine). Sierra On-Line had a game interpreter, AGI, that was used for a number of retrogames, among them *King's Quest* (1984). It had 256 eight-bit global variables as part of its game state that acted as registers, from an instruction set design point of view.[17] Its design favored a two-operand approach; Fig. 4.14 shows two example AGI instructions manipulating global variables (there were separate instructions to add or assign a number to a variable). For the addition instruction in particular, one of the source operands *had* to be the destination operand.

Example 4.11 (RobotWar, 1981). *RobotWar*'s interpreted code was exclusively one-operand, with the exception of the ENDSUB (return) instruction.[18] Robot code could refer to any of 34 global registers, some of which had special semantics related to robot control. The instructions made heavy use of an internal accumulator register, and an addition like a = b + c would need three instructions: load accumulator with b; add c to accumulator; store accumulator to a. For each of these three instructions, the use of the accumulator was implied and not explicitly specified.

---

[16] Verified in source code.

[17] Information here cross-checked in the source code for two different, modern AGI interpreters.

[18] This example's information is from [25], along with reverse engineering of (and writing a disassembler for) the object code files.

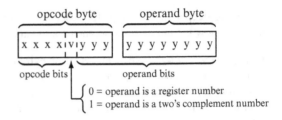

Fig. 4.15 Format of a
RobotWar instruction

One quirk of the instruction set encoding was where an operand was placed relative to the instruction. Figure 4.15 shows the instruction format that *RobotWar* used. The two bytes of the instruction were split apart: if the opcode byte was at address *i*, the operand byte would be at address $256 + i$ (object code programs were limited to a maximum of 256 instructions). This was likely because numbers and labels could then be used interchangeably, and this design trivially gave each instruction a known location and avoided having to convert a number into an instruction address.

4.2.3 Case Study: Level 9

Level 9 was a UK company that produced text adventure games, like *Colossal Adventure* (1983). Their games were implemented with an interpreted 'A-code' (not to be confused with Dave Platt's A-code). Their interpreted architecture was little-endian and had 256 global variables that could be referenced, each of which could hold a 16-bit value.[19] In addition, there were so-called "lists" which were in fact one-dimensional data arrays. An internal call stack existed but wasn't referenced directly from A-code programs; this was not a stack-based interpreter.

Opcode bytes were in one of two formats, shown in Fig. 4.16. The *c* and *a* bits were only used when warranted: for example, a variable-variable assignment would use neither of them, but a variable-constant assignment would use the *c* bit. Operand byte(s), if needed, were placed inline following the opcode byte.

Operations supported by the A-code interpreter are listed in Tables 4.1 and 4.2. Words in italic indicate operands that follow the opcode byte. Some, but not all, instructions have variants for constant and variable operands, and the range of arithmetic operations is very limited. Opcode 6 permits the instruction set to be extended indefinitely and gradually without altering the existing instruction format (something that would potentially require extensive modification of the interpreter and toolchain).

---

[19] Information gleaned statically and dynamically from the Level 9 interpreter, plus writing and using a framework to construct and inject interpreted programs into existing games.

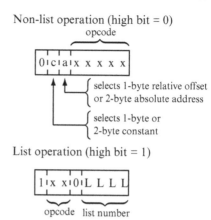

Fig. 4.16 Level 9 opcode
formats

Table 4.1 Selected Level 9 non-list opcodes

Opcode	Operation
0	goto *address*
1	call *address*
2	return
3	print number in *variable*
4	print message whose number is in *variable*
5	print message number *constant*
6	call function *n*, where *n* is
	1 quit game
	2 *variable* = random number
	3 save game
	4 restore game
7	input $variable_1$ $variable_2$ $variable_3$ $variable_4$
8	*variable* = *constant*
9	$variable_1$ = $variable_2$
10	$variable_1$ = $variable_1$ + $variable_2$
11	$variable_1$ = $variable_1$ - $variable_2$
14	dispatch via *jump table* with index *variable*
16	if $variable_1$ = $variable_2$ goto *address*
17	if $variable_1$ ≠ $variable_2$ goto *address*
18	if $variable_1$ < $variable_2$ goto *address*
19	if $variable_1$ > $variable_2$ goto *address*
24	if *variable* = *constant* goto *address*
25	if *variable* ≠ *constant* goto *address*
26	if *variable* < *constant* goto *address*
27	if *variable* > *constant* goto *address*

Opcodes 7 and 14 are essential to a game's input loop. The input instruction reads
user input and parses it, returning up to three word values in the first three registers
specified (the fourth is used to return the word count). Words are mapped to values
using an internal dictionary, part of which is shown in Fig. 4.17. The typewriter font
indicates an ASCII character, and the characters in gray boxes have their high bits

Table 4.2 Level 9 list opcodes

Opcode	Operation
0	L[*constant*] = *variable*
1	*variable* = L[*variable*]
2	*variable* = L[*constant*]
3	L[*variable*] = *variable*

N	O	R	T	H	$1	N	E	A	S	T	$2	N	O	R	T	H	E	A	S	T	$2

Fig. 4.17 Level 9 dictionary structure

set to flag the end of the word. The value in the byte immediately following a word is the value the parser returns; note that this scheme allows synonyms, like NEAST and NORTHEAST in the figure. Once the input is parsed, the verb number is used in conjunction with opcode 14 to jump to the appropriate handler for a verb.

Overall, the A-code interpreter presents a fairly clean design. Obviously it was tailored for the genre of games Level 9 was producing, and was not intended for general computation.

4.2.4 Case Study: Infocom

Infocom's Z-machine, by comparison, has a general enough design that it has been used as the target of a C compiler.[20] There were multiple versions of the Z-machine over Infocom's lifetime, but the core design remained much the same.[21] It was a big-endian machine, with 240 global variables, up to 15 local variables, and it had the ability to use a stack. All variables could hold 16-bit values.

A good way to tour the Z-machine's design is by examining its instruction formats, of which there were four types where the most significant bits were 'arranged to make decoding easy' [26, p. 6]. This was not empty rhetoric: the easy-decoding structure is reflected in the Z-machine interpreter code, which also reveals it to be a classical interpreter.[22]

---

[20] No, really: [20].

[21] Unless otherwise stated, information in this section is from [26, 34] with examples and statistics based on disassembly with txd. For examples, I have used the Infocom instruction format names and mnemonics along with txd's more readable assembler syntax.

[22] As seen in a third-party annotated disassembly of Infocom's Apple II Z-machine [32, pp. 1-26–1-27] and, using that as a guide, verified firsthand in the Apple II *Zork I* disassembly.

Fig. 4.18 Infocom Z-machine
0-operand instruction format

The first instruction format is the 0-operand one. As Fig. 4.18 shows, it was a straightforward affair supporting up to 16 operations. Even a few 0-operand instruction examples begin to hint at how the Z-machine was inclined both towards text adventure games and code size reduction. CRLF outputs a newline sequence, and is the harbinger of many other text output instructions that would be needed for these games. RFALSE and RTRUE return the values 0 and 1, respectively, and here we already see some specialization as opposed to only having a generic "return" instruction requiring an operand (which existed as well). The PRINTI instruction printed an inline string that followed the opcode byte; it was classified as 0-operand because, as will become apparent, the 1-operand instructions had a much different format. As a last example combining output and specialization, PRINTR behaved like PRINTI, but was followed by an implied CRLF and RTRUE, thus abbreviating this common instruction sequence by two bytes.

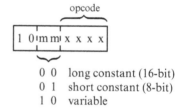

Fig. 4.19 Infocom Z-machine
1-operand instruction format

The 1-operand instruction format (Fig. 4.19) included two bits, mm, to describe the type of operand that accompanied the instruction. Excluding the bits $mm = 11$, which couldn't be used due to overlap with 0-operand encoding, the operand could be a one- or two-byte constant value, or a variable. The latter is of particular interest, because a variable was specified in one byte that married both stack and register operands. A "variable" value of 0 used the top of the stack, values from 1 to 15 referred to local variables, and values 16 and up referenced global variables (explaining why there were only 240 global variables). 1-operand instructions included an unconditional JUMP, and more text output instructions: PRINTB to print a string at the operand's (unadulterated) address, and PRINT to print the string at the operand's address (adjusted for alignment).

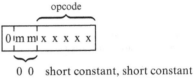

opcode

0 ｜m m｜x x x x

0 0	short constant, short constant
0 1	short constant, variable
1 0	variable, short constant
1 1	variable, variable

Fig. 4.20 Infocom Z-machine
2-operand instruction format

In the 2-operand instruction format (Fig. 4.20), besides allowing up to 32 operations, the 2 bits of operand type must now describe two operands and not only one. The sacrifice is long constants – any ostensibly two-operand instructions needing greater constant range must use extended format instructions instead. Examples of 2-operand instructions include the arithmetic operators, like ADD, SUB, MUL, DIV, and MOD. At first glance, this would suggest that one source operand doubled as a destination, but in fact "2-operand" only includes *input* operands. A one-byte variable specification following the input operands gave the destination where the result should be stored.

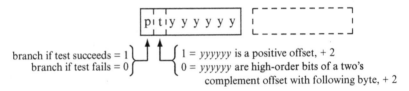

p｜t｜y y y y y

branch if test succeeds = 1
branch if test fails = 0

1 = *yyyyyy* is a positive offset, + 2
0 = *yyyyyy* are high-order bits of a two's
complement offset with following byte, + 2

Fig. 4.21 Infocom Z-machine predicate format

Another thing that did not count as a source operand was a predicate specification. For example, the 2-operand EQUAL? instruction had the semantics

if *operand₁* = *operand₂* then *predicate*

A predicate specification was very elaborate and could take one to two bytes. As Fig. 4.21 shows, the sense of the test could be flipped using the predicate's high bit, and its neighboring bit selected between two kinds of offset used to specify the destination address. The shorter one-byte predicate form only allowed a positive (forward) offset, reflecting a bias in ZIL programs, where loops were infrequent, but there were often forward branches to handle special cases. Jump offsets 0 and 1 were reserved to mean RFALSE and RTRUE respectively. To help illuminate this complex scheme, some example instructions from *Zork I* (1980) are deconstructed in Fig. 4.22. The first example is a test for *in*equality, because the test is negated by the predicate. The byte encodings for the two local variables are each offset by one (e.g., L01 is encoded as $02) to compensate for the value $00 referring to the stack. Similarly, the offset encoded as 5 ends up being an offset of 3, to adjust for the RTRUE and RFALSE special cases. Example (b) uses the RFALSE special case for its *eq*uality test, and also employs a global variable ($87 − 16 gives 77 in base 16) and a short constant value. Example (c) is another inequality test, but pops the top-of-stack value as its first operand, and its predicate holds a long branch value − as a two's complement number, the branch offset is −11, and subtracting 2 to adjust it yields the −13 final offset.

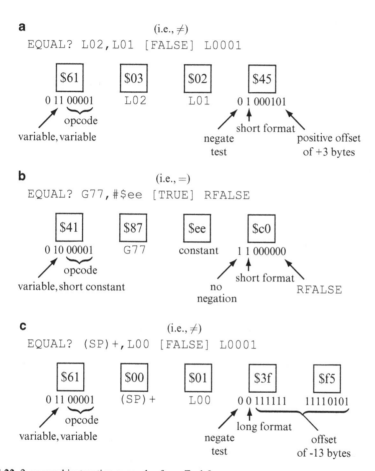

Fig. 4.22 2-operand instruction examples from *Zork I*

Last, in the extended instruction format (Fig. 4.23), the bits describing operand types migrate to a separate byte, making room for up to four operands to be specified. A special "end of operand" code flags when no more operands are to be found. Figure 4.24 has an example from *Zork I*. Two operands are supplied: the first is the address of the function to be called, the second is the constant argument to pass to the function. The final $00 byte indicates that the function's return value should be

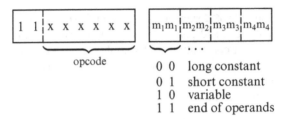

Fig. 4.23 Infocom Z-machine extended instruction format

pushed on the stack; notice that this output operand's presence is not reflected in the input operand encoding, as was mentioned for 2-operand instructions.

```
CALL R0235 (#$a3) -> -(SP)
```

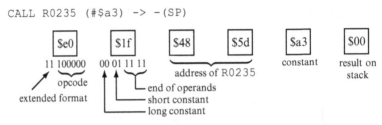

Fig. 4.24 Extended format instruction example from *Zork I*

The Z-machine certainly possesses an intricate design. To assess whether or not it paid off, we can look at how well it optimized for the common case. Here a static analysis suffices, because optimizing for size was the goal. Statically, *Zork I* had 6797 instructions, employing 59 distinct opcodes. The most frequent instruction was RTRUE with 205 appearances. Of the 2083 predicates, 1793 were only one byte, which includes 436 special-case returns (jump offsets 0 and 1). The numbers were similar for *Zork II* (1981), *Zork III* (1982), and *Planetfall* (1983). It does appear that the extravagant Z-machine design admirably captured common usage.

Interpreters are widely used to implement popular programming languages today, for some of the same reasons that retrogames used them: portability is still a concern, and a basic interpreter is easy to construct. Building an *efficient* interpreter is another matter entirely, and is an area of ongoing research even now (e.g., [12, 35]). What lies beyond interpretation? Once a language has sufficient momentum and resources, interpretation may give way to just-in-time compilation [7] for the sake of speedier program execution. Alternately, a language may be compiled into another language that already has a just-in-time compiler, in order to leverage the nontrivial effort that goes into building one.

On modern CPUs, interpreters with centralized instruction dispatch can fare noticeably worse because of branch misprediction [14, 18]. This by itself suggests some advantage in returning to a threaded interpreter model with multiple dispatch points, as in Fig. 4.7. Threaded code is seeing a Renaissance for quite a different reason, however. "Return-oriented programming" is a recent development in terms of attacks on computer security [30], but it is really a variant on threaded code where the program's threaded code addresses are placed in the stack, the stack pointer acts as the pc, and instruction dispatch is done with `return` instructions. This approach allows certain security defenses to be bypassed.

References

1. Adams, S.: An adventure in small computer game simulation. Creat. Comput. 5(8), 90–97 (1979)
2. Adams, S.: Pirate's adventure. Byte 5(12), 192–212 (1980)
3. Adobe Systems Incorporated: PostScript Language Reference Manual, 2nd edn. Addison-Wesley, Reading (1990)
4. Adobe Systems Incorporated: PDF Reference, 6th edn. Adobe Portable Document Format, version 1.7, Adobe Systems Incorporated, San Jose (2006)
5. Altice, N.: I AM ERROR: The Nintendo Family Computer/Entertainment System Platform. MIT, Cambridge (2015)
6. Apple Computer, Inc.: Applesoft II BASIC Programming Reference Manual. Apple Computer, Inc., Cupertino (1978)
7. Aycock, J.: A brief history of just-in-time. ACM Comput. Surv. 35(2), 97–113 (2003)
8. Bala, V., Duesterwald, E., Banerjia, S.: Dynamo: a transparent dynamic optimization system. In: ACM SIGPLAN'00 Conference on Programming Language Design and Implementation, Vancouver, pp. 1–12 (2000)
9. Bell, J.R.: Threaded code. Commun. ACM 16(6), 370–372 (1973)
10. Bernstein, R.L.: Producing good code for the case statement. Softw.: Pract. Exp. 15(10), 1021–1024 (1985)
11. Brodie, L.: Starting Forth, 2nd edn. Prentice-Hall, Englewood Cliffs (1987)
12. Brunthaler, S.: Efficient interpretation using quickening. In: 6th Symposium on Dynamic Languages (2010). doi:10.1145/1869631.1869633
13. Carmack, J.: readme.txt (Undated). https://github.com/id-Software/Quake-Tools/blob/master/qcc/readme.txt
14. Casey, K., Ertl, M.A., Gregg, D.: Optimizing indirect branch prediction accuracy in virtual machine interpreters. ACM Trans. Program. Lang. Syst. 29(6), Article 37 (2007)
15. Debaere, E.H., Van Campenhout, J.M.: Interpretation and Instruction Path Coprocessing. MIT, Cambridge (1990)
16. Dewar, R.B.K.: Indirect threaded code. Commun. ACM 18(6), 330–331 (1975)
17. doppelganger: SMBDIS.ASM – a comprehensive Super Mario Bros. disassembly (Undated, probably 2007 or earlier)
18. Ertl, M.A., Gregg, D.: The structure and performance of *efficient* interpreters. J. Instr. Level Parallelism 5, Paper 12 (2003)
19. Ertl, M.A., Gregg, D., Krall, A., Paysan, B.: Vmgen – a generator of efficient virtual machine interpreters. Softw.: Pract. Exp. 32(3), 265–294 (2002)

20. Given, D.: vbccz: A C compiler that targets the Z machine. http://cowlark.com/vbcc-z-compiler/
21. Klint, P.: Interpretation techniques. Softw.: Pract. Exp. **11**(9), 963–973 (1981)
22. Leventhal, L.A.: 6800 Assembly Language Programming. Osborne & Associates, Berkeley (1978)
23. McNeil, A.: Résumé. http://a9k.info/Resume.html
24. Mesztenyi, C.K.: Applesoft internal structure. CALL–A.P.P.L.E., pp. 9–13 (January 1982)
25. Muse Software: RobotWar manual (1981)
26. PKWARE, Inc.: APPNOTE.TXT – .ZIP file format specification (2014). https://pkware.cachefly.net/webdocs/casestudies/APPNOTE.TXT. Version 6.3.4
27. Retro Gamer staff: Lode Runner. Retro Gamer (111), 20–27 (2013)
28. Ritter, T., Walker, G.: Varieties of threaded code for language implementation. Byte **4**(9), 206–227 (1980)
29. Sale, A.: The implementation of case statements in Pascal. Softw.: Pract. Exp. **11**(9), 929–942 (1981)
30. Shacham, H.: The geometry of innocent flesh on the bone: return-into-libc without function calls (on the x86). In: 14th ACM Conference on Computer and Communications Security, Alexandria, pp. 552–561 (2007)
31. Shi, Y., Casey, K., Ertl, M.A., Gregg, D.: Virtual machine showdown: stack versus registers. ACM Trans. Archit. Code Optim. **4**(4), Article 21 (2008)
32. Smith, E.L.: Infocom INTERLOGIC interpreter disassembly, Apple II/6502 version, release 3 (1984). https://www.brouhaha.com/~eric/if/zip/
33. Various contributors: Definition. Included file in ScottFree v. 1.14
34. Various contributors: The Z-machine standards document (1997)
35. Würthinger, T., Wimmer, C., Wöß, A., Stadler, L., Duboscq, G., Humer, C., Richards, G., Simon, D., Wolczko, M.: One VM to rule them all. In: ACM International Symposium on New Ideas, New Paradigms, and Reflections on Programming & Software, Indianapolis, pp. 187–204 (2013)
36. Zilog: Z80 family CPU user manual (2004). Document UM008005-0205

Chapter 5
Data Compression

It is almost inevitable that data compression would arise in the context of retrogames. With limited memory space combined with limited secondary storage space (like floppy disks), space was at a premium for retrogames in multiple dimensions. We would expect to see compression schemes in retrogames that strike a balance between the size of the resulting data and the complexity of the encoding, for two reasons. First, the effectiveness of compression depends not only on how small the data gets, but on how large the decompression code needs to be. Any data can be trivially shrunk to zero bytes in size, after all, given decompression code of a gigantic print statement that blindly regurgitates the original data. An overly complex compression scheme demanding elaborate decompression code would not have been a good choice for a retrogame. Second, some retrogame platforms and types of retrogame had timing constraints, and decompression that took too long to run on slow CPUs would not have been viable either.

The last chapter was already quietly looking at compression methods, because interpreters specialized for a game or a game genre could represent game code more concisely than generic native code for a CPU. In this chapter, we shift the focus to data rather than code, and use a selection of retrogames to lead an exploration through techniques for compressing text, static images, and moving images (i.e., video).

Some techniques could be quite subtle. As a general rule, seemingly odd things in retrogame implementations were often done for speed or size. For instance, why would game data values be multiplied by strange amounts like 150 and 20?

Example 5.1 (Scott Adams). Each guarded statement in Scott Adams' game interpreter needed 16 pieces of data to be stored: the verb and noun; five conditions, each with an argument; four actions.[1] All of these were represented as positive numbers and, in the TRS-80 BASIC that Adams started with, integers were the most natural fit to store these values in. The integers in BASIC were 16-bit, though, meaning that

---

[1] Game database information from [1, 2, 30]. The use of TRS-80 BASIC is mentioned in [2], and its data types and memory requirements are detailed in [21].

© Springer International Publishing Switzerland 2016
J. Aycock, *Retrogame Archeology*, DOI 10.1007/978-3-319-30004-7_5

each guarded statement would consume 32 bytes of precious memory. Adams cut this by half. The verb and noun were packed together in one integer by multiplying the verb number by 150 and then adding the noun number; both values individually were comfortably less than 150.[2] This can be seen as treating the values as two digits of a base 150 number, or it can be viewed as a way of packing two values together in lieu of bit-shifting operators in BASIC. The exact same scheme was used to encode the four actions into two integers. A condition and its associated argument became one integer, with the argument value multiplied by 20 and added to the condition number (there were only 20 condition types provided).

5.1 Text Compression

Text-heavy retrogames like text adventures clearly had reason to consider ways to squeeze as much text as possible into limited memory.

Example 5.2 (Infocom). The case study of Infocom's Z-machine in the last chapter shied away from discussing text encoding, because their method lies firmly in the realm of data compression.[3]

   String encoding in the Z-machine was based conceptually on pre-ASCII Baudot codes used for teletypes [9], but we can also see it as a furtherance of the Z-machine design optimizing for the common case. For an (English) text adventure game, the common case in strings would be lowercase alphabetic characters, of which there are 26. The encoding of a single "common" character would therefore fit into five bits, and leave six extra encoding values to spare. Other, less-frequently used characters were separated into different "banks" that the extra encoding values could select, similar to using the shift key on a keyboard before typing an uppercase letter or a punctuation symbol. The net result is that each visible character in a string takes approximately 5.5 bits to encode [9].

   The fact that five bits, much less five and a half, don't divide nicely into a convenient byte boundary has probably not gone unnoticed. In practice, a two-byte word in the Z-machine held three character codes, with one bit to spare that was used as a flag to indicate the end of the string (EOS). Figure 5.1 shows three examples. For "the," the EOS bit is set indicating that the string does not continue beyond the three codes in the word, i.e., seeing EOS does not cause decoding to stop immediately. The default character set contains lowercase alphabetic characters, which are arranged in alphabetic order starting at 6, explaining why e has the code 10 even

---

[2] In theory, this could have risen to 181 before exceeding the maximum positive 16-bit integer value but, as confirmed in Adams' game editor source code and [2], these values were wired fairly deeply into the game infrastructure.

[3] This section is based on [20, 34] unless otherwise noted, along with constructing a `strings` program for Z-machine data files. Some minor details are omitted for clarity; we focus on version 3 of the Z-machine for the same reason.

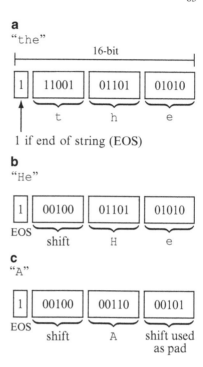

Fig. 5.1 Text encoding in the
Z-machine

though it is not the tenth character in the alphabet. In the second example, "He"
uses one of the shift codes – code 4 shifts into the bank of uppercase characters
temporarily – and apart from this context, the code for H is identical to the code
for h. The third example shows what happens when a 16-bit word has extra codes
left over. "A" only needs two codes, one to shift into uppercase and one for the letter
itself; extra shift codes, which have no visible effect, are used to pad out the string.
The space character is code 0 in all character sets.

At this point, of the 32 possible five-bit codes, 26 are taken by alphabet characters, two are shift codes, and one is the space character. That only accounts for 29
codes... what about the other three?

Z-machine games supplied three groups of what Infocom called 'frequent words'
but a better name is probably 'abbreviations.' The three extra codes 1, 2, and 3 signal
that the next code refers to an abbreviation Z-string in the corresponding group. The
abbreviations were decoded starting in the default lowercase character set, and they
could not use abbreviations themselves, meaning that recursion when decoding was
limited.

Table 5.1 shows a brief sample of the abbreviations from *Zork I* (1980). The
spaces, shown explicitly with the ␣ symbol, were part of the abbreviations. Because
abbreviations all decoded started in lowercase, we see both the␣ and The␣, and
you␣ and You␣. It may also seem unusual that two-character strings like I␣ and
A␣ are abbreviations, but in fact they would take *three* codes otherwise: one to shift

"A‿thief‿!"

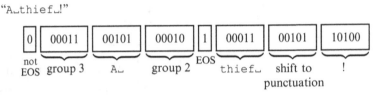

Fig. 5.2 Z-machine text encoding using *Zork I* abbreviations

Table 5.1 Sample of *Zork I* abbreviations

Abbreviation group	Abbreviation number within group	Abbreviation
1	0	the‿
1	1	The‿
1	2	You‿
1	3	,‿
1	4	your‿
1	5	is‿
1	6	and‿
1	7	you‿
	...	
2	2	his‿
2	3	thief‿
2	4	It‿
	...	
2	27	I‿
	...	
3	5	A‿

into uppercase, one for the letter, and one for the space. The abbreviations were automatically chosen at game build time [18], and they were different for each game released.[4] Figure 5.2 has a more extensive example that includes abbreviations; there is no way to suppress or delete the space that ends many abbreviations, explaining the extra space before the exclamation mark in this example.

Put together, Infocom's text encoding scheme could give some substantial space savings. Consider the following text, that shows (*Zork I*) abbreviations using angle brackets:

```
<You ><are ><in ><the >bed<room >when<, ><with >
a <grating >sound<, >a secret <door ><in ><the >
<north ><wall >opens <and >a <troll >appears.
```

---

[4] It is unclear if the metric for choosing abbreviations was word frequency, as internal Infocom documentation suggests [20, p. 62], or abbreviations that would result in the most space savings [18], although there would be a natural overlap. The different abbreviations per game were observed by comparing *Zork I*, *Zork II* (1981), *Zork III* (1982), and *Planetfall* (1983); I suspect the automated abbreviation output was ordered, given that the‿, The‿, and You‿ always made the top five.

An abbreviation could be used, when appropriate, as only part of a word, as in bed<room >. Ignoring the EOS indicator, a straightforward encoding of this text using one byte per ASCII character would consume 109 bytes. In contrast, a Z-machine encoding using *Zork I* abbreviations would take 72 five-bit codes or 45 bytes, again ignoring EOS bits.

Infocom games did have one technical advantage in that their target systems included floppy drives. While floppy storage was not capacious by any stretch of the imagination, it did mean that not everything had to be in RAM all at once. On the other hand, other producers of text adventures had to load their game and data fully into memory once, from cassette tape.

Example 5.3 (Level 9). Level 9 was one of these lucky companies: its primary audience was the cassette-happy UK market [23]. Non-dictionary text in Level 9 games was encoded and compressed using easy-to-manipulate bytes.[5] The value $01 was the EOS indicator. Byte values from $03...$5d represented ASCII values from $20...$7a, which includes space, digits, upper- and lowercase letters and all but the most obscure punctuation.[6]

That left the byte values from $5e...$ff. These served as references to entries in an abbreviation table. As with Infocom games, the abbreviations were automatically selected at game build time [23] but Level 9's compressor could select fragments of words and phrases, as Table 5.2 shows. What is not obvious from the table is that the encoding was fully recursive, and abbreviations could include other abbreviations. Figure 5.3 illustrates how the abbreviation the␣ was recursively encoded; this saved two bytes in the abbreviation table over a non-recursive representation, keeping in mind that the abbreviations used recursively would also have been used by other strings and abbreviations.

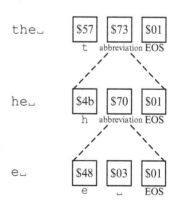

Fig. 5.3 Recursion in Level 9 abbreviations

---

[5] Information gleaned by writing a program to print the strings and abbreviations in *Colossal Adventure* (1983), using the Level 9 interpreter as a guide.

[6] The temptation is overwhelming to include an ASCII table here, like nearly every single computer reference manual from the 1970s and 1980s.

Table 5.2 Sample of Level 9's *Colossal Adventure* abbreviations

Abbreviation byte encoding in string	Abbreviation
$5e	␣a
$5f	!␣
$60	's␣
$61	,␣
$62	-west␣
$63	.␣
$64	0␣feet
$65	A␣
$66	Hall␣of␣
$67	It␣
$68	Mists
$69	Please␣
$6a	The
$6b	You␣are
$6c	as
$6d	be
$6e	ch
$6f	d␣
$70	e␣
$71	f␣
$72	g␣
$73	he␣
...	
$85	ze␣of␣twisty␣little␣passages,␣all␣

Text compression was not only a consideration for text adventures. Games in other retrogame genres hit the upper limits of memory capacity and had to condense their text too.

Example 5.4 (Elite, 1984). It is probably fair to characterize *Elite*'s text compression as more of an *ad hoc* affair. The scheme only needed to work for the one game, and the phrasing of text in the game was even manually tweaked to reduce the byte count under compression [11, 38:28].

The strings in *Elite* were NUL-terminated, i.e., the EOS indicator was a $00 byte.[7] All other bytes in the string were exclusive-ORed with 35, and then interpreted as shown in Table 5.3. The ability to interpolate certain game state values into a string was a nice feature, potentially avoiding extra subroutine calls to achieve the same effect. The range of ASCII values that could be directly encoded was comparatively restricted and did not include lowercase letters; the game determined which letters to convert to lowercase at run time. *Elite* did not keep a separate abbreviation table, and any string could recursively include any other string,

---

[7] Information here is from reverse engineering the source code statically (after writing a program to reformat and increase legibility of the dense BBC BASIC plus 6502 assembly) and dynamically in-emulator, then writing a program to reconstruct the text from the game.

Table 5.3 *Elite*'s text encoding

Byte value in string (n)	Interpretation
$00...$0d	Include value from game state, e.g.,
	$02 present system's name
	$03 hyperspace system's name
	$04 commander's name
$0e...$1f	Recursively include string $n + \$72$
$20...$5f	ASCII value of character
$60...$7f	Recursively include string n
$80...$9f	Include digram, using n & $7f as index into digram table
$a0...$ff	Recursively include string $n-\$a0$

which were numbered from 0...145. Finally, any of a select set of 32 digrams –
two-letter combinations – could be specified. The digrams were an arrangement of
convenience and were present for an entirely different reason that we revisit later.

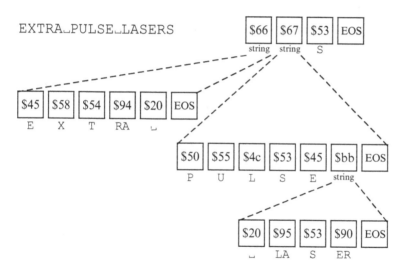

Fig. 5.4 Example *Elite* string encoding

Figure 5.4 shows a complete example. For simplicity, the byte values given have
been exclusive-ORed already.

One commonality with all these text compression methods is that they replace
long, often-repeated sequences by shorter codes that represent the sequences, thus
saving space. This is a theme we will see often repeated for other types of media in
retrogames.

5.2 Static Image Compression

As a bridge between text compression and static image compression, we begin with static images rendered using text.

Fig. 5.5 *Spook House* screenshot (Image copyright Roger Schrag, used with permission)

Fig. 5.6 TRS-80 graphic characters producing a stepped line

Example 5.5 (Spook House, 1982). Figure 5.5 shows a screenshot of *Spook House* for the TRS-80. The TRS-80, along with other home computers of the time, had extensions to ASCII that provided a graphic character set, meaning that text characters could be used to draw low-resolution pictures.[8] The angled line in the upper left corner of the screenshot, for example, is comprised of the three graphic characters shown in Fig. 5.6.

---

[8] Graphic character set information is from [21]; game information is from reverse engineering the image format and writing a program to reconstruct the images from the game data.

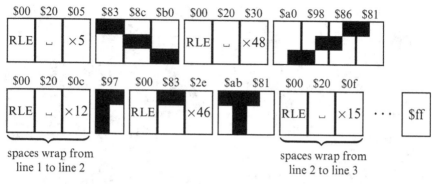

spaces wrap from
line 1 to line 2

spaces wrap from
line 2 to line 3

Fig. 5.7 Decoding *Spook House*'s RLE data

The text-based images in *Spook House* were 64 × 12 characters, or 768 bytes in total per image. With 52 screens in total, the uncompressed size would be almost 40,000 bytes, but the game stored it in under 9000 bytes using run-length encoding (RLE). The idea behind RLE is to replace repeated sequences of the same value, a repeated byte value in this case, with an abbreviated code that only stores the byte value to repeat and the number of times it does so. *Spook House*'s RLE decompressor thus went through the bytes of the compressed images looking for three cases. First, a $ff byte signaled the end of the image. Second, a $00 byte indicated RLE data: the following two bytes were the byte value and the repeat count, respectively. Third, any value besides $00 and $ff was taken as a literal byte value to be copied directly into the image being decompressed. Figure 5.7 partially decodes the data for the image in Fig. 5.5.

Other retrogames also compressed images by representing the image data in shorter form, but a shorter form that allowed the images to be not so much decompressed as reconstituted. Hearkening back to the last chapter, retrogames would store images as instructions to be interpreted that would reproduce the images at run time.

Example 5.6 (Mystery House, 1980). The images in *Mystery House* were all line-based drawings, as illustrated by a screenshot (Fig. 5.8). The Apple II's high-resolution graphics mode (leaving the four lines on the bottom in text mode) was 280 × 160.[9] Or, to put it another way, a vertical coordinate would easily fit in a byte, and a horizontal coordinate could be *slightly* larger than a byte, slight enough that the excess 24 pixels could be safely ignored by the game.

Each image was a sequence of byte pairs, with $ffff marking the end of the image. It is easiest to imagine their scheme in terms of paper and a physical pen that can be either up off the paper (moving but not drawing) or down on the paper (moving

---

[9] Resolution from [4]. The image information here is from reverse engineering, and then writing a program to reconstruct the images from the game data. Levy's *Hackers* hints at the method, but gets the technical details incorrect [17, p. 298].

Fig. 5.8 *Mystery House* screenshot

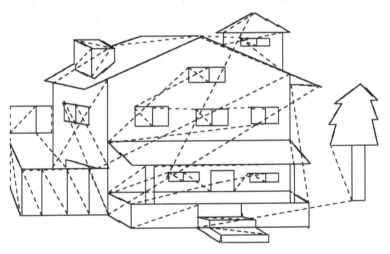

Fig. 5.9 Drawing *Mystery House* images

and drawing). The byte pair $0000 says to lift the pen up; the byte pair $xxyy moves the pen to the given (absolute) coordinate and put the pen down if it is not already down. This can be seen as optimizing for the common case of a continuous line, and storing only the next endpoint's coordinate rather than the two coordinates needed to fully describe an arbitrary line. Figure 5.9 shows the rendering of the screenshot, where the dashed lines indicate movement with the pen up.

In *Mystery House*, there was no explicit instruction set for drawing images, but other retrogames went to this extent, especially once the complexity of images expanded beyond line drawings.

Fig. 5.10 *Emerald Isle* screenshot (Image copyright Mike and Pete Austin, used with permission)

Example 5.7 (Emerald Isle, 1984). Level 9's *Emerald Isle* was a text adventure game that incorporated static images to add to the textual gameplay. Figure 5.10 shows one of the game images, which graphically is a fairly typical example of image-enhanced text adventures of the era. The most striking addition is color, that in many adventure games would seem to be an afterthought, because the player would see the outlines of the image rendered onscreen before the color was flood-filled into place. This hints at how the image was stored, however.

In the case of Level 9 games, their interpreted game instruction set had an additional instruction not mentioned in Table 4.1: draw an image whose number was supplied in a variable. Images were described using a *different* interpreted instruction set. Structurally, their interpreted graphics instruction set had subroutine calls that allowed graphics routines to be reused, but otherwise included no conditionals or other control flow.[10]

Table 5.4 Selected *Level 9* interpreted graphics instructions

Bit encoding	Bytes	Interpretation
00 *xxx yyy*	1	Draw line to $\Delta xxx, \Delta yyy$ from current position
01 *xxx yyy*	1	Move[a] from current position by $\Delta xxx, \Delta yyy$
10 *nnnnnn*	1	Call graphics routine #*nnnnnn* (0...63)
11000 *xxxxx yyyyy*	2	Draw line to $\Delta xxxxxx, \Delta yyyyy$ from current position
11001 *xxxxx yyyyy*	2	Move[a] from current position by $\Delta xxxxxx, \Delta yyyyy$
11100 *ccc*	1	Flood fill current location
11101 *nnnnnnnnnnn*	2	Call graphics routine #*nnnnnnnnnnn*
11111011 *xxxxxxxx yyyyyyyy*	3	Move to absolute location
11111111	1	Return from subroutine

[a]Without drawing

Table 5.4 gives a sampling of the graphics instructions. There were three different formats, distinguished by the most significant two to five bits. The design supports keeping the image descriptions small through graphics subroutine re-use: the smallest drawing and moving commands are relative to the current drawing location, allowing an object to be drawn in multiple locations using the same code, and there are one-byte call and return instructions. Curved lines in images are actually composed of short line segments, explaining the one-byte move and draw instructions. And of course, there is an instruction to fill an area with color.

Emerald Isle has 405 graphics routines occupying 7597 bytes in total, with a median routine size of 13 bytes. A subroutine call analysis shows that over 64 % of the routines are called by other ones, suggesting a fairly high degree of re-use. In the screenshot, for example, all the rocks are drawn by one routine; that routine is also called by 14 other game images. In turn, it directly calls three routines – one draws the three round rocks together, one draws a chipped rock (called twice), and one draws a flat-top rock (called three times, and revealing that the graphics instruction set also had scaling operators).

What is striking when comparing graphical text adventure retrogames is that their static images had a substantively similar look, platform differences apart. And yet at the implementation level, there were a number of different ways of describing how the images were drawn, even considering an element as simple as a line.

---

[10] Information from Level 9 interpreter source, which I used to write a program that partially reconstructs game images and also performs call analysis.

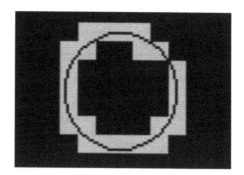

Fig. 5.11 ZX Spectrum color
attribute granularity

Example 5.8 (The Hobbit, 1982). The Hobbit drew its images in the ZX Spectrum's standard graphics mode, which boasted 256×192 resolution.[11] Each of those pixels could be turned on or off individually, but the foreground and background colors could only be set for 8×8 blocks, leading to odd color clashes extensive enough that some Spectrum games were monochrome to sidestep the issue.[12] It is hard to show the full effect in print, but Fig. 5.11 illustrates the difference in granularity: the screen's background was originally black, and then a circle was drawn in black on a gray background, a clear contrast between the pixels and the blocks.

This information about the Spectrum is not an idle digression; elements of the Spectrum's graphics echo throughout *The Hobbit*'s image format. Each of the 22 game images began with a two-byte header setting global image properties. The first byte's low three bits controlled the screen's border color, and was blasted verbatim into a memory-mapped I/O port. The second byte became the default initialization value for the image background.

From there, the image was described using an interpreted instruction set. Table 5.5 shows the full set of instructions, with several of note. The end of image and flood fill are self-explanatory, of course, and a coordinate fit perfectly in a byte with the maximum horizontal resolution of 256. The movement instruction changed the current position, but was co-opted at times for a different purpose entirely. Some images' data "fell through" onto other images to save space; this was implemented by placing a dummy $08 move instruction opcode at the end of one image, which would cause the header bytes of the second image to be harmlessly treated as coordinates.

---

[11] The Spectrum's technical specifications are nicely contextualized by Collins [12]. Game information is from reverse engineering, starting with a partial disassembly [36] (which unfortunately didn't tackle any of the graphics code), and then writing a program to reconstruct the images from the game data.

[12] Kindly confirmed by Spectrum retrogame programmers Jon Ritman (*Batman*, 1986; *Head over Heels*, 1987) [24] and Shahid Ahmad (*Chimera*, 1985) [3]. Ahmad observes that any color clashes are worse in isometric games because the color blocks don't align with the coordinate axes as they would in 2D games.

Table 5.5 Interpreted graphics instructions from *The Hobbit*

Bit encoding	Bytes	Interpretation
00000000	1	End of image
00001000 $xxxxxxxx$ $yyyyyyyy$	3	Move to new x, y position without drawing
01000 ccc $xxxxxxxx$ $yyyyyyyy$	3	Flood fill color $\#ccc$ starting at x, y
00100 ccc $aaaaaaaa$ $aaaaaaaa$ $nnnnn$ dd ... 11111111	4+	Set background color attributes
1 $rrrr$ $z_1z_2z_3$ rr $nnnnnn$	2	Draw line from current x, y position

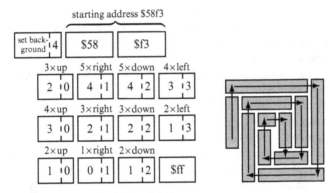

starting address $58f3

Fig. 5.12 Setting background color in *The Hobbit*

The background color instruction demands a close inspection. The best way to imagine its operation is as a set of instructions describing directions to apply a continuous stroke of paint. The two $aaaa$... bytes are an absolute address in the Spectrum's color attribute memory to begin at (given in big-endian order despite the Spectrum's little-endian Z80). What followed was a list of bytes, terminated by the value $ff, each of which contained a direction dd (0...3 stood for up, right, down, and left respectively) and the number of 8×8 color blocks to paint the background of while moving in that direction (-1, because a repeat count of 0 would make little sense). This instruction is thus arguably using run-length encoding rather than separately specifying each color block.

Figure 5.12 shows an example setting the background color. In *The Hobbit*'s opening game image, the player is in a room with a green door. The green (color #4) appears courtesy of the background color instruction in the figure, and the figure's diagram shows the length and movement described by the individual bytes in the list. (The color blocks have been separated in the diagram for exposition, but would fit snugly together in the game image.)

Last and definitely not least is the line-drawing instruction. The slope of a line between two endpoints can be described in terms of Δy and Δx, and it may be expressed equivalently in terms of rise and run (Fig. 5.13). The latter maps nicely into physical reality: when walking up a hill, how much vertical elevation gain (rise)

Fig. 5.13 Describing a line

occurs for a given amount of horizontal travel (run)? In *The Hobbit*, the rise of a line is always fixed to 1 and therefore does not need to be specified in the instruction. However, there is still a need to describe the line's direction, which is where three control bits come in.

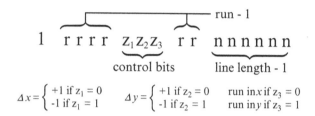

Fig. 5.14 *The Hobbit*'s line-drawing instruction

The format of the line-drawing instruction is broken down in Fig. 5.14. The run and line length values are both decreased by 1 to get slight additional range, since zero values again wouldn't be useful. Together, this information says how many total steps to move in the "run" direction (line length), and how many "run" movements (run) to make before a "rise" movement. The drawing of a line can be seen as a side effect of the movement.

The control bits, meanwhile, provide the amounts to change x and y by, and whether the run is done on the x or y coordinate. Their values have a big impact. Figure 5.15 shows the result of three line-drawing instructions, all starting at (100, 50) with a run of 3 and a length of 10. The only difference is in how the control bits are set.

Between *Emerald Isle* and *The Hobbit*, we see two markedly distinct instruction set designs. Subroutines versus no subroutines, many instruction types versus few instruction types, one line representation versus another. For this final example we move even further afield as we transition from the line as the atomic drawing unit to jigsaw puzzle pieces: tiles.

Example 5.9 (Return to Pirate's Isle, 1983). In an interview, Scott Adams said of *Return to Pirate's Isle* (henceforth *RPI*) 'Getting a full graphic adventure into a TI-99/4A game cartridge was an amazing feat' [22, p. 39], and it was indeed an interesting scheme.[13]

---

[13] Information here is from reverse engineering the image format and writing a program to reconstruct the images from game data.

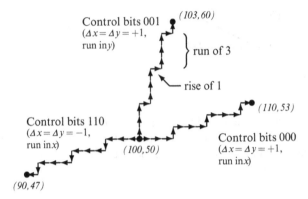

Fig. 5.15 Line control bits in *The Hobbit*

Game images were comprised of 8 × 8 tiles, arranged in 12 rows of 32 columns each. Unlike the Spectrum's 8 × 8 color blocks, this was not a hardware-based limitation; the use of square tiles was essential to *RPI*'s image representation, and choosing a width of eight bits meant that a tile's entire bitmap (without color) fit in eight consecutive bytes. Under normal circumstances, the tile granularity was not starkly apparent.

Figure 5.16 shows a screenshot fragment of the same area under both normal and abnormal circumstances. *RPI* started with the player not wearing glasses, and the images were distorted until the player located and donned their glasses. The effect was cleverly achieved. Without glasses, the game started reading the image two bytes after its actual start address, offsetting tiles in an almost-but-not-quite recognizable manner, and the way that color was applied enhanced the effect. This simple implementation also meant that the player could remove their glasses at any point in the game and the image would be similarly distorted – it wasn't limited to the one image.

It is hardly a surprise at this point to learn that images in *RPI* were described by a set of interpreted instructions. All the details of the 16-bit instructions and their interpretation are not terribly enlightening, but a higher-level view is. The 384 tiles of an image were produced one by one, starting at the upper left corner. There was thus always an implicit "current tile" destination location that did not need to be stored in image data, a location that was advanced automatically as instructions produced tiles for the image.

The basic instruction format is shown in Fig. 5.17. The first two fields mutually influenced one another's interpretation:

- *Count* = 0. *Function* selects one of a small set of operations, such as ending the image data or supplying the eight bytes of a nonstandard tile. In the latter instance, *argument* is treated as the first byte of tile data, and the instruction is followed by the remaining seven bytes.

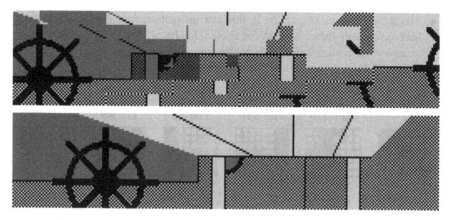

Fig. 5.16 *Return to Pirate's Isle* image excerpt, without glasses (*top*) and with glasses (*bottom*)

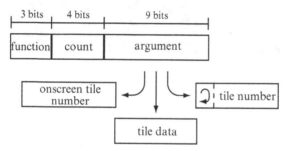

Fig. 5.17 *Return to Pirate's Isle* image instruction format

- *Count* > 0 and *function* ≠ 6. *Non*standard tiles implies that there is such a thing as standard tiles, and in fact that is what underlies *RPI*'s scheme. This instruction field interpretation takes *count* as a repeat count for the given *function*, a separate set of operations from the *count*=0 case above. These operations fall roughly into two categories. First, tiles that have already been placed onscreen can be copied to the destination location; all nine bits of the *argument* may be used to identify an onscreen starting tile. Second, one of a set of 64 standard tiles can be placed at the destination location. Here, eight bits of the *argument* are used: six bits give the standard tile's number, and the remaining two say how many clockwise rotations to apply to it, allowing a small set of standard tiles to become many more.

  Figure 5.18 shows how the top of the ship's wheel (Fig. 5.16) is constructed from standard tiles with rotations. Tile #6, in particular, gets reused in this short sequence; more subtly, the presence of tile pairs #8 and #11, and #9 and #10, reveals that the instruction set has no operation to flip a tile horizontally.

- *Count* > 0 and *function* = 6. In this last instruction field combination, *count*
  becomes a (sub-)function specifier itself. This batch of operations allows more
  extensive tile manipulations, where tiles are not output immediately, but may be
  ANDed, ORed, and exclusive ORed with other tiles first.

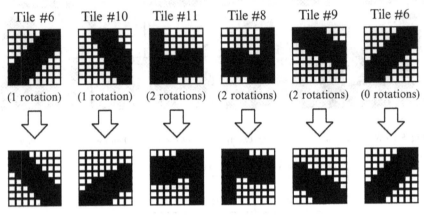

Tile #6	Tile #10	Tile #11	Tile #8	Tile #9	Tile #6
(1 rotation)	(1 rotation)	(2 rotations)	(2 rotations)	(2 rotations)	(0 rotations)

Fig. 5.18 Tile usage in *Return to Pirate's Isle*

Following the rendering instructions was the color data. It was stored run-length
encoded as a sequence of two-byte pairs, each a repeat count and a color value to
repeat, where an all-zero pair signaled the end of data. Each repeated color value
byte (one nibble foreground color, one nibble background color) was applied to an
entire 8 × 8 block, reducing the amount of color data that needed to be stored. There
was a way to override the mechanism to supply color values for all eight bytes of a
block individually, however.

The static image compression schemes here are for retrogames where space is
important, but performance less so: a bit of extra time spent producing an image
when the player moves from one location to another in a text adventure can be
ignored. The same principle applies to static images in faster-paced games, though,
where a static image appears after an arbitrarily-long level loading process, or during a pause as the player moves from one screen to another. Moving pictures are
different.

5.3 Video Compression

With CD-ROM drives came a wave of full-motion video retrogames. The problem,
at least for the first retrogames to make use of them, is that the drives at the time
were really no different than those playing audio CDs; these drives were optimized
for delivering Bananarama to humans, not high-speed data transfers to a computer.

While maximizing storage capacity would be a concern, it was secondary compared to getting video data from the CD-ROM to the computer in time to play it. And here time is definitely at issue, because media playback has soft real-time requirements. Early CD-ROM retrogames had to run on the least common denominator of equipment available, meaning what would now be derisively called a 1× speed CD-ROM, able to transfer 150 K per second [27]. An *extremely* modest frame rate is 15 frames per second, and a single uncompressed 640 × 320 black and white image is 25 K. To transfer 15 of these every second is already well past the capability of a 1× drive, not to mention the extra data requirements of audio and color. Clearly some data compression was at work.

Example 5.10 (The 7th Guest, 1993). It seems fitting to examine retrogame video compression by delving into one of the pioneering CD-ROM games, *The 7th Guest.*[14]

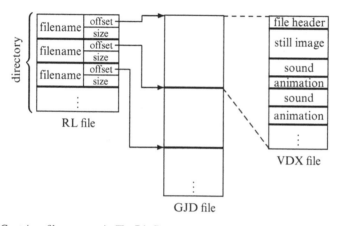

Fig. 5.19 Container file structure in *The 7th Guest*

One of the first questions, when creating a game with literally thousands of animation sequences, is how to organize them all. *The 7th Guest* had container files similar to *Doom* WADs, except the directory information was broken out into separate files. There was quite a size discrepancy: "GJD" files containing data had a median size of over 30 M, whereas the median size was just over 2 K for the "RL" directory files indexing into GJD files.[15] Figure 5.19 shows how the files related to

---

[14] Game information based on writing a program to list GJD file contents, reconstruct still images from VDX files, and visualize VDX animation deltas, using information from [31–33].

[15] Through a remarkable coincidence, "RL" and "GJD" happen to be the initials of *The 7th Guest* developers Rob Landeros and Graeme J. Devine, respectively [32].

one another. Each RL directory entry was a fixed size, with 12 bytes for the filename
(enough for an MS-DOS-like $8 + 3$ filename format) and a four-byte offset and size
pinpointing a location in the GJD file.

Each entry in the GJD file, in turn, was a "VDX" file, and it is here that the journey into video compression begins. Following an unexciting VDX file header, the
VDX file consisted of a sequence of blocks. Each block possessed its own header,
identifying the block type, its size, and whether or not the block's data was compressed; after the block header came the block's (possibly compressed) data. As
Fig. 5.19 shows, the block types included still frames – static images – as well as
sound and animation data. Setting sound aside, *The 7th Guest*'s video was produced
by the combination of still frames and animation data.

A video sequence began with a still image, which was the only complete representation of one of the 640×320 full-color images. The fact that this happened
at the start of a sequence, often in response to a player action, also allowed some
timing slack in case the still image took extra time to load. From that point, the moving portion of the video sequence was described by animation blocks. These were
shorter (read: faster to load) blocks that simply described the differences, or deltas,
between the last video frame and the current video frame.

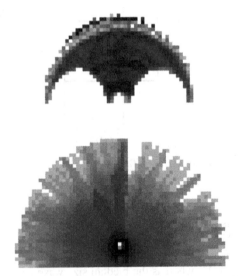

Fig. 5.20 Heat map (log scale) showing change frequency for inanimate object

That *The 7th Guest* exists substantiates the idea that this video compression was
effective, but how effective was it for full-motion video? We can get some sense of
this using (grayscale) heat maps showing the frequency that areas in a video clip
changed, where white means no changes and progressively darker colors indicate

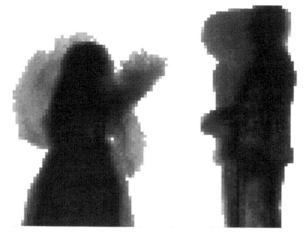

Fig. 5.21 Heat map (log scale) showing change frequency for two people

more changes.[16] Figure 5.20 shows the heat map for an inanimate object, an eight-second video clip of a clock whose hands and mechanism are moving to show the passage of time (the clock hands are faintly visible in the 11:00 position). The changes in the video are both small in proportion to the whole image, and restricted to certain areas. This can also be true for animate objects: Fig. 5.21 shows the change heat map for a 14-second clip of two actors and, even here, small focused changes occur. On average, animation deltas changed barely over 20 % of the total image, and the largest changes in the game's animation deltas corresponded not to animate or inanimate objects' movement, but to camera motion.

We are seeing two types of compression at work for video. First, each still or animation block may be compressed with the "LZSS" algorithm – more on this below – that applies compression to each individual point in time. Second, there is compression across time through the use of deltas that only store differences between frames. The deltas themselves are expressed in a way that returns to an underlying theme: they are commands in a simple interpreted instruction set.

Instead of seeing yet another interpreted instruction set, the LZSS algorithm that *The 7th Guest* uses for blocks needs a closer look. Throughout this chapter, there have been many game-specific compression methods but few generic methods apart from run-length encoding. Furthermore, run-length encoding is restricted in scope to a local sequence of bytes. LZSS, on the other hand, is generic enough to apply to all types of data and operates with a more global view to spot better compression opportunities.

---

[16] Both still frames and animation deltas in *The 7th Guest* are decomposed in terms of 4×4 squares, explaining the chunky look of the heat maps. The color of each pixel within a square could be individually set, however.

LZSS stands for Lempel-Ziv-Storer-Szymanski and is an improvement to Lempel and Ziv's 1977 compression algorithm ([37], usually called LZ77) by Storer and Szymanski described in a fairly impenetrable journal paper [28].[17] LZSS is a so-called 'adaptive dictionary' scheme [25]. Whereas the text compression schemes discussed earlier would have a static, unchanging set of abbreviations – i.e., a dictionary – LZSS' dictionary references refer to a window of the most recent decompressed output. The dictionary thus adapts with the data being decompressed over time and can take advantage of redundancy with a broader view than run-length encoding.

Fig. 5.22 Sixteen-bit LZSS dictionary reference from *The 7th Guest*

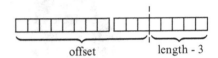

offset   length - 3

Like the text compression methods, LZSS has a mix of literal bytes and dictionary references. Literal bytes are stored as bytes, true to their name; dictionary references are two bytes long and encode an offset into recently-decompressed data along with the length to copy from that location. The division of bits between these two fields in a dictionary reference is controlled by a parameter which, in *The 7th Guest*, is located in a VDX block's header. The parameter value could (and did) vary on a per-block basis. Figure 5.22 shows an example dictionary reference from the game, with five length bits specified in the VDX block header. The length value is adjusted by 3 to get additional range, because lengths of 0, 1, and 2 cannot exist (two bytes is the break-even point for a two-byte dictionary reference, therefore a length of at least three bytes is needed for compression).

Dictionary references are distinguished from literal bytes by expending one more bit. LZSS uses the eight bits of a "flag byte" to identify the disposition of the following compressed data. In *The 7th Guest*, a 1 bit in the flag byte means a literal byte, and a 0 bit is a dictionary reference; the *least* significant bit in the flag byte regulates the first compressed value following the flag byte, i.e., the bits in the flag byte are read backwards.

Figure 5.23 shows an example from some of *The 7th Guest*'s compressed data. The bits in the flag byte (backwards) tell the decompressor to expect four literal bytes, a dictionary reference, a literal byte, a dictionary reference, and a literal byte. The dictionary references are stored in little endian format, and need to be byte-swapped before splitting into an offset and length; in this example, there are four length bits. Notice that the initial $16 $16 sequence, although a repeated byte value, falls below the compression threshold and is left as two literal bytes.

---

[17] Bell provides a mercifully more coherent description [6].

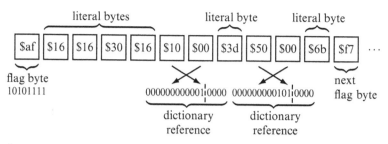

Fig. 5.23 LZSS example from *The 7th Guest*

Table 5.6 traces through the decompression process. Steps 1–4 are just literal byte copies. At step 5, the first dictionary reference is reached: offsets are applied backwards in the decompressed output (the copy source is highlighted) and the stored length of 0 has 3 added to it. Effectively, because the −1 offset selects the last decompressed output byte, LZSS becomes run-length encoding for this first dictionary reference. For the second dictionary reference (steps 9–11) the offset is −5, and LZSS shows its ability to refer back to earlier parts of the decompressed output.

Table 5.6 Decompressing the LZSS example

Step	Decompressed output	Explanation
1	$16	Literal byte
2	$16 $16	Literal byte
3	$16 $16 $30	Literal byte
4	$16 $16 $30 $16	Literal byte
5	$16 $16 $30 **$16** $16	Offset −1, 3 left to copy
6	$16 $16 $30 $16 **$16** $16	Offset −1, 2 left to copy
7	$16 $16 $30 $16 $16 **$16** $16	Offset −1, 1 left to copy
8	$16 $16 $30 $16 $16 $16 $16 $3d	Literal byte
9	$16 $16 $30 **$16** $16 $16 $3d $16	Offset −5, 3 left to copy
10	$16 $16 $30 $16 **$16** $16 $16 $3d $16 $16	Offset −5, 2 left to copy
11	$16 $16 $30 $16 $16 **$16** $16 $3d $16 $16 $16	Offset −5, 1 left to copy
12	$16 $16 $30 $16 $16 $16 $16 $3d $16 $16 $16 $6b	Literal byte

Data compression is a continually ongoing concern. The amount of data generated now is astronomical and, while network throughput has increased dramatically over the years, it invariably lags behind demand. Data still needs to be compressed for storage and for moving from one place to another.

It may seem as if there are sufficiently good generic compression methods now, and that the data-specific techniques that dominate this chapter are antiquated. In program optimization, often the biggest gains result from effective choices of data structures and algorithms [7], not fiddling with compiler options: a good programmer can understand and take advantage of properties that a good but generic compiler cannot discern or safely take advantage of. Similarly, while generic compression schemes can perform some transformations of their input to improve compression (e.g., Burrows-Wheeler or move-to-front coding [25]), these are superficial transformations that are dependent on the original input byte sequence; they have no understanding of what those bytes *mean*. A good data-specific technique still has the potential to win out over a generic method. Arguably, the lossy JPEG algorithm applies this principle by carefully considering the input (images) and how it will eventually be perceived (by humans with limited perceptual capability). Other more specialized application areas exist where a deep understanding of input data yields better compression (e.g., [5, 29]), possibly in concert with an existing generic method.

The generic methods mentioned here, and relatives thereof, are still in active use. Run-length encoding is an easy-to-implement compression method when data indicates its use, and it is found buried inside bzip2 [26] and JPEG [35]. LZSS' siblings on the LZ77 family tree see extensive use. In particular, LZ77-based DEFLATE [15] is used by gzip [16], PNG [10], and zip [8] (and by extension Java's JAR files [19]).

One last application introduces one last constraint: a physical one. Related to modern "autocomplete" functionality, predictive compression models can be applied to generate likely text input sequences as assistive technology for people who would otherwise have difficulty typing [13, 14]. How some retrogames generated content is the topic of the next chapter.

References

1. Adams, S.: An adventure in small computer game simulation. Creat. Comput. **5**(8), 90–97 (1979)
2. Adams, S.: Pirate's adventure. Byte **5**(12), 192–212 (1980)
3. Ahmad, S.: Email Communication (1 Mar 2015)
4. Apple Computer, Inc.: Apple II Reference Manual. Apple Computer, Cupertino (1978)
5. Aycock, J.: What's in a name... generator? J. Comput. Virol. **8**(1–2), 53–60 (2012)
6. Bell, T.C.: Better OPM/L text compression. IEEE Trans. Commun. **34**(12), 1176–1182 (1986)
7. Bentley, J.L.: Writing Efficient Programs. Prentice-Hall, Englewood Cliffs (1982)
8. Berez, J.M., Blank, M.S., Lebling, P.D.: ZIP: Z-Language Interpreter Program. Infocom Internal Document, Draft (1989)
9. Blank, M.S., Galley, S.W.: How to fit a large program into a small machine, or how to fit the great underground empire on your desk-top. Creat. Comput. **6**(7), 80–87 (1980)

10. Boutell, T. (ed.): PNG (portable network graphics) specification version 1.0. RFC 2083 (1997)
11. Braben, D.: Classic game postmortem: Elite. Game Developer's Conference 2011. http://www. gdcvault.com/play/1014628/Classic-Game-Postmortem (2011)
12. Collins, S.: Game graphics during the 8-bit computer era. ACM SIGGRAPH Comput. Graph. **32**(2), 47–51 (1998)
13. Darragh, J.J., Witten, I.H.: The Reactive Keyboard. Cambridge University Press, Cambridge/New York (1992)
14. Darragh, J.J., Witten, I.H., James, M.L.: The reactive keyboard: a predictive typing aid. IEEE Comput. **23**(11), 41–49 (1990)
15. Deutsch, P.: DEFLATE Compressed Data Format Specification Version 1.3. RFC 1951 (1996)
16. Deutsch, P.: GZIP File Format Specification Version 4.3. RFC 1952 (1996)
17. Levy, S.: Hackers: Heroes of the Computer Revolution. Dell, New York (1984)
18. Meretzky, S.: Email Communication (22 Nov 2013)
19. Oracle: JAR File Specification (Undated). http://docs.oracle.com/javase/6/docs/technotes/guides/jar/jar.html
20. PKWARE, Inc.: APPNOTE.TXT – .ZIP File Format Specification. https://pkware.cachefly.net/webdocs/casestudies/APPNOTE.TXT (2014). Version 6.3.4
21. Radio Shack: LEVEL II BASIC Reference Manual. Radio Shack (1979). Catalog number 26-2102
22. Retro Gamer staff: Great Scott. Retro Gamer (3), 36–41 (2010)
23. Rigby, P.: Level 9. Retro Gamer (57), 22–27 (2008)
24. Ritman, J.: Email Communication (1 Mar 2015)
25. Sayood, K.: Introduction to Data Compression, 2nd edn. Morgan Kaufmann, San Francisco (2000)
26. Seward, J.: Bzip2 Source Code, version 1.0.6. http://www.bzip.org/ (20 Sept 2010)
27. Stan, S.G.: Compact disc standards and formats. In: Origins and Successors of the Compact Disc: Contributions of Philips to Optical Storage, chap. 4, pp. 137–176. Springer (2009)
28. Storer, J.A., Szymanski, T.G.: Data compression via textual substitution. J. ACM **29**(4), 928–951 (1982)
29. The Chromium Projects: Software updates: Courgette. http://dev.chromium.org/developers/design-documents/software-updates-courgette (c. 2009)
30. Various contributors: Definition. Included file in ScottFree v. 1.14
31. Various contributors: LZSS. http://wiki.xentax.com/index.php?title=LZSS&oldid=9437
32. Various contributors: The 7th Guest GJD. http://wiki.xentax.com/index.php?title=The_7th_Guest_GJD&oldid=7933
33. Various contributors: The 7th Guest VDX. http://wiki.xentax.com/index.php?title=The_7th_Guest_VDX&oldid=4606
34. Various contributors: The Z-Machine Standards Document (1997)
35. Wallace, G.K.: The JPEG still picture compression standard. Commun. ACM **34**(4), 30–44 (1991)
36. Wild, C., Irvine, S.: The Hobbit Disassembly (Undated). http://www.icemark.com/downloads/files/hobbitsrc.zip
37. Ziv, J., Lempel, A.: A universal algorithm for sequential data compression. IEEE Trans. Inf. Theory **23**(3), 337–343 (1977)

Chapter 6
Procedural Content Generation

Procedural content generation (PCG), using algorithms to produce game content, is in some ways the limit case of data compression. At one extreme is uncompressed, pre-existing game data, which was completely satisfactory for many retrogames. Not all. Hence data compression, but what if the game data is still too big? Instead of having compressed, pre-existing data along with code to decompress it, a retrogame could have next to no data and have code to generate the necessary content on demand as the game was played. Obviously this would be an attractive option when memory or storage space was tight.[1] An ideal PCG result should approach what a human game designer would create, and not just be a jumble of random things in random locations.

PCG does imply the use of randomness to give scalability and diversity, though, and that's where we begin. There must be a source of random numbers for a retrogame to use. Computer games often channel the late interior decorator Dorothy Draper, who declared 'If it looks right it is right' [34]. While applications like cryptography have very stringent requirements for randomness [32], games can get away with "random-ish" or "random enough" numbers so long as the end result appears random to the player.

One source of randomness in retrogames was bytes that were not random at all; just the opposite, in fact. These particular bytes were chosen with painstaking precision: the bytes of the game code.

Example 6.1 (Yar's Revenge, 1981). As Fig. 6.1 clearly shows, the object of the game was for Yar to destroy the Qotile with the Zorlon Cannon [2].[2] The interesting thing about *Yar's Revenge* from an implementation point of view is not the gameplay or the comic book that accompanied its release, but the colorful vertical

---

[1] There have been complementary treatments of procedural content generation whose focus is on the state of the art rather than history. See, for example, [18, 33].

[2] I'm being facetious, of course. *Yar's Revenge* frequently finds itself on lists of the best games for the Atari 2600, and its gameplay holds up extremely well decades after its release.

J. Aycock, *Retrogame Archeology*, DOI 10.1007/978-3-319-30004-7_6

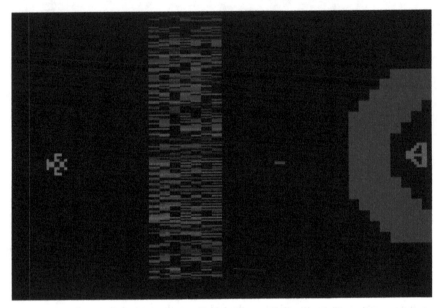

Fig. 6.1 *Yar's Revenge* on the Atari 2600 (Image ©Atari Interactive, Inc., used with permission)

strip near the middle of the screen. This is the 'Neutral Zone' [2], and its seemingly-random color and fluctuating pattern are derived from the game's code bytes being treated as data.

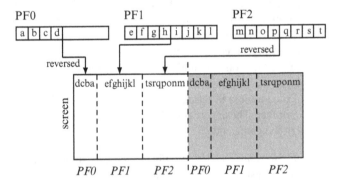

Fig. 6.2 Conceptual view of the Atari 2600 playfield

The placement of the Neutral Zone is a reflection of the Atari 2600's hardware. The 'playfield' basically consists of foreground objects that do not correspond to the player, NPC, and any shooting activity they may be engaged in; the Atari reference manual describes it as 'walls, clouds, barriers, and other seldom moved objects' [41]. Conceptually, the screen is divided in half, and the playfield contents within the left half-screen are controlled by 20 bits spread over three graphics chip registers: PF1, PF2, and half of PF0 (Fig. 6.2).[3] A playfield bit set in one of those registers results in an (elongated) pixel in the corresponding playfield area onscreen; the right half-screen is a copy of the left half. In practice, the programmer was responsible for setting the graphics chip registers for each individual scan line on the screen, meaning that the playfield's bit patterns could change from one line to the next. Here, the Neutral Zone's bit pattern is derived from code bytes and placed in PF2; the color is similarly set. Figure 6.1 depicts the Neutral Zone with seven bits because the value has been ANDed with $fe prior to being stored in PF2 (since PF2's bits are reversed, the remaining seven bits are right-aligned with the center of the screen).

Fig. 6.3 Code as "random" data in *Yar's Revenge*

```
1  A = M[M_w[$e9] + Y]
2  M[PF0] = A
3  M[PF1] = A
4  M[PF2] = A
5  M[COLUPF] = A
```

The purest expression of code as data in *Yar's Revenge* is the full-screen explosion seen when the player succeeds in destroying the Qotile. Figure 6.3 shows the pseudo-assembly code. Line 1 reads a (code) byte from memory, which is blasted into the memory-mapped PF0, PF1, and PF2 registers (lines 2–4) and finally into the playfield's color register at line 5.

Interestingly, for both the explosion and the Neutral Zone, a code byte used as data could be drawn from the exact location being executed. This allowed the player to glimpse a representation of the currently running instruction, if only for an instant.

Yar's Revenge was not the only Atari 2600 game using its code as data. Dan Oliver's *Laser Gates* (1983) used "random" code bytes to color force fields (Fig. 6.4). It would be easy to label his use of the technique as being derivative, had he not used code bytes to produce random sounds in a game two years earlier: *Space Cavern* (1981).[4]

A different approach to randomness in retrogames would be to use some physical, real-world event that occurs unpredictably to generate random numbers; this is an approach used by random number generators that have security aspirations.[5] For games, the time a game was started, the movement and button presses on a joystick, or the delay between keystrokes on a keyboard are all unpredictable enough to be

---

[3] Atari 2600 technical information in this chapter is from [41]. Game information for *Yar's Revenge* was obtained through dynamic analysis and cross-checked where possible with Montfort and Bogost [25].

[4] Information for Oliver's games from dynamic analysis, with the tip-off regarding *Space Cavern* from [15].

[5] Eastlake et al. [13] has a good general discussion, and [21] itemizes how the entropy pool is filled on Linux.

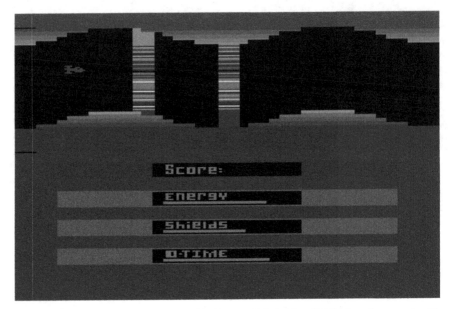

Fig. 6.4 *Laser Gates* on the Atari 2600 (Image ©Activision Publishing, Inc., used with permission)

used for randomness. A related method is for a game to sample some physical event that changes predictably, but frequently enough that its value will appear random.

```
1    random:    A = M[FRMCNT]
2               c‖A = A + M[RNDM] + c
3               c‖A = A + M[RNDM+1] + c
4               push A
5               A = M[RNDM]
6               M[RNDM+1] = A
7               pop A
8               M[RNDM] = A
9               return
```

Fig. 6.5 *Dig Dug*'s random number generator

Example 6.2 (Dig Dug, 1987). On the Atari 7800 port, *Dig Dug* had a FRMCNT variable whose one-byte value was incremented once every display frame,[6] which would equate to 60 times a second for NTSC and 50 for PAL/SECAM. The pseudo-assembly code for the random number generator itself is shown in Fig. 6.5. The two-byte random value in RNDM and RNDM+1 is updated using FRMCNT, somewhat unpredictably: at line 2, the state of the carry flag is unknown and it is added

---

[6] Usage observed in source code; increment rate confirmed in emulator.

anyway (a normal sequence of addition instructions on the 6502 would clear the carry flag first). Lines 4–8 swap the two random bytes around before returning the most-changed byte as the random number.

A typical usage of a returned random number is to mask off some number of bits. At one point in *Dig Dug*, the random value is ANDed with 1, and that single remaining bit is used to decide rock placement. It may therefore not be sufficient for the random number as a whole to appear random – the changes in individual bits of the random number from one call of the random number generator to the next may need to occur randomly as well.

Table 6.1 PRNG seeding and output

Action	Random number sequence produced
Seed PRNG with 42	64, 2, 27, 22, 74, 68, 90, 8, 42, 3, ...
Seed PRNG with 1234	97, 44, 0, 92, 94, 58, 67, 8, 77, 23, ...
Re-seed PRNG with 42	64, 2, 27, 22, 74, 68, 90, 8, 42, 3, ...

Other approaches to randomness would technically be called *pseudo*-random. A pseudo-random number generator (PRNG) is a deterministic algorithm which, given the same initial seed value as input, produces the exact same sequence of random numbers.[7] Table 6.1 briefly illustrates seeding and re-seeding a PRNG, and the random number sequences it produces. Retrogames could use PRNGs in two ways. First, PRNGs happen to be a good way to produce random numbers, and some retrogames would use them in PCG to produce a vast amount of unrepeated content. Second, because PRNGs can reproduce the same random number sequence given the same seed, they can be used in PCG to concisely regenerate the same content over and over. We will see both types – and different PRNG algorithms – as we progress through examples of procedural content generation.

6.1 Name Generation: *Elite* (1984)

Elite uses a pseudorandom number generator based on Tribonacci numbers.[8] Unlike Fibonacci numbers, where the nth term in the series is based on the previous two terms, Tribonacci numbers use the previous three terms:

$$T(n) = T(n-1) + T(n-2) + T(n-3)$$

---

[7] Strictly speaking, pseudo-random numbers. These terms will be used interchangeably here to avoid excessive awkwardness. Table 6.1 is using `random.randint(0,100)` from Python 2.7.5.

[8] Game information here is based on reverse engineering as mentioned previously, and cross-checked against [5]. Their PRNG is usually only loosely described as Fibonacci-based [7, 35].

But, unlike the formal mathematical definition of the Tribonacci sequence [39], *Elite* doesn't start with the initial values $F(0) = F(1) = 0$ and $F(2) = 1$.

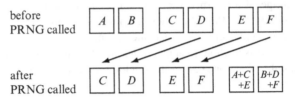

Fig. 6.6 Pseudo-random number generation in *Elite*

The three 16-bit values are stored in six bytes that change from one call of the PRNG to the next as shown in Fig. 6.6 (the addition's carry is handled correctly but not shown in the figure). By extracting bits from these six bytes in various ways, this gives enough information to produce and deterministically reproduce all the characteristics of eight galaxies, each with 256 planets.

```
1   N = 4
2   if bit 6 of A is 0:
3       N = N - 1
4   while N > 0:
5       index = F AND $1f
6       if index ≠ 0:
7           output digram[index]
8       call PRNG
9       N = N - 1
```

Fig. 6.7 Name generation in *Elite*

Elite's algorithm for name generation is shown in Fig. 6.7. It uses six bits of the six bytes that the PRNG shuffles around, along with the set of digrams mentioned in Chap. 5. The maximum number of digrams in a name is four (N, line 1), although that can be decreased at the outset (lines 2–3) and digrams can be skipped (line 6, if index is 0). Special cases aside, the low five bits of F are used as an index into the digram table, relevant parts of which are shown in Table 6.2. *Elite*'s code skips question marks in digrams such as the one at index 15, allowing some generated names to have an odd number of characters.

Figure 6.8 illustrates how some names used in *Elite* are generated. RIEDQUAT produces the full four digrams; LAVE, the starting location, has only three digrams, one of which is skipped due to a digram index of 0. Finally, USZAA has an odd number of characters because its generation uses the specially-handled A? digram.

Table 6.2 *Elite* digram table excerpt

Index	Digram	Index	Digram
1	LE	16	ER
2	XE	17	AT
3	GE	18	EN
4	ZA	19	BE
5	CE	20	RA
6	BI	21	LA
7	SO	22	VE
8	US	23	TI
9	ES	24	ED
10	AR	25	OR
11	MA	26	QU
12	IN	27	AN
13	DI	28	TE
14	RE	29	IS
15	A?	30	RI

Elite's name generation is directly related to the generation of random, but pronounceable words for passwords, which can be traced back to the mid-1970s [16], and the same ideas can be applied now to generate passwords and other "words" like usernames and CAPTCHA challenges. There are a number of different approaches to pronounceable word generation, varying in quality and scalability. Good results can be obtained by learning the probability with which one syllable follows another in a dictionary, and using that as a guide to generate words [11].

One modern application of name generation is a malicious one. Malicious software wanting to "phone home" to get new commands or send stolen data to its creator needs an address to connect to, like a domain name or a network IP address. If the malicious software is preprogrammed with one address, or a small set of addresses, then defenders can block access to those locations or even take control of the malicious software. The solution is procedural content generation, which is called "domain flux" in this context [37]. Malicious software produces a large number of domain names using a domain generation algorithm and attempts to connect to them all; there are too many for defenders to block, and yet the malicious software's creator need only register one of these domain names temporarily to control their progeny. Malicious software can up the ante by incorporating an unpredictable element like closing stock prices or social media trends as an input to the domain generation algorithm [23, 38], meaning that knowing the algorithm is insufficient to know in advance what domain names will be generated.

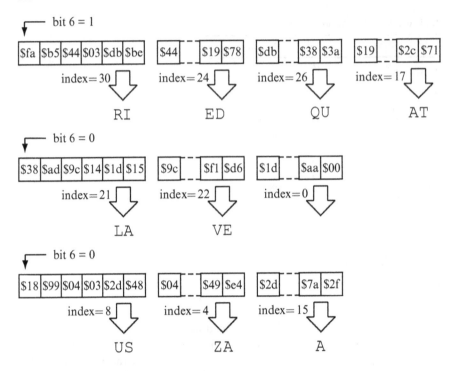

Fig. 6.8 *Elite* name generation examples

6.2 Room Wall Generation: *Berzerk* (1980) and *Frenzy* (1982)

Rooms in the arcade game *Berzerk* and its sequel *Frenzy* used essentially the same algorithm for procedural generation of the walls within rooms, and they used exactly the same PRNG to do it with.[9]

The PRNG in question is an instance of a linear congruential generator, the general form of which is [22]

$$X_{n+1} = (aX_n + c) \bmod m$$

It is not immediately obvious that this maps to the PRNG in *Berzerk*, however, looking at the Z80 pseudo-assembly code in Fig. 6.9. The constant c and its value of $3153 can be spotted easily enough; the "mod m" doesn't appear at all, but there is an implied modulo 65,536 thanks to the 16-bit arithmetic. The Z80's lack of a

---

[9] *Frenzy* game information is from the source code, *Berzerk* information is from disassembly guided by [29]. The algorithm given here simplifies by blending the two games: *Frenzy* had more pillars, *Berzerk* had an extra call to the PRNG.

```
 1   RANDOM:    push H‖L
 2              H‖L = M_w[Seed]
 3              D = H
 4              E = L
 5              H‖L = H‖L + H‖L
 6              H‖L = H‖L + D‖E
 7              H‖L = H‖L + H‖L
 8              H‖L = H‖L + D‖E
 9              D‖E = $3153
10              H‖L = H‖L + D‖E
11              M_w[Seed] = H‖L
12              A = H
13              pop H‖L
14              return
```

Fig. 6.9 Pseudo-assembly code for *Berzerk*'s PRNG

multiplication instruction requires some cleverness when it comes to a. The value of a is 7, and it is incrementally computed by the additions in lines 5–8, adding values to themselves to multiply by two:

$$2 \times (2 \times \text{seed} + \text{seed}) + \text{seed}$$
$$= 2 \times (3 \times \text{seed}) + \text{seed}$$
$$= 6 \times \text{seed} + \text{seed}$$
$$= 7 \times \text{seed}$$

Equipped with this PRNG, *Berzerk* generates walls using the algorithm in Fig. 6.10, which is simple and gives good results. A 4×2 grid of pillars is conceptually located in the room, and each is considered in turn. Two bits from the PRNG's value are used at each pillar to determine which direction to draw a wall in. A full example is given in Fig. 6.11, showing the pillars as dots; the pillar being processed is circled. Notice that it is possible for a single wall to be generated two ways, as the example shows, although this does no harm to the end result.

How random is random? Great batteries of tests exist to check statistical properties of PRNGs [22, 30]. Given a common usage of PRNG output in retrogames was extracting a handful of bits, one concern is that all bits may not be equally random. Knuth points out, for example, that linear congruential generators using the machine's word size for m have right-hand bits that are 'much less random' [22, p. 13]. *Berzerk*, of course, uses this $m = 2^{16}$ optimization along with the two least-significant bits of the PRNG's output.

Another measure of a PRNG is its period, the number of times it may be called before the same sequence of output numbers is repeated. Of three tests for a linear congruential generator to have a period of length m [22], *Berzerk*'s PRNG passes two of them, the ramifications of which are that it only has a period of 16,384 regardless of its initial seed.

```
NROWS = 2
NCOLS = 4
for row in 1...NROWS:
    for col in 1...NCOLS:
        r = RANDOM() AND 3
        if r = 0:
            up()
        else if r = 1:
            down()
        else if r = 2:
            right()
        else:
            left()
```

Fig. 6.10 Pseudocode for wall generation in *Berzerk*

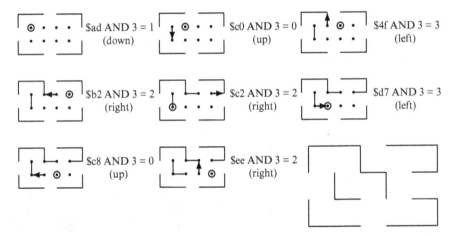

Fig. 6.11 *Berzerk* wall layout example

The linear congruential generator in *Prince of Persia* (1989),[10] by contrast, does pass all three period tests with its computation of seed $= (5 \times \text{seed} + 23) \bmod 256$. This is probably a good thing, given that it is only an eight-bit PRNG to begin with. Figure 6.12 shows its 6502 pseudo-assembly for the Apple II, where it makes use of left shifts to multiply by two (adding a register's value to itself was not an option on the 6502, in contrast to the Z80). Having a full-length period does not necessarily translate into good randomness by itself, though. The least-significant bit output by *Prince of Persia*'s PRNG just alternates back and forth incessantly between 1 and 0. At one place in the code, the PRNG is called twice in a row and the two low-order bits are used for a random star. Unfortunately the double call doesn't make the PRNG output more random: with one call, the two least-significant bits cycle

---

[10] Verified in source code. Empirical testing of the PRNGs in *Berzerk* and *Prince of Persia* was done using separate programs I wrote.

```
RND:    A = M[RNDseed]
        c‖A = shiftleft(A)
        c‖A = shiftleft(A)
        c = 0
        c‖A = A + M[RNDseed] + c
        c = 0
        A = A + 23
        M[RNDseed] = A
        return
```

Fig. 6.12 Pseudo-assembly
code for *Prince of Persia*'s
PRNG

through the four-value sequence 3,2,1,0,3,2,1,0,..., whereas only two values alternate predictably with a double PRNG invocation. It's enough to make a programmer
go berserk.

Returning to *Berzerk*, the PRNG seed was very deliberately chosen, as programmer Alan McNeil explains in an interview [14, p. 114]: 'I used the XY coordinate
of the room as a 16bit [sic] number to seed my random number generator. That way
you could exit, run back and see the same room.' In other words, the PRNG was
used for both its usefulness for random number generation but also its ability to
deterministically regenerate a random number sequence. The example in Fig. 6.11,
for instance, corresponds to the actual PRNG output *Berzerk* uses when seeded with
$x = 104$ and $y = 63$.

This repeatability trick was used by other retrogames. One example of this was
Telengard (1982) on the Commodore PET, a "dungeon-crawling" game that would
regenerate the same dungeon each game (thus avoiding the space needed to save
the dungeon data) by seeding its PRNG with the player's (x, y, z) coordinates.[11] Of
course, *Telengard* was not the only dungeon crawler.

6.3 Dungeon Generation: *Rogue* (1980)

Procedural dungeon generation for dungeon-crawling games conjures up an entire
family of games, modern and retro, but the grandfather of them was *Rogue*, so much
so that games of this ilk are referred to as 'roguelikes.' One of the selling points *is*
the lack of repeatability: each game sports a different randomly-generated dungeon.
But first we prorogue *Rogue* to discuss a roguelike that was pre-*Rogue*.

Beneath Apple Manor (1978) for the Apple II had classic roguelike characteristics, despite its earlier appearance.[12] Figure 6.13 shows a screenshot of the game
and one of its generated dungeons. This is a top-down view; the larger squares
and rectangles are rooms, and the spidery tentacles connecting them are corridors.

---

[11] Mentioned in an interview with *Telengard*'s author [4], and verified in the source code with
guidance from [6, 8].

[12] Game information from static analysis and a visualization I constructed.

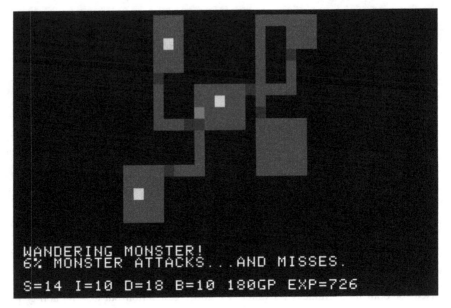

Fig. 6.13 *Beneath Apple Manor* screenshot

The handful of differently-colored blocks represent doors, treasure chests, the player, and the wandering monster accosting the player, but those are incidental to this discussion and will be ignored.

The dungeon was generated in a series of steps whose progression was pointedly marked by the game – the PCG code was written in BASIC, making this a non-instantaneous process. The user selected the number of rooms per dungeon level at the start of the game (five was recommended) and an entry into a new/lower dungeon level was heralded by an incremental display of:

```
CONSTRUCTING A DUNGEON LEVEL
NOW BUILDING:
ROOMS
CORRIDORS...1 2 3 4
DOORS
MONSTERS AND TREASURE
MAGIC ITEMS
```

We will focus on the first two. The requisite number of rooms were produced by randomly selecting a location and a (bounded) size and checking to see if those map cells were unoccupied. If not, new random values were chosen, and this repeated indefinitely until a suitable placement was found. In practice, the room size bounds were small enough that this task was not onerous. Figure 6.14 shows what this intermediate stage would look like, along with room numbers.

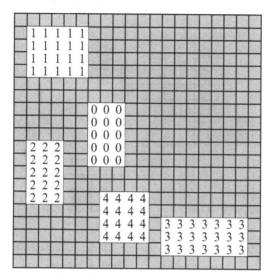

Fig. 6.14 Example room layout in *Beneath Apple Manor*

The random room placement obviously can scatter the rooms in no particular order. The second step, corridor generation, does treat the rooms in order and ensures that all rooms are reachable. The overall goal is to connect consecutively-numbered pairs of rooms: room 0 to room 1, 1 to 2, 2 to 3, and so on, hence the numbers following the CORRIDORS... message above.

It is easiest to illustrate corridor layout with an example, and the connection of room 2 to room 3 is a good one. A room's location is represented internally by its upper-left corner and, starting at the upper-left corner of room 2, the target is the upper-left corner of room 3. In the absence of other rooms, there are two options. Either move horizontally until directly over room 3's corner then down, or move vertically until directly to the left of 3's corner then right. The corridor layout algorithm randomly chooses one of these options and starts mapping out the corridor's path cell by cell in the chosen direction. If another room is encountered, directly or in an immediately adjacent cell to the growing corridor, the layout restarts from *that* room's upper-left corner.

Figure 6.15 shows this play out when connecting room 2 to room 3. At room 2, horizontal movement is randomly chosen and eventually runs into room 0 (a), and the algorithm is now trying to connect room 0 to room 3. Vertical movement is randomly chosen, which passes beside room 4 (b); the goal is now to connect room 4 to room 3. An initial vertical movement is again chosen randomly (c), and the final corridor routing is shown in Fig. 6.15d.

Rogue took a more intricate approach to its dungeon level generation.[13] A dungeon level had nine rooms, always. This sounds less than random, but it was done

---

[13] Based on *Rogue* 3.6, game information from static source code analysis and construction of an algorithm visualization. Empirical PRNG testing was done with a separate program I wrote.

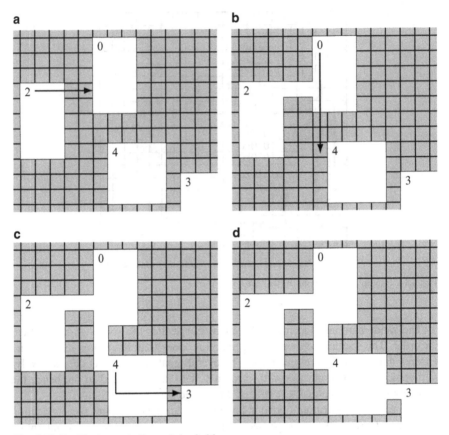

Fig. 6.15 Corridor layout in *Beneath Apple Manor*

for good reason: the screen was conceptually divided into a 3 × 3 grid, and each box on the grid contained one room, whose size and placement within its box was random. Up to three randomly-selected rooms were labeled as "gone," meaning they would be assigned a location but would otherwise be treated as points rather than full-fledged rooms; their usefulness came later. Figure 6.16 shows an example room layout. The grid is represented by dashed lines, and rooms 1, 2, and 8 are gone rooms.

The next step is creating corridors. Connectivity is randomly made between immediately adjacent rooms – for instance, room 6 can be connected to room 3 and room 7, but not any others. Two rooms may be connected unidirectionally or bidirectionally, which makes no difference in gameplay, but results in the rooms being connected by two corridors that may be routed differently due to randomness.

Other parts of level generation were straightforward, like placing items randomly, making room and corridor layout the most interesting part to examine.

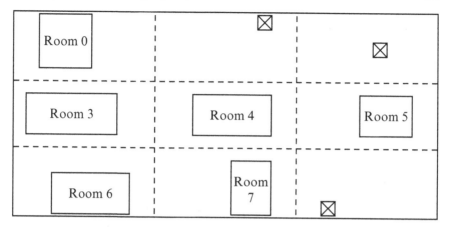

Fig. 6.16 Example room layout in *Rogue*

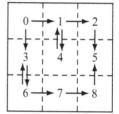

Fig. 6.17 Example room
connectivity

Also, gone rooms are included in connectivity, because corridors to and from (non-visible) gone rooms look like interesting winding corridors in the finished level. Figure 6.17 shows the connectivity generated for the running example.

Once the connectivity is decided, the corridors are created. Each pair of connected rooms is sorted such that there are only two cases to consider. Either a corridor is being created from one room above another in the grid, or from one room to the room in the grid cell on its right. In other words, the corridor layout is moving down, or moving right. Breaking down the corridor creation in this way makes reasoning about the process straightforward. For example, it is now apparent that for a downward layout, a door will need to reside on the bottom of one room along with one on the top of the other room.

Figure 6.18 illustrates the two cases, overlooking a minor exception for handling gone rooms. Locations for doors (denoted ×), the start and end points of the corridor, are chosen randomly on the appropriate walls. Each corridor is composed of three segments: one straight out from the start location; one perpendicular to that segment, possibly of zero length; one straight from the perpendicular segment to the end location. The final corridor layout is shown in Fig. 6.19. The gone rooms have become connection points for corridors, and of the bidirectionally connected rooms, rooms 1 and 4 simply retraced the same corridor twice, whereas rooms 3 and 6 ended up with two separate corridors.

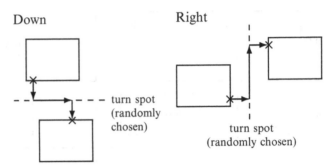

Fig. 6.18 The two corridor layout cases in *Rogue*

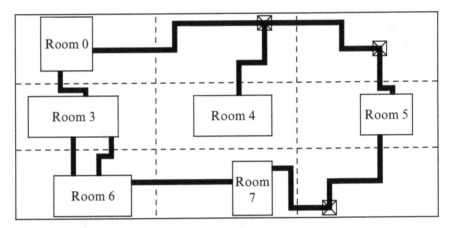

Fig. 6.19 Final *Rogue* room and corridor layout

The PRNG that *Rogue* uses is again a linear congruential generator. It computes seed $= (11,109 \times$ seed $+ 13,849)$ mod $65,536$ and shifts the result right by one bit, perhaps to help mitigate Knuth's 'much less random' problem. Indeed, without the shift, the rightmost bit simply alternates between 0 and 1. Obviously choosing a PRNG, or values to use for a PRNG, has its pitfalls, but there are other algorithms for generating pseudorandom numbers.

6.4 Jungle Generation: *Pitfall!* (1982)

A number of retrogames used an alternative approach for pseudorandom number generation, the linear feedback shift register.[14] Given a bit-shift operation in hardware or software, there is a one-bit vacuum that must be filled, and the value that fills that empty location changes the nature of the operation.

---

[14] Information on linear feedback shift registers is from [28].

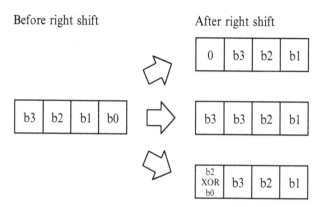

Fig. 6.20 Nature abhors a bit vacuum

For example, Fig. 6.20 demonstrates three different ways that the high bit may be populated after the (one-bit) right shift of a four-bit value. Always setting the high bit to 0 corresponds to a logical shift operation that divides an unsigned integer value by two. Duplicating the old high bit's value as the new high bit's value – essentially a form of feedback – results in an arithmetic shift, dividing a signed integer by two.[15] The feedback preserves the sign of the two's complement result. Finally, if the high bit always becomes a specific linear combination of previous bit values, then the shifting results in what is called a linear feedback shift register (LFSR). The bit positions that are combined are referred to as taps, making *b2* and *b0* taps in this example. This idea is not restricted to right shifting, either, and works equally well in the other direction. Among other applications, an LFSR can have all or part of its value interpreted as a pseudorandom number.

On now to the game. While *Pitfall!*'s PCG has been well described in Montfort and Bogost [25] and by the game author himself [9], they have nonetheless failed to capture all the subtle nuances of how cleverly this scheme functioned.[16]

Figure 6.21 shows a screenshot from *Pitfall!*, the code for which coincidentally was written using a line editor on one of the ADM-3A terminals mentioned in Chap. 3 [10]. *Pitfall!*'s jungle had 255 screens, the content of which was procedurally generated. It might seem odd to do PCG on the Atari 2600, where the CPU was occupied 'racing the beam,' but to store 255 screens' worth of information would have been prohibitive in a 4 K cartridge. The mechanism needed to be lightweight in terms of both size and processing requirements, however.

The game contained not one, but two LFSRs. The simpler one produced an eight-bit value in a memory location we'll call R2, and that LFSR provides a nice introduction to how they were implemented on the 6502. Figure 6.22 gives the pseudo-assembly for this LFSR (writing M[R2] as R2 for simplicity) along with

---

[15] With caveats about rounding [36].

[16] Game information from static and dynamic analysis, with much assistance from [19].

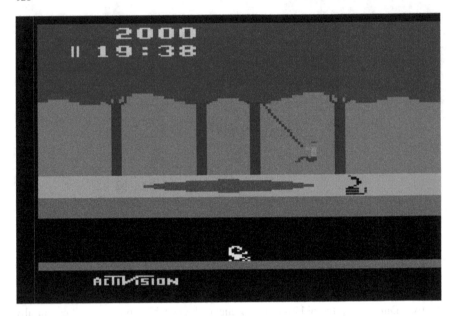

Fig. 6.21 *Pitfall!* on the Atari 2600 (Image ©Activision Publishing, Inc., used with permission)

a diagram showing the information flow. The net result sees R2's bits shifted left, and its leftmost bit replaced with the XOR of two original bits; this is an LFSR with taps *b6* and *b7*. The key idea is to align the tap bits together, combine them with XOR (other bit combinations are created as a side effect), and then move the final combination into the carry bit, enabling it to be rotated into place in R2. Despite all the activity, at each stage there is really only one bit position that holds the value of importance: the gradually-building XOR combination for the LFSR.

With that in mind, we turn to the second LFSR in *Pitfall!*, which we'll call R1. It too is an eight-bit value, initialized to $c4 at the start of a game. Figure 6.23 shows the pseudo-assembly code for this LFSR, and traces in condensed form the progression of the XORed bit through the computation.

This LFSR's design has two important properties. First, the LFSR is bidirectional, meaning that it is possible to move forward *and* backward through the sequence of pseudorandom numbers. To understand how this is possible, consider the final value of R1 in Fig. 6.23 versus the initial value. Seven of the original bits are directly present in R1's final value; the only one missing is *b7*. However, *b7* is present in XORed form, and because of how XOR works, the original value of *b7* can be retrieved. In particular, $(a \text{ XOR } b) \text{ XOR } a = b$: taking an XORed value and XORing it again by one of its original operands yields the other operand. Extending this to the situation at hand:

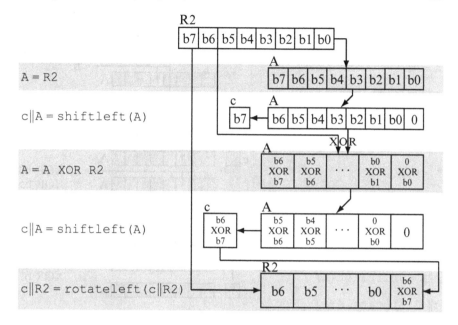

Fig. 6.22 One of *Pitfall!*'s LFSRs

$(b3 \text{ XOR } b4 \text{ XOR } b5 \text{ XOR } b7) \text{ XOR } b3 \text{ XOR } b4 \text{ XOR } b5$

$= (b3 \text{ XOR } b3) \text{ XOR } (b4 \text{ XOR } b4) \text{ XOR } (b5 \text{ XOR } b5) \text{ XOR } b7$

$= 0 \text{ XOR } 0 \text{ XOR } 0 \text{ XOR } b7$

$= b7$

Different code (not shown) is needed to implement this, obviously, but it is feasible to move either direction in the PRNG sequence.

The second important property R1 has is that it is a maximal-length LFSR. Moving in one direction through the PRNG sequence, all 255 values will be produced by the LFSR before returning to the original seed value. (There are 255 values and not 256 because an LFSR value with all zeroes cannot occur.) This is the reason why R1 has so many taps compared to R2. Not all taps are created equal, and there are a small number of tap combinations that will result in a maximal-length sequence. R2, by contrast, does not use a maximal-length set of taps, and its PRNG sequence repeats after only 63 values.

How is this used? *Pitfall!* has 255 screens, after which the player finds themself back at the starting screen. Now it is apparent that this number is not coincidental at all. *Pitfall!* performs PCG using the value of R1 to produce the contents of each screen in a repeatable fashion. The appropriate LFSR code is called to advance R1 either forwards or backwards through the PRNG sequence depending on whether the player moves offscreen to the left or to the right.

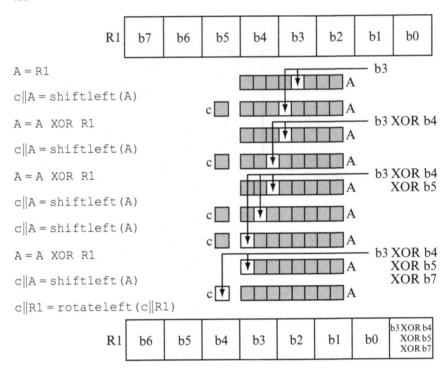

Fig. 6.23 Left-shifting LFSR in *Pitfall!*

Bits of R1 are carved out to perform the PCG, as shown in Fig. 6.24. At a glance, not all screen combinations are possible: blue quicksand cannot appear in conjunction with the swinging vine, for example. On the topic of vines, vine control shifts to *b1* on a crocodile screen, but the remainder of the object type bits are ignored. This may seem like an odd bit choice – why *b1* instead of *b0*, for instance? – but the object type's value is stored directly into the Atari 2600's graphics ENABL register to enable the vine, which ignores all bit positions except *b1* [41]. The efficient implementation of *Pitfall!*'s PCG is thus intimately linked to the Atari 2600.

Other bits are multiply used or otherwise repurposed. For the two screen types having holes, *b7* is used to locate an underground wall on those screens, the left side if *b7*=0 and the right side otherwise. Treasure screens look to *b1–b0* to determine the type of treasure: the four possible combinations select one of a money bag, a ring, a silver bar, or a gold bar.

While the presence of treasure and its type are produced using PCG, game screens don't restock. *Pitfall!* therefore needs to keep track of which treasures have been picked up by the player, and this bookkeeping involves one last clever usage of the LFSR. There are 32 treasures in total, and they are tracked using a four-byte bitmap, one bit per treasure. To index this bitmap, *b7–b6* of R1 select one of the four bytes, and the three object type bits choose one bit within that byte.

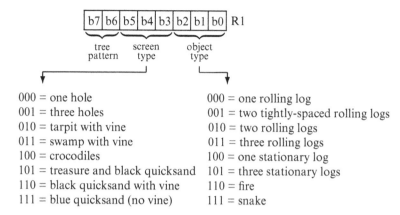

Fig. 6.24 *Pitfall!*'s jungle generation scheme

This uniquely tracks each treasure. On a treasure screen, the screen type bits are always 101, and the remaining five bits of R1 (*b7–b6* and *b2–b0*) must assume all the possible $2^5 = 32$ values exactly once because the LFSR is maximal-length.

Using PCG for an application leaves the programmer at the mercy of the PCG algorithm they devised and the PRNG that drives it, to a certain extent. Instead of a programmer directly controlling their code and data, they must indirectly steer their algorithm. *Pitfall!*'s author, David Crane, observed this with relation to game design. He had to vet the 255 generated screens to decide on the best initial LFSR seed from the gameplay point of view, picking a seed that would start the player at screens where they could learn gameplay skills gradually [9, 27:34].

Pitfall!'s PCG extended beyond the Atari 2600. Crane's port of *Pitfall!* to the Intellivision was extremely faithful, and in fact the same eight-bit LFSR algorithm can be found in the code.[17] This would be fairly unremarkable, except that the Intellivision had a 16-bit CPU and a dazzling *eight* general-purpose registers, r0–r7; the 16-bit processor had to be made to implement an eight-bit algorithm.

The pseudo-assembly code in Fig. 6.25 shows how this was accomplished; this Intellivision LFSR code corresponds to the Atari 2600 code in Fig. 6.23. The byte at $150 holds the value of R1, and the same sequence can be seen at lines 3–8: shift, XOR, shift, XOR, shift, shift, XOR. Line 7 takes advantage of a feature of the Intellivision's CPU, where it could shift by either one or two bits in a single instruction. Lines 9–10 handle setting the carry bit in the same way that the 6502's left shift would. Retaining only the low-order eight bits (line 9), line 10 subtracts the value $80 so that the carry reflects the subtraction's borrow, which is precisely the carry bit value required here. Line 11 finally rotates the carry bit into place just as the eight-bit version did.

---

[17] Game information from static and dynamic analysis, with Intellivision's CP1600 CPU information from [17, 40].

```
1   r0 = M[$150]
2   r1 = r0
3   r0 = shiftleft(r0)
4   r0 = r0 XOR r1
5   r0 = shiftleft(r0)
6   r0 = r0 XOR r1
7   r0 = shiftleft(r0) ; r0 = shiftleft(r0)
8   r0 = r0 XOR r1
9   r0 = r0 AND $ff
10  if r0 < $80 c = 0 else c = 1
11  r1 = rotateleft(c‖r1)
12  M[$150] = r1
```

Fig. 6.25 *Pitfall!*'s LFSR on the Intellivision

6.5 Riverbank Generation: *River Raid* (1982)

River Raid was a vertically scrolling game (Fig. 6.26) whose riverbanks and islands were generated using PCG.[18] Like *Pitfall!*, it had two LFSRs, although they were different ones. One of *River Raid*'s LFSRs was eight-bit, with taps $b4$ and $b7$, and the other was a 16-bit LFSR that was used for PCG.

The reason *River Raid* scrolls vertically is related to yet another feature of the Atari 2600's graphics hardware. The 2600 could be set to mirror the left half of the playfield's contents on the right side, explaining the symmetry in *River Raid*. Figure 6.27 illustrates how this worked conceptually; the ordering on the right-hand side is flipped compared to the playfield's earlier appearance in *Yar's Revenge* (see Fig. 6.2, page 110).

Regardless of how wide the river becomes, there is always a thin strip of riverbank present, which corresponds to the four bits of PF0 always being set. From the 20 playfield bits on one half of the screen, that means at most 16 bits remain to describe the rest of the riverbank's width on any given line, minus a few bits of width to allow the player's plane to fly through. Now imagine having a set of riverbank tiles to choose from with widths from 0...13. Figure 6.28 shows how these tiles, randomly selected, could be placed to make a crude riverbank of sorts.

The problems with this are twofold. First, an aesthetic problem: it's ugly. Second, the maneuvering capability of the plane is limited, and the player would not be able to turn sharply enough to avoid any approaching riverbank, nor could they direct the plane into the riverbank's extreme crevices. There needs to be a taper from tile to tile. *River Raid*'s riverbank tiles are thus defined to taper up to, and down from, their maximum width. The PCG code must offset its pointers into the tiles to ensure a smooth taper when they are adjoined.

There is one extra complication. The 16 bits of playfield width for the riverbank are spread across two of the 2600's graphics registers, PF1 and PF2, and as a result

---

[18] Game information from static and dynamic analysis, assisted by [20], along with writing a program to reconstruct the riverbank generation algorithm.

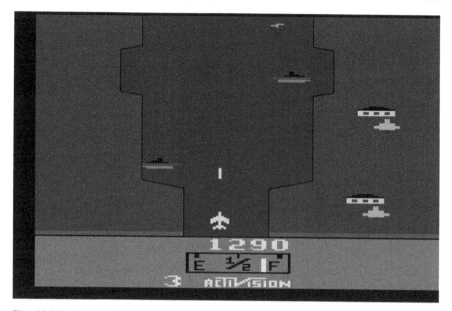

Fig. 6.26 *River Raid* on the Atari 2600, with riverbank outlined for clarity (Image ©Activision Publishing, Inc., used with permission)

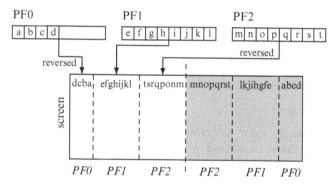

Fig. 6.27 Conceptual view of the Atari 2600 playfield, with mirroring

the tiles need to be pieced together both vertically *and* horizontally. In other words, there is no such thing as a tile of width 11; it is the combination of a width-8 tile and a width-3 tile.

The PCG algorithm manages these constraints by choosing a random riverbank width to aspire to ("current"), and comparing it to the previous width ("previous") to distinguish each individual case. Figure 6.29 shows the tree of checks that are performed, and result in values for PF1 and PF2 being chosen. Because PF2's bits are reversed, however, some tiles need to be stored reversed in the game's ROM. For example, to make a width-11 riverbank, the two tiles required are shown in Fig. 6.30.

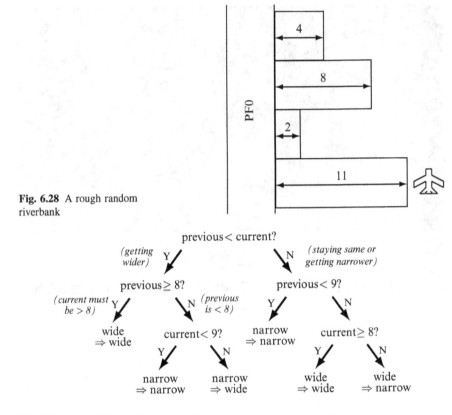

Fig. 6.28 A rough random riverbank

Fig. 6.29 *River Raid* tile selection algorithm

Although none appear in the screenshot, the other feature of *River Raid*'s water-way is the occasional island, and this is the final bit of cleverness. Thanks to the tile arrangement and the Atari 2600's hardware, to make an island simply requires exchanging the PF1 and PF2 values around (Fig. 6.31).

6.6 Intermezzo: Strange Pseudorandom Number Generators

Several retrogames had PRNGs unusual enough to justify a closer look.[19]

As previously mentioned, *Telengard* seeded its PRNG with the player's (x, y, z) coordinates. How those coordinates are manipulated is rather mysterious, how-ever. In an interview, game author Daniel Lawrence described *Telengard*'s PCG this way [4]: 'Take your character's X/Y/Z position, do some math involving prime

---

[19] Unless otherwise stated, game information here is from static analysis, with Integer BASIC's RND code isolated using [31].

In memory On screen

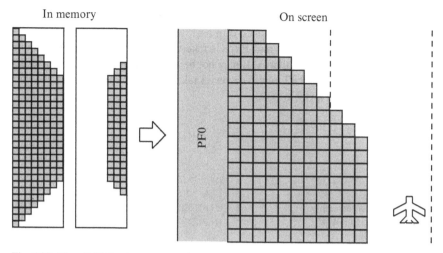

Fig. 6.30 *River Raid* tiles in memory and on screen

PF1 and PF2 values exchanged

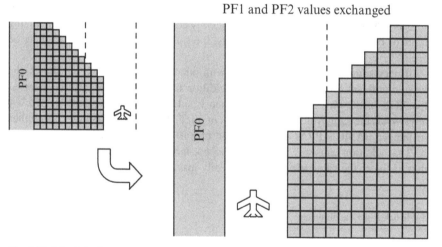

Fig. 6.31 Islands in the stream

numbers, pick out a few internal bits of the result and there you have a description of the current location!' One would therefore expect to see prime numbers as part of the PRNG. One would be disappointed.

There are three floating-point constants defined in *Telengard*'s code, specified to four decimal places and used in the calculation of a floating-point number Q:

$$XO = 1.6915$$
$$YO = 1.4278$$
$$ZO = 1.2462$$
$$Q = x \times XO + y \times YO + z \times ZO + (x + XO) \times (y + YO) \times (z + ZO)$$

Q's fractional part is then taken and scaled, to yield an integer between $0\ldots4693$. This computation has the appearance of a hash function rather than a PRNG, and insofar as both hash functions and PRNGs take their input and scramble it into a new value, there is some similarity. It may not be overdramatic to say that the exact nature of *Telengard*'s PRNG may be a secret taken to the grave; Daniel Lawrence unfortunately passed away in 2010.

<table>
<tr><td>1</td><td>A = M[RNDH]</td></tr>
<tr><td>2</td><td>c‖A = shiftleft(A)</td></tr>
<tr><td>3</td><td>c = 0</td></tr>
<tr><td>4</td><td>c‖A = A + $40 + c</td></tr>
<tr><td>5</td><td>c‖A = shiftleft(A)</td></tr>
<tr><td>6</td><td>M[RNDL] = rotateleft(c‖M[RNDL])</td></tr>
<tr><td>7</td><td>M[RNDH] = rotateleft(c‖M[RNDH])</td></tr>
</table>

Fig. 6.32 Pseudo-assembly code at the heart of Woz' PRNG

Beneath Apple Manor used the PRNG in Apple's Integer BASIC, which was written by none other than master engineer Steve Wozniak himself. At the core of Integer BASIC's PRNG is the pseudo-assembly code in Fig. 6.32. It bears tantalizing hints of being a 16-bit LFSR – the shifts, the rotates – but there is no XOR to be seen.

Binary addition is intimately linked with binary logic. As Table 6.3 shows, the least-significant bit resulting from the addition of two bits is exactly the same as the XOR of the bits. Notice too that when $y = 1$, the most-significant bit of $x+y$ always has the same value as x. With this in mind, Table 6.4 shows how this applies to Integer BASIC's PRNG. The addition of $40 potentially affects $b6$ and $b7$ of A. That addition causes 1 to be added to $b6$, meaning the most-significant bit of that addition, the value added to $b7$, is really just $b6$'s original value. And, because

Table 6.3 Binary addition and XOR

x	y	x + y	x XOR y
0	0	0 0	0
0	1	0 1	1
1	0	0 1	1
1	1	1 0	0

Table 6.4 Integer BASIC's addition, deconstructed

b7	b6	b6 + 1	b7 + MSB(b6 + 1)	b7 XOR b6
0	0	0 1	0 0	0
0	1	1 0	0 1	1
1	0	0 1	0 1	1
1	1	1 0	1 0	0

that being added to *b7* is the same as XOR, line 4 of the pseudo-assembly code is revealed to be a sneaky way to XOR *b6* and *b7* together, leaving the result in *b7*. Integer BASIC's PRNG is indeed based on an LFSR.

The PRNG for the last retrogame example, *Fort Apocalypse* (1982) for the Atari 800, has all the hallmarks of a locked room mystery.[20] Its source code defines a location called RANDOM, and the assembly code contains multiple instructions that read from that location. Observing the code running, RANDOM offers differing values when read, and yet no code ever changes the location. No need to alert Sherlock Holmes, however: the Atari 800 hardware used LFSRs for audio generation, and eight bits of a 17-bit LFSR are readable at $d20a – the location RANDOM was defined as in *Fort Apocalypse*'s source code.

A point worth reiterating is that the pseudorandom number generation methods discussed in this section, and throughout this chapter, must be taken in the context of retrogames. Recall that games' randomness requirements are not necessarily strong ones, and PRNG algorithms exist that are much better suited for use in critical applications like security and science.

6.7 Maze Generation

Finally, we indulge in some comparative retrogame archeology by exploring three different maze generation algorithms used by three different games. The ability to compare different PCG algorithms was alluded to in dungeon generation, and here we have multiple algorithms all with the same intent, but with quite distinct results. It will surely astound and amaze.

```
def maze(row, column):
    directions = [UP, DOWN, LEFT, RIGHT]
    repeat 10 times:
        20% chance of swapping pairs of
            entries in "directions" list
    MAP[row][column] = TUNNEL
    for direction in directions:
        if canmove(direction):
            newrow, newcolumn = row, column adjusted
                                to reflect direction
            maze(newrow, newcolumn)
```

Fig. 6.33 Pseudocode for *Rogue* maze generation

---

[20] Game information from static analysis of source code along with dynamic analysis. Atari hardware information is from [1, 26]; they use the term 'polynomial counter' which is an LFSR.

Later versions of *Rogue*, like the 1993 edition that shipped with 4.4 BSD, had the ability to include randomly-generated mazes in dungeons.[21] The mazes were created using a recursive depth-first search process, pseudocode for which is in Fig. 6.33. The algorithm was initially passed a starting row and column position along with rectangular bounds to fill in the dungeon MAP, which was a 2D array indexed by row and column numbers.

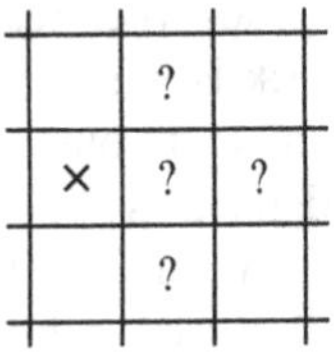

Fig. 6.34 Deciding where to move in *Rogue*

When can the algorithm move and dig a portion of tunnel in a given direction? The details are abstracted away in the function canmove. The idea is to avoid moving to a spot that would cause an accidental connection to an existing TUNNEL. Figure 6.34 shows the locations in the map that must be checked for a move to the right, for instance; the current location is denoted × and the checked locations with question marks. If a tunnel is found in any of those locations, the move cannot be made.

Fig. 6.35 *Rogue* mazes with direction randomization (*left*) and without (*right*)

The rounds of scrambling that the algorithm did on the ordered direction list were essential to the final look of the maze. Figure 6.35 compares two mazes generated with the algorithm, where one omits this step. Starting at the lower right corner, the unrandomized algorithm is at the mercy of the direction list's ordering: moving up until blocked at the top right corner, then left until downwards movement becomes possible, and so on, forming a snakelike tunnel. The version with randomized directions exhibits far more variety, although the underlying movement structure is still apparent.

Especially compared to *Rogue*'s depth-first-generated mazes, the mazes in *3D Labyrinth* (1982) for the Commodore VIC-20 looked good and seemed to have a

---

[21] Game information from static analysis and building an algorithm visualization.

Fig. 6.36 Maze generated the *3D Labyrinth* way

much more random, irregular look (Fig. 6.36).[22] Pseudocode for the maze-generation algorithm is given in Fig. 6.37, which performs gradual modifications to a map area that starts with half walls and half open space.

It would be reasonable to ask why this algorithm always results in a solvable maze, with a path between the two randomly-chosen entry and exit points. It doesn't. The game had a selection of 18 mazes that could be randomly generated; a curious-looking string in the code, 18 characters long, acted as a lookup table:

```
" [BFK?TV$YL1/P>Q37<"
```

Each maze corresponded to one ASCII character in the string, whose value was used as a PRNG seed to generate that maze.

Already there is a notable difference in these algorithms' approaches and their results, from the regimented depth-first generation to a more ad hoc PCG. The final maze generation algorithm takes a third approach.

Amazing Maze (1978) on the Bally Astrocade composed mazes using the set of four tiles shown in Fig. 6.38, which can be thought of as having attributes describing what movements they permit.[23] Overall, the object of the game is for player 1 to move from their randomly-located door on the left side of the maze to player 2's door on the right side of the maze, before player 2 makes the opposite trek. Maze

---

[22] Game information from static analysis and building an algorithm visualization. The game author, Jeff Minter, kindly pointed out the nature of the mystery string [24].

[23] Game information based on static analysis of disassembly [12], plus writing an algorithm visualization. This is the tileset from the game's 'easy' setting.

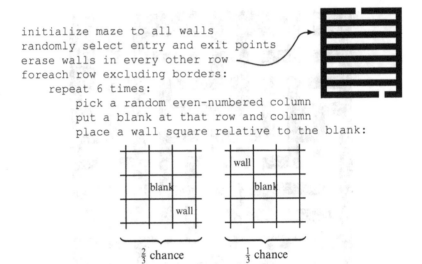

```
initialize maze to all walls
randomly select entry and exit points
erase walls in every other row
foreach row excluding borders:
    repeat 6 times:
        pick a random even-numbered column
        put a blank at that row and column
        place a wall square relative to the blank:
```

Fig. 6.37 *3D Labyrinth* maze generation algorithm

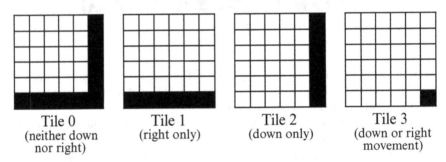

Tile 0 (neither down nor right)   Tile 1 (right only)   Tile 2 (down only)   Tile 3 (down or right movement)

Fig. 6.38 Maze tileset from *Amazing Maze*

generation in this game is interesting to watch, because the Astrocade's video RAM was also used as scratch space, and the temporary data used for maze construction is visible as random-looking colored pixels while the generation algorithm runs.

The generation method used by *Amazing Maze* is a variant of the 'hunt and kill' algorithm [27]. The code is a bit more extensive than the other maze generators and is perhaps best understood starting at the main generation routine in Fig. 6.39. Each (x,y) location in the maze has a tile number associated with it, along with a flag indicating whether or not that location has been marked as being visited by the generation algorithm. Initially, the algorithm tries to find a path from player 1's door across to the right side of the maze, with some built-in assistance to transform a right-edge contact point into player 2's door location. The `else` clause at lines 6–10 is what happens when this search hits a dead end: give up and start anew if the right side hasn't been reached (line 8), or hunt for a new place to resume the path creation (line 10). The latter option is what eventually fills in the whole maze area once a valid path across it has been discovered.

```
1  initialize()
2  while not all cells marked visited:
3      directions = getdirections(x, y)
4      if len(directions) > 0:
5          x, y = pickdirection(directions, x, y)
6      else:
7          if p2door not found:
8              initialize()
9          else:
10             x, y = hunt(x, y)
```

Fig. 6.39 Pseudocode for *Amazing Maze*'s main maze generation

There are four subroutines that lend assistance to the process:

- `initialize()`. This sets all maze locations to Tile 0 and clears all "visited" flags. The initial (x, y) location is set to a random location on the maze's left-hand side that serves as player 1's door, and this location is marked as visited.
- `getdirections(x, y)`. Returns a list of directions from (x, y) to adjacent unvisited locations. If (x, y) is on the right-hand edge of the maze and player 2's door has not been found yet, the subroutine quietly adds "right" into the direction list.
- `hunt(x, y)`. Starting at (x, y), this scans subsequent columns and rows, wrapping around if necessary, until a previously-visited location is found; its (x, y) location is returned.
- `pickdirection(directions, x, y)`. This is the most complex of the four. A direction is chosen at random from the `directions` list, and updates occur as shown in Table 6.5. The new location is marked as visited and its (x, y) is returned.

Table 6.5 Handling movement in *Amazing Maze*

Direction	Add to current (x, y) tile attribute	Δx to apply	Δy to apply	Add to new (x, y)'s tile attribute
Up	–	0	−1	Down
Down	Down	0	+1	–
Left	–	−1	0	Right
Right	Right	+1	0	–

Figure 6.40 shows one run of the algorithm at three points. First, a dead end is reached, forcing a reinitialization; visited locations are marked in gray. Second, a path across the maze is found, but the remainder has yet to be visited. Third, the final form of the maze once all locations have been completely visited.

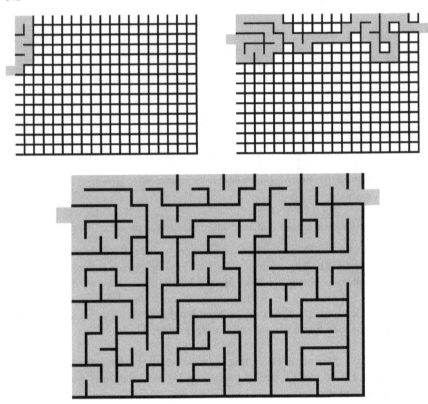

Fig. 6.40 Three snapshots of *Amazing Maze*'s generation algorithm

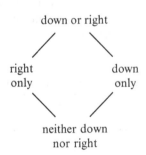

Fig. 6.41 Tile movement
attribute lattice

Does this algorithm always work and, if so, why? The process loops continuously until a path across the maze is discovered; it will eventually succeed.
That path is not destroyed during the hunt that follows, despite the changes made by
pickdirection, because the tiles' movement attributes form a lattice (Fig. 6.41).
Alterations to the maze tiles' attributes can only move locations up the lattice, serv-
ing to open the maze walls up more, not block any existing paths. This retrogame's
PCG algorithm must therefore always work.

At the beginning of this chapter, procedural content generation was initially presented as an extreme form of data compression, but in fact it is much more. Compression implies that the content all exists to begin with, whereas it is now clear that PCG can be employed to produce an always-differing variety of content that may never all exist, or use pseudorandomness to concisely make a large amount of content that is always the same.

Repeatable PCG content can be viewed within the broader context of lazy computation: only computing something (in this case, producing content) when it is actually required. Even in a modern environment, it is not always feasible or efficient to compute things, nor is it always possible to precompute and store massive amounts of data. Modern environments do still have limits, even if they are much higher limits than existed during the retrogaming era.

As an example, we built a simulator that would simulate a million domains' worth of Internet content on a single computer [3]. It was neither possible nor necessary to store all of the simulated web pages. Instead, a request for a web site in the simulator passed through two PCG stages. The first stage used the hash of the web site's domain name to seed a PRNG, which was used to generate the web site's hierarchy of web pages, so it would be consistent throughout the entire simulated web site. The second stage re-seeded the PRNG with the hash of the full URL requested and randomly generated the web page's content using the first stage information. This approach also guaranteed the repeatability of the content across simulated web site visits, a requirement of the application.

Experience with this and other examples has shown that procedural content generation is far from a trivial undertaking, then or now. Good PCG results can involve endless repeated tweaking and experimentation; seeing simple, elegant PCG algorithms such as the ones in these retrogames – especially operating under tight constraints – may belie tremendous effort that went into them.

References

1. Atari, Inc.: De Re Atari: A Guide to Effective Programming. Atari Program Exchange (1982)
2. Atari, Inc.: Yar's Revenge Atari Game Program Instructions (1982)
3. Aycock, J., Crawford, H., deGraaf, R.: Spamulator: the Internet on a laptop. In: 13th Annual Conference on Innovation and Technology in Computer Science Education, Madrid, pp. 142–147 (2008)
4. Barton, M.: Interview with Daniel M. Lawrence, CRPG Pioneer and Author of Telengard. http://armchairarcade.com/neo/node/1366 (22 June 2007)
5. Bell, I.: Text Elite 1.4. http://www.iancgbell.clara.net/elite/text/index.htm (Date unclear, 1999 or later)
6. Boris, D.: Telengard, Avalon Hill (1982), Comments by Dan Boris (2008), DSKTEL.BAS (2008)

7. Braben, D.: Classic Game Postmortem: Elite. Game Developer's Conference 2011. http://www.gdcvault.com/play/1014628/Classic-Game-Postmortem (2011)
8. Bush, G.: The Dungeon. http://elm-telengard.blogspot.ca/2014/03/the-dungeon.html (24 Mar 2014)
9. Crane, D.: Classic game postmortem: Pitfall! Game Developer's Conference 2011 (2011). http://www.gdcvault.com/play/1014632/Classic-Game-Postmortem-PITFALL
10. Crane, D.: Email Communication (25 June 2014)
11. Crawford, H., Aycock, J.: Kwyjibo: automatic domain name generation. Software: Pract. Exp. **38**(14), 1561–1567 (2008)
12. Degler, R.C.: Reverse-Assembly of the File "AMAZMAZE.BIN" (2010)
13. Eastlake, D., III., Crocker, S., Schiller, J.: Randomness recommendations for security. RFC 1750 (1994)
14. Edge Staff: The Making of… Berzerk. Edge mag. (225), 112–115 (2011)
15. Ferg: Q & A with Atari 2600 programmer Dan Oliver. Atari 2600 Game by Game Podcast. http://2600gamebygamepodcast.blogspot.ca/2014/03/q-with-atari-2600-programmer-dan-oliver.html (2 Mar 2014)
16. Gasser, M.: A random word generator for pronounceable passwords. MITRE Technical Report MTR-3006 (also listed as ESD-TR-75-97) (1975)
17. General Instrument: CP1610 16-bit Microprocessor Data Sheet (undated)
18. Hendrikx, M., Meijer, S., Van Der Velden, J., Iosup, A.: Procedural content generation for games: a survey. ACM Trans Multimed. Comput. Commun. Appl. **9**(1), Article 1 (2013)
19. Jentzsch, T.: Pitfall! Annotated Disassembly, v0.9 (2001)
20. Jentzsch, T.: River Raid Annotated Disassembly, v0.9 (2001)
21. Kaplan, D., Kedmi, S., Hay, R., Dayan, A.: Attacking the Linux PRNG on Android. In: 8th USENIX Workshop on Offensive Technologies, San Diego (2014)
22. Knuth, D.E.: The Art of Computer Programming. Volume 2: Seminumerical Algorithms, 3rd edn. Addison-Wesley, Boston (1998)
23. Lee, H.H., Chang, E.C., Chan, M.C.: Pervasive random beacon in the Internet for covert coordination. In: 7th International Workshop on Information Hiding, Barcelona, pp. 53–61 (2005)
24. Minter, J.: Email Communication (27 Mar 2014)
25. Montfort, N., Bogost, I.: Racing the Beam: The Atari Video Computer System. MIT, Cambridge (2009)
26. Patchett, C., Sherer, R.: Master Memory Map for the Atari. Reston Pub. Co, Reston (1984)
27. Pullen, W.D.: Think Labyrinth: Maze Algorithms. http://www.astrolog.org/labyrnth/algrithm.htm (12 Feb 2015)
28. Rader, C.: Using shift register sequences. In: Lyons, R.G. (ed.) Streamlining Digital Signal Processing: A Tricks of the Trade Guidebook, pp. 311–318. Wiley, Hoboken/IEEE Press, Piscataway (2007)
29. Riddle, S., Hoff, M.: Code — Robotron 2084 Guidebook. http://www.robotron2084guidebook.com/home/games/berzerk/mazegenerator/code/ (Undated, 2012 copyright year given)
30. Rukhin, A., Soto, J., Nechvatal, J., Smid, M., Barker, E., Leigh, S., Levenson, M., Vangel, M., Banks, D., Heckert, A., Dray, J., Vo, S.: A Statistical Test Suite for Random and Pseudorandom Number Generators for Cryptographic Applications. NIST Special Publication 800-22, Revision 1a. U.S. Department of Commerce, Technology Administration, National Institute of Standards and Technology, Gaithersburg (2010)
31. Santa-Maria, P.R.: Integer BASIC Disassembly. http://www.easy68k.com/paulrsm/6502/INTLST.TXT (2000)
32. Schneier, B.: Applied Cryptography, 2nd edn. Wiley, New York (1996)
33. Shaker, N., Togelius, J., Nelson, M.J.: Procedural Content Generation in Games: A Textbook and an Overview of Current Research. Springer, Forthcoming (2015)
34. Simpson, J.: Dorothy Draper: a penchant for bold gestures and audacious scale. Archit. Dig. **57**(1), 156–159 (2000)
35. Spufford, F.: Backroom Boys: The Secret Return of the British Boffin. Faber and Faber, London (2003)

36. Steele, G.L., Jr.: Arithmetic shifting considered harmful. SIGPLAN Not. **12**(11), 61–69 (1977)
37. Stone-Gross, B., Cova, M., Cavallaro, L., Gilbert, B., Szydlowski, M., Kemmerer, R., Kruegel, C., Vigna, G.: Your Botnet is My Botnet: analysis of a Botnet takeover. In: 16th ACM Conference on Computer and Communications Security, Chicago, pp. 635–647 (2009)
38. UCSB Computer Security Group: Your botnet is my botnet: taking over the Torpig botnet. https://seclab.cs.ucsb.edu/academic/projects/projects/your-botnet-my-botnet/ (24 Sept 2011)
39. Various Contributors: A000073 (Tribonacci numbers). The On-line Encyclopedia of Integer Sequences. http://oeis.org/A000073
40. Various Contributors: CP1610. IntelliWiki: Intellivision Wiki. http://wiki.intellivision.us/index.php?title=CP1610&oldid=15006
41. Wright, S.: 2600 (STELLA) Programmer's Guide (3 Dec 1979). Updated by D. May, 1988

Chapter 7
Protection

(Copyright 2008, Penny Arcade, Inc., http://www.penny-arcade.com, used with permission.)

Protection is a broad term that covers unauthorized access to software, guarding against software copying and cracking, and preventing unauthorized software from running on a platform. Because retrogames were a favorite target for copying and cracking, we begin with copy protection.

No copy protection method is foolproof. Given sufficient motivation, and sometimes sufficient technology, all the methods described here can be broken. The challenge is to raise the bar high enough to keep the inevitable illegitimate copies to an acceptably low level, yet hopefully not inconvenience legitimate users. Some methods strike this balance better than others.

Computer security has studied user authentication extensively, and it provides a helpful lens through which to view copy protection. Basic authentication traditionally relies on one of three methods to validate a user's identity to the computer,[1] and

---

[1] See, for example, [48]. There are at least two more methods, *where you are* and *who you know*, but they are less well known.

© Springer International Publishing Switzerland 2016
J. Aycock, *Retrogame Archeology*, DOI 10.1007/978-3-319-30004-7_7

in the context of copy protection this task can be seen as validating that the user has a legitimate, properly authorized copy of the software.

The first authentication method is *what you know*. In user authentication terms, this implies a password; in retrogame terms, a registration code to unlock the full functionality of a "shareware" game (or at least silence nagging registration prompts) acted as a password.

Example 7.1 (Scorched Earth, 1991). Scorched Earth was an artillery game for MS-DOS. Any doubts about its shareware status were dispelled up front, because running the game caused some initial text to appear that read in part:

```
Scorched Earth is shareware.  If you enjoy playing Scorch,
you are encouraged to take part in its developement by
registering with the author!  To register, send $10 to:
```

This was a typical example of shareware software. Registering (via physical mail) would yield a registration code that could be entered into the game at a prompt that notably said 'Please enter your password.'

Technically, the game author's generation of the registration code and its verification by the game would seem to need sophisticated cryptographic algorithms. The actual mechanism used by *Scorched Earth* relied more on psychology and the relative difficulty of spreading information in the retrogame era: there was a password, but everyone got the same one [23]. The password was hardcoded into the game for verification purposes, although the characters were not all located together as a single string – that would have been too easy to find in the binary. The individual password characters were checked, one at a time, with separate comparison instructions for each character.[2] Most password characters were subject to light obfuscation prior to comparison so, for example, a password character of X might be incremented twice and instead compared with Z.

The second user authentication method is *what you have*. In security terms, this could mean a physical door key or possessing a mobile phone with a specific number. Much the same idea carries through to retrogames that would ship with physical objects, and having a copy of the software alone would be insufficient to run it past a certain point. As a simple example, a game could challenge a user to enter the word appearing in a certain place in the game's physical instruction manual. *King's Quest IV* (1988) would issue demands like 'On page 3, what is the third word in the second paragraph?' even before deigning to show the Sierra splash screen.[3]

Infocom famously bundled physical 'feelies' with their games that could be used for this purpose, but there was no need for a blatant copy-protection challenge: solving the mystery in *Deadline* (1982) was 'aided by evidence packaged with the computer disk' [52] that was 'vital to the success of the investigation' [9]. There were other copy protection methods using physical objects too.

---

[2] Game information from static and dynamic analysis. I'll leave finding the password as an exercise for the interested reader.

[3] Verified on, and quote taken from, the DOS version in-emulator.

Fig. 7.1 Lenslok

Fig. 7.2 Lenslok prisms

Example 7.2 (Lenslok). Lenslok was a copy-protection device that involved holding an exotic device containing vertically-aligned plastic prisms against the screen to reveal the secret distorted code displayed by the software. The size of Lenslok was such that it would comfortably fit in software's cassette tape boxes [15]. Figure 7.1 shows one of these devices for *ACE* (1986) sitting atop a Lenslok instruction sheet,

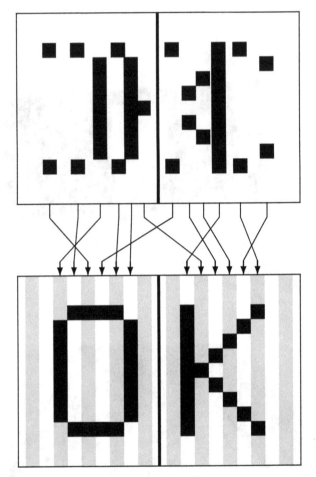

Fig. 7.3 Scrambled and unscrambled Lenslok code for *Elite*

and Fig. 7.2 gives a close-up view of its prisms. As as example, Fig. 7.3 shows how the code "OK" would be seen with and without Lenslok.[4] This particular code was shown for calibration before the program would issue the real code challenge to the user. It was critical, as part of the calibration process, for the user to adjust the size of the Lenslok image appropriately: the ideal on-screen image width, cleverly, matched the unfolded length of the physical Lenslok device.

Deployment of Lenslok for retrogames and other software was not without incident. Correct display of Lenslok images required the user to calibrate the software to the television [15]. A release of *Elite* had Lenslok instructions that were 'less than perfect' to the extent that the publisher offered updated instruction sheets [57].

---

[4] I wrote a program to generate the encoded images, using the prism data from LensKey, and verified the images using LensKey and real Lenslok devices; for clarity, the generated image does not include any extra obfuscating blocks that a real Lenslok implementation could add.

Later games had not only the Lenslok instructions proper but 'Lenslok hints' that included gems like [36] 'Slightly moving the Lenslok, or your head, can make the characters more recognisable.' Computer magazine letter columns of the time are brimming with vitriol:

> As for the LensLok, it took me 35 minutes, 5 reloads, 80% eye strain and 80% guess work to start the game. [50, p. 45]

> The larger scale resolution of the family 23in TV, coupled with the need to hold the Lenslok device on the screen whilst operating the keyboard and working against the clock, make for an interesting challenge, though not the one I thought I was purchasing. [60, p. 16]

Example 7.3 (Code wheels). A code wheel is similar in nature to a secret decoder ring that children might once have found in cereal boxes. With this copy protection scheme, the software would present a challenge to the user in the form of words or symbols present on the code wheel. The user would need to align the code wheel accordingly and enter the revealed code into the software for verification. Figure 7.4 shows the code wheel for the Amiga's *SideShow* (1989), a game that a reviewer says [6, p. 68] 'can get on your nerves [...] You must enter codes from a copy-protection wheel several times.' This particular code wheel had three layers, and if the game's challenge was POPCORN-RINGMASTER-HIPPOS, then aligning those words in the wheel would yield the response code HCIO, as shown in Fig. 7.4a. Figure 7.4b shows the bottom layer of the code wheel separated, revealing its single ring of response letters; Fig. 7.4c shows the discs of the top two layers, whose response rings have both letters and physical holes.

Also for the Amiga was *F/A-18 Interceptor* (1988) that needed the correct response from a code wheel before embarking on a mission [27]. This too is a three-layer wheel, and Fig. 7.5a shows that a variety of response codes could result from aligning 1-F-C. Figure 7.5b shows the bottom layer separated, and that it held many response codes as opposed to *SideShow*'s single ring; Fig. 7.5c highlights the holes in the second layer.

While production of the code wheel added additional cost for the retrogame publisher, it was partially offset by alleviating the need for other protection. *Pool of Radiance* (1988) for the Commodore 64/128 came with a beautifully designed two-layer code wheel; it is partially shown in Fig. 7.6 along with the instructions the user was supplied for its use. Here, the game's 'Quick Start Card' explicitly encouraged copying all four of the game's disks and playing the game using the backup copies.

Example 7.4 (Dongles). A dongle is a physical device that plugs in to one of the computer's ports, like a cassette port, parallel port, serial port, joystick port, or (now) a USB port. The theory behind basic dongles is that resistors or other circuitry inside the dongle provide a "secret" or at least hard-to-duplicate value that copy protection code can read and verify for correctness. The dongle's casing would be sealed and tamper-resistant to discourage casual physical inspection, but of course the value from the dongle could be read by other software equally well [42].

Fig. 7.4 *SideShow* code wheel and component layers

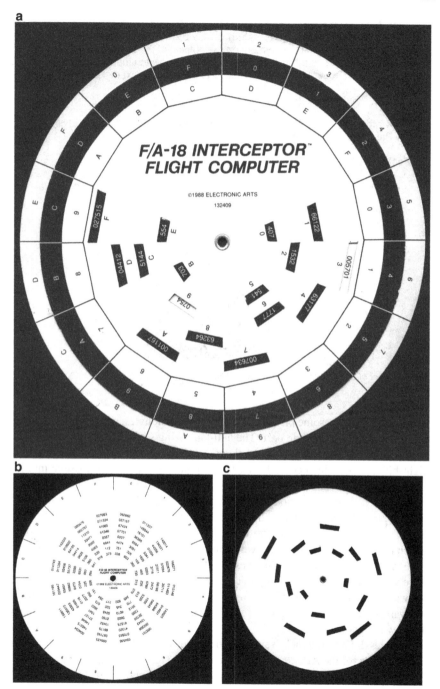

Fig. 7.5 *F/A-18 Interceptor* code wheel and component layers

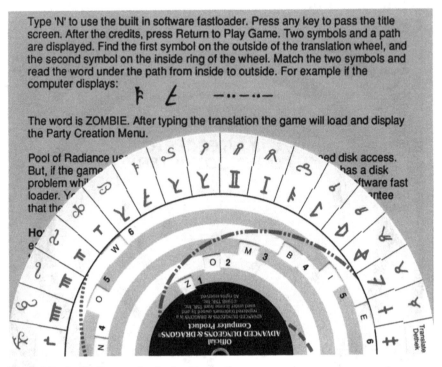

Type 'N' to use the built in software fastloader. Press any key to pass the title screen. After the credits, press Return to Play Game. Two symbols and a path are displayed. Find the first symbol on the outside of the translation wheel, and the second symbol on the inside ring of the wheel. Match the two symbols and read the word under the path from inside to outside. For example if the computer displays:

The word is ZOMBIE. After typing the translation the game will load and display the Party Creation Menu.

Fig. 7.6 *Pool of Radiance* code wheel and instructions

Figure 7.7 shows some pictures of one of the first dongles, which plugged into the Commodore PET's cassette port. The anti-tampering sealing resin is clearly visible in the end view. This particular dongle contained a parallel-load shift register,[5] the eight-bit value of which could be shifted in a bit at a time via the cassette interface and verified. The values these dongles produced could vary from one to the next, interestingly; their production was farmed out, effectively forming a small cottage industry, and the people wiring up the shift register would choose randomly which of the chip's eight inputs to wire to the supply voltage (resulting in a 1 bit) and which to wire to ground (0). This would appear to wreak havoc with the verification code, unless each dongle's value was checked, and each shipped copy of the software was modified accordingly – not a scalable prospect. Instead, the first time the software was run by the user, the dongle value would be read and embedded into the software at that time, making the software unusable thereafter unless that particular dongle was attached.

Dongles did not find their way into retrogames frequently. One example is *Robo-Cop 3* (1992) for the Amiga, which came with a dongle that plugged into one of the Amiga's joystick ports (Fig. 7.8) – a sticker on the game box said 'FOR YOUR SE-

---

[5] There seems to be no available authoritative source for dongle history. Information here is from Wikipedia [66] that I have verified with one of the dongle's creators [35]; chip information is from [61]. Figure 7.7 is a composite image created from pictures taken by Mike Lake.

Fig. 7.7 One of the first dongles created

CURITY, THIS GAME IS PROTECTED WITH AN ELECTRONIC KEY.' Another example is the dongle for *Leaderboard Pro Golf Simulator* (1986) on the Commodore 64. This spartan dongle (Fig. 7.9 shows front and back views) plugged into the cassette port; the program itself was on floppy disk. Because this dongle simply grounded the "cassette sense" pin, it was possible to bypass security by connecting a Commodore cassette player to the computer and playing a tape when the game checked the dongle.[6]

The third user authentication method is *what you are*, which typically refers to biometrics like fingerprints or iris recognition, properties inherent to humans. This initially seems inapplicable to copy protection; no retrogame would have demanded a DNA sample of the player prior to running.[7] But insofar as a game's protection code was trying to spot illegitimate copies, it would take advantage of properties

---

[6] Thanks to numerous Internet forums for the tip; verified with game on real hardware.

[7] Actually, a few retrogame authors might have considered that, but they wouldn't have been serious about it.

Fig. 7.8 *RoboCop 3* dongle

Fig. 7.9 *Leaderboard Pro Golf Simulator* dongle

inherent to the game's storage medium and common methods of duplication. The game collectively treated the user and the media as the "you" in "what you are," in essence. With that framing, we will examine protection specific to different media types.

7.1 Cassette Tapes

Conceptually, protection options for cassette tapes would seem to be fairly limited. A magnetic signal on the tape saunters linearly past a stationary read head, the same technology as found in audio cassette tape players. In fact, some computers of the time like the Apple II and the ZX Spectrum assumed that a commodity audio cassette player would be used [2, 67].

Certainly code obfuscation was a possibility to deter cracking, as was wearing down the patience of someone trying to monitor the tape loading process by loading in many parts. Freeload, a tape loader for the Commodore 64, could load a game in *fourteen* parts.[8]

---

[8] Hughes [26], confirmed in cassette mastering source code.

(Would-be software pirates were not the only people whose patience was tried by tape loading. Mastertronic's 1988 release of *Ghostbusters* for the Commodore 64 went so far as to have a mini-game to play while the real game was loading. Early in the loading process, a screen would appear saying 'JUST WHEN YOU THOUGHT IT WAS SAFE TO MAKE A CUP OF TEA... IT'S.. INVADE-A-LOAD!' and a clone of *Space Invaders* could be played to pass the time.[9] Other tape loading mini-games existed at that time but were unreleased due to licensing concerns [24, 26].)

The copying problem still remained: tape-to-tape copies were trivially possible, especially given the prevalence of dual-cassette players with dubbing capability built in. One approach to make tape copying more challenging took advantage of the "what you are" notion. As the Apple tape loading documentation notes, [2, p. 4] 'Cassette tape recorders in the $40 – $50 range generally have ALC (Automatic Level Control) for recording from the microphone input. This feature is useful since the user doesn't have to set any volume controls to obtain a good recording.' A tape copy protection mechanism for the Commodore 64 was to insert a loud tone in between parts of the program on tape; the goal was to trick the ALC circuit in a would-be copier's tape recorder into lowering the recording volume temporarily, hopefully to the level where the following data was too quiet to be re-read properly on the tape copy [25, 26].[10]

7.2 Cartridges

For a cartridge-based retrogame, the cartridge is implicitly "what you have." It *is* possible, for example, to copy a cartridge's contents from its ROM into a writable EPROM, but as it requires the proper equipment, skills, and knowledge, it raises the copying bar substantially [42]. A similar argument can be made for cartridges that contain additional components besides ROM, like the Atari Super Chip.

Computer systems that accepted cartridges and had banked RAM behind the cartridge address space (e.g., the Commodore 64 [8] and Atari 400/800 [47]) had another option. A cartridge's contents could be copied onto tape or disk, and later restored into the RAM to run without the cartridge present. Countering this, some cartridge's code would copy garbage into its own memory addresses: this would have no effect on the cartridge's code in ROM, but a copy in RAM would be corrupted [42, 56].

---

[9] Verified in emulator.

[10] While this technique sounds plausible, and I have no reason to doubt it, it has been hard to verify. I acquired a working *Uridium* (1986) on cassette for the Commodore 64 (which should have this protection [26]) and two dual-tape decks; copies from one deck worked, copies from the other didn't. The only firm conclusion is that tape-to-tape copies of retrogames didn't always work.

Example 7.5 (Star Ranger, 1983). Star Ranger on the Commodore 64 uses this protection scheme.[11] For example, the game code contains a set of subroutine addresses, and a store instruction writes the value $ff to the high byte of one of these, located at $878d in the cartridge's address space. This write has no effect if the game is running from the cartridge ROM, and when the game uses the subroutine address, it goes to the original address of $8045. On the other hand, if the game code has been copied to RAM, execution finds its way to $ff45 instead.

The net effect of this and similar writes to cartridge addresses is that the game shows blocky lines on the screen, plays the brief level starting tune (a distinctly funereal piece), and hangs if run from RAM.

Example 7.6 (Pole Position, 1983). The Atari 400/800 version of *Pole Position* contains a number of code sequences that write to the cartridge's address space, of the form:

```
A = $60
M[$ae5a] = A
```

Different sequences write to different memory locations, all of which correspond to the start of subroutines in the game code. The value $60 happens to be the opcode for a `return` instruction, meaning that an in-RAM copy of the game code is surgically altered. The resulting changes create what amounts to a demo version of the game, where the player drives down a perpetually straight road.[12]

End users' copying was not the only thing that concerned game producers when it came to protection; other game producers making their own cartridges could be a threat as well. Cartridge production can provide a revenue stream for a game company, and the ability to control licensing of game titles for a platform provides both revenue and the ability to perform quality control (dubious game quality being a factor in the North American video game market crash of the 1980s) [46]. How does a computer verify that a cartridge plugged into it is permitted to run? With readily available Internet access, a modern game console could periodically download a "whitelist" with cryptographic hashes of allowed cartridges, for instance, but that would not have been broadly feasible in the retrogame era. Some other mechanism was called for.

Example 7.7 (Sega Genesis III). Starting in 1990 with the Genesis III, Sega's Genesis game consoles had protection measures to guard against unlicensed game cartridges running on their platform.[13] First, the console looked for the string SEGA at a specific location in a cartridge's ROM. This would be fairly unremarkable by itself, but the other part to this (patented) technique was that the console would automatically display a copyright message in response to finding the string. The reasoning is elaborated in the patent [58]:

---

[11] Tip from [70], behavior verified in emulator.

[12] Not unlike traveling through the Canadian province of Saskatchewan. Game behavior found and verified in emulator.

[13] The legal bunfight between Sega and Accolade over Sega's protection measures is interesting reading but outside the scope of this book; for details, see [32, 46].

The unauthorized vendor must, therefore, not only breach the security system, but also publish a misrepresentation that its work is authorized and that the copyright resides in the authorized vendor [...] the vendor of unauthorized units will have misrepresented to the user that he is an authorized vendor, thus subjecting such vendor to risk of violation of the law respecting copyright and/or unfair competition or illegal trade practices.

Presciently, the patent provides assembly source code for its implementation on the Vectrex, which contains the inline comment 'DISPLAY LEGAL MESS.' A legal mess did indeed result from the Genesis III's 'PRODUCED BY OR UNDER LICENSE FROM SEGA ENTERPRISES LTD' [43, 65] message, and illustrates that protection need not be purely technical.

A second protection method used by Genesis consoles built on the above by also requiring the game code to write the value SEGA to a particular memory location in the video display processor [43]. Taken together, Sega's protection measures can be viewed as authenticating a cartridge based on what it is (the static signature) and what it knows (the video display processor code).

From a security point of view, having a hardcoded static signature seems like an extremely weak protection mechanism to rely on. Any technical judgment on Sega should take into account that the Intellivision II beat them to it by about eight years, though.

```
if bit 6 of M[$500c] is 0:
    y = last two digits of copyright year in cartridge
    if y < 78 or y > 82:
X:      goto X
```

Fig. 7.10 Intellivision II authentication pseudocode

Example 7.8 (Intellivision II). As a review of the Intellivision II put it [39, p. 82]: 'For some reason, the game cartridges currently manufactured by Coleco Industries do not work with the *Intellivision II*.' It has been alleged that this was a very deliberate effect, and that the Intellivision II's ROM code had been modified specifically to prevent third-party games from running [4, 29]. While no definitive proof of the rationale seems to exist, the fact remains that some Coleco games don't work on the platform. For example, *Donkey Kong* (1982) and *Mouse Trap* (1982) both show only a blank, avocado green screen when run on the Intellivision II.[14] The culprit is some code in the Intellivision II whose pseudocode is shown in Fig. 7.10: the combination of a flag bit not being set in the cartridge and the last two digits of the year being outside a narrow range results in an infinite loop. (The code in question implements the year check in two parts, each with its own infinite loop, making it hard to dismiss this as an inadvertent bug.) The bit and year values, taken together, act as a static signature for authentication.

---

[14] Verified in emulator. Technical information from static and dynamic analysis.

158

7 Protection

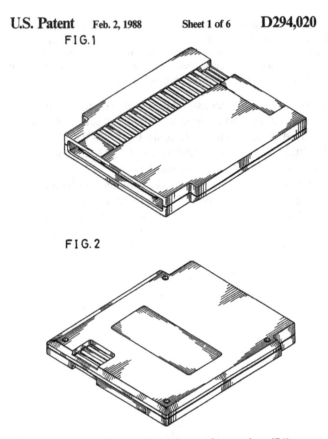

U.S. Patent Feb. 2, 1988   Sheet 1 of 6   D294,020
FIG.1

FIG.2

Fig. 7.11 Cartridge design for the Nintendo Entertainment System, from [74]

Authentication that uses a combination of different methods is referred to as multi-factor authentication. For instance, the Sega protection can be seen as two-factor authentication for cartridges. The Nintendo Entertainment system had two-factor authentication as well.

Example 7.9 (Nintendo NES). The Nintendo NES' cartridge protection began with a very distinctive patented design (Fig. 7.11) that provided some physical and legal protection as to what cartridges could be inserted into the console [45, 46]. Additional protection came in the form of the '10NES,' a small four-bit microprocessor. One of these chips was placed in the NES itself, and another in each cartridge; the processors did some arithmetic operations with the same timing, and a mismatch in the results would reset the console's CPU [44, 45]. The 10NES' calculate-and-check cycle could be repeated indefinitely throughout execution of the game [44, 45]. As with the Sega protection, this can again be seen as cartridge authentication based on what it is (physical design) along with what it knows (10NES).

7.3 Floppy Disks

Floppy disks offered an enormous amount of flexibility when it came to protection.[15] It was not uncommon for software to have very direct control over the floppy drive's operation, and lack of memory protection meant that the operating system did not enjoy exclusive access to the floppy drive's hardware. Depending on the platform, the disk operating system may have been read from the floppy disk when booted anyway, making it a simple matter to modify or replace for protection purposes.

Some floppy protection methods relied on using "what you are" authentication with the floppy disk itself to distinguish between an original disk and a copy.

Example 7.10 (Physical damage). There seems no end to the stories about copy protection methods that involved intentional physical damage to the disk surface. The general principle [5, 19, 68] is that randomly-chosen areas on the disk surface are damaged, and the exact locations of those areas are discovered and stored on the damaged disk, along with the copy protection code and the program being protected. The copy protection code will attempt to write to the damaged areas when run and, in an appropriately *1984* way, success is failure and failure is success. If the write fails, the disk is the original damaged one and the copy protection check succeeds; if the write succeeds, the disk is a copy and the check fails.

How was the physical damage created? It is here that the story takes on the feel of an urban legend. Various sources claim pinpricks [42], a hole punch [19, 56], scratching or scraping [18, 19, 68], heating [18], cutting [18], radiation [18], lasers [51, 64], and drops of acid.[16] Regardless of the means of destruction, indirect evidence suggests that this protection method was successful. An advertisement for a board to create 'ARCHIVAL BACKUPS OF PROTECTED SOFTWARE!' says that it 'can easily backup almost all protected diskettes for the IBM PC (except those "protected" by physical disk damage)' [7], and Defendisk – holder of some of the patents on this technique – ran a contest offering to 'pay **$10,000** to the first person to defeat our system' [12, emphasis theirs].

Other protection methods we encounter later extend "what you are" to the floppy drive, specifically the ability of expensive disk duplicating equipment to write in ways that low-cost commodity drives could not mimic [68]. However, not all software publishers used such equipment: Brøderbund disks were duplicated on stock Apple II drives connected in parallel to write two disks at once [20]. Even in this case, the floppy drives had certain physical limitations that could be (and were) exploited for copy protection.

---

[15] Unfortunately, there are too many creative floppy protection schemes to cover in full. This section's sampling tries to give a flavor of the variety of methods used without getting too lost in the weeds.

[16] I recall hearing in the 1980s that someone had done this with acid as a science fair project.

There is a natural overlap here with "what you know" authentication. Protection that did nonstandard things might slow down copying and cracking efforts, but booting a protected floppy required the boot code on disk to know the secrets of reading the data. Ultimately this is the Achilles heel that allowed such protections to be broken.

Example 7.11 (Moving the directory). Apple floppy disks had 35 tracks, concentric circles on the disk surface where data would reside; the floppy drive's read/write head would be positioned at a track's location to read or write its magnetically encoded signal as the floppy drive rotated the disk's surface underneath the head. The disk directory was located at track 17, in the middle of the disk to minimize the head movement required to access it.[17] As a very simple "protection" method, the directory could be moved to another track, and the DOS on disk suitably modified to locate it. Standard DOS would not be able to list a protected disk's directory, not knowing this secret, and the protected floppy would have to be booted (and its modified DOS loaded) to access the contents. Beyond this inconvenience, the technique's value is mostly didactic – nothing prevented a DOS disk with a relocated directory from being copied.

Tracks on a disk were logically divided into sectors. On the Apple II, for example, DOS 3.3 and ProDOS disk tracks contained 16 sectors, each holding 256 bytes of data [71, 72]. The space occupied by a sector on disk is not solely devoted to storing the sector's data; a certain amount of overhead is necessary.[18] The data is sandwiched between meta-data: a sector prologue preceding the data would store the sector and track number; an epilogue would hold a data checksum for verification. Furthermore, expendable gap bytes are placed to buy time for the CPU to process the prologue information – the spinning disk presents a soft real-time constraint – and also "wiggle room." Due to physical variance even on the same disk drive, a modified and rewritten sector was unlikely to be written to the precise physical location as the old data, and the gap bytes provided padding that could be overwritten to compensate for this. Even for sectors, however, the formatting could be programmer-controlled if desired.[19]

Example 7.12 (RW18). Prince of Persia (1989) for the Apple II used Roland Gustafsson's "RW18" disk routines, which managed to cram the equivalent of 18 sectors onto each disk track instead of only 16.[20] Cracked versions of *Prince of Persia* in standard Apple DOS format were forced to use one additional floppy to store the

---

[17] This example is based on DOS 3.3; information from [71]. There's one slight simplification here, in that some drives would support more than 35 tracks [72].

[18] The exact details vary with the system, of course. References used are [28] (Commodore 64) and [71] (Apple II).

[19] This assumes the more common "soft sectored" disks. Hard sectored disks, by contrast, had physical index holes denoting the start of sectors.

[20] RW18 information from [16, 21, 53]; some of the RW18 source code appears in the released *Prince of Persia* code, and a commented disassembly of the $5\frac{1}{4}''$ RW18 code [17] was used for verification.

extra data; a 16-sector version occupying the same number of disks as the original game did not appear until a quarter century later [14].

RW18 optimized for the common (retrogame) case of reading. Assuming that a disk track was written in its entirety, i.e., when creating the game disk, meant that no gap byte allowances needed to be made for sector writes. In addition, larger 768-byte sectors reduced the amount of per-sector overhead required, with the result that RW18's six sectors per track could hold 512 more data bytes than a standard 16-sector track.

A programmer's control over the floppy disk could also extend to the bit encoding within the track.

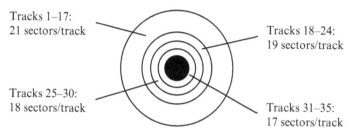

Tracks 1–17:
21 sectors/track

Tracks 18–24:
19 sectors/track

Tracks 25–30:
18 sectors/track

Tracks 31–35:
17 sectors/track

Fig. 7.12 Zones on a standard Commodore 64 floppy disk

Example 7.13 (Changing bit rates). Commodore 64 disk drives spun at a constant speed, but the hardware allowed the rate at which bits were clocked in and out to be changed. This permitted more bits, and ultimately sectors, to be stored on areas of the disk that were further out and thus had more physical space. A standard floppy would be divided into "zones" based on the track number, where each zone held a different number of sectors (Fig. 7.12) [28]. One protection method involved changing tracks' bit density to nonstandard values [56, 59] in an attempt to throw off copy programs.

Finally, the programmer could even control the physical positioning of drive elements like the read/write head. The location of tracks was not a requirement of the floppy disk's media itself; their location was a reflection of the disk drive head positioning mechanism, physical drive limitations on reading and writing, and convention. Commodore 64 disk drives, for instance, could have their read/write head stepped in half-track increments [28]. This ability to read and write half tracks was used for copy protection on the Commodore 64 [56, 59], but since the same tricks (and more) were possible on Apple II drives, we will focus on them instead.

Apple II drives have four electromagnets controlling head stepping: phase 0, phase 1, phase 2, and phase 3.[21] The magnets, when energized, attract cogs on a

---

[21] This discussion is based on [30, 54], and Fig. 7.13 was inspired by the representation in [54, Figure 9.4].

rotor that moves the drive head when the rotor turns. Cogs being aligned with an even-numbered phase correspond to a whole-track head position, and odd-numbered phases are half-track positions.

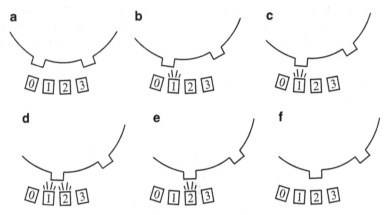

Fig. 7.13 Disk drive read/write head stepping on the Apple II

Figure 7.13 illustrates the sequence of steps required to move the head from one whole track to the next. From the initial state with no magnets energized (a), phase 1 is turned on (b) and the head eventually moves to the half-track position (c). Energizing phase 2 (d) continues the head movement, which results in the head positioned on the next whole track once phase 1 is shut off (e). Finally, after allowing sufficient time for the head to arrive, phase 2 can be shut down as well (f).

Whole track and half-track positioning was clearly possible. Positioning the head on quarter tracks was also possible, albeit not with complete accuracy. If both phases are shut down after step (d) above – essentially the two phase magnets are participating in a tug-of-war with the rotor cog – then the head will roughly be positioned in between two half tracks.

```
                                0 1 1 1 1 0
              track N−1    ···  0 1 1 1 1 0 ···
                                0 1 1 1 1 0
              N−1/2             ? ? ? ? ? ?
              N−1/4             1 0 1 0
              track N     ···   1 0 1 0              write
              N+1/4             1 0 1 0              head
              N+1/2             ? ? ? ? ? ?
                                1 1 0 1 0 1
              track N+1   ···   1 1 0 1 0 1 ···
                                1 1 0 1 0 1
```

Fig. 7.14 Writing track N, et al.

The catch to using half tracks and quarter tracks for protection is that writing on floppy drives is not a precision operation. When writing data, the magnetic field bleeds onto adjacent physical locations: as Fig. 7.14 shows conceptually, the data from writing track N also appears in the quarter tracks beside track N. Adjacent half tracks will pick up some of the content of track N, but also receive cross-talk from the data written to adjacent whole tracks. The net result is that writes of adjacent tracks must be separated by at least a track's width. However, this does not preclude writing on fractional tracks, so long as this constraint is met, and it does also not require that tracks be written in their entirety; this opens up interesting protection options.

From a disk copying point of view, a copy program that is not privy to knowledge of which track positions are in use will fail. For example, a copy program that only copies whole tracks, when part of the floppy uses half tracks, will duplicate the noisy crosstalk instead of the actual data. Protection results from the combination of "what you know" along with the physical writing limitations of floppy drives.

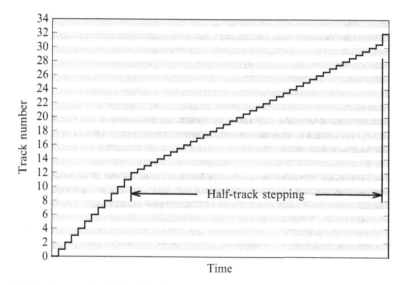

Fig. 7.15 Track read plot of *Choplifter* boot

Example 7.14 (Choplifter, 1982, and Lode Runner, 1983). Choplifter combined the use of half tracks with partial track writes, a scheme that made a straightforward copy challenging: it required the ability to copy half tracks *and* know when to skip from one half track to the next.[22] Figure 7.15 plots the location of disk reads when *Choplifter* is booted, showing that it steps by whole tracks at first, then graduates to half-track stepping starting at track 12.

---

[22] Emphasis on straightforward – at least one set of copy program parameters does this [41]. However, [30, 62] assert that this scheme can be copied by reading and writing quarter tracks, and a different set of copy program parameters follows that advice [41]. I gathered data for the disk read plots from a specially-instrumented emulator.

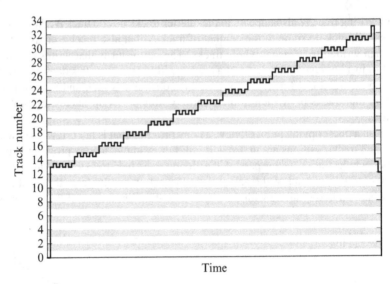

Fig. 7.16 Track read plot of *Lode Runner* boot

Lode Runner extended this idea, by bouncing back and forth between bands of whole and half tracks. The net effect, when plotted (Fig. 7.16), is reminiscent of a castle's battlements.

This technique of using part of a track, then stepping the disk head a half track, using part of that track, stepping the head another half track, and so on is referred to as track arcing [30, 41, 56] or spiral tracking [62, 68].[23] The terminology is apt, because track arcing causes the movement of the disk head to trace out a spiral pattern on the rotating disk's surface. One notable drawback to this protection scheme is loss of storage space on an already space-challenged medium; to avoid interference between data on adjacent half-tracks, only a quarter to a third of the normal track capacity can be written before moving the heads [30, 62]. When the disk hardware permits, there is no reason to limit track arcing's steps to half-track increments, and an extreme form of track arcing would use quarter tracks instead.

Example 7.15 (Spiradisc). The story of the Spiradisc protection scheme was captured in the book *Hackers* [38].[24] Only a handful of programs are known to be protected using this scheme, like an early release of *Frogger* (1982) [31, 40]. One of the programs protected with Spiradisc was *Maze Craze Construction Set* (1983), and its disk read plot during boot is shown in Fig. 7.17. The Spiradisc track arcing activity in quarter-track increments is clearly visible.

---

[23] Some sources suggest that the data is read and written as the disk heads are moving (e.g., [68]) but this may be platform-dependent: as Sather notes [54, p. 9–8], 'phase-1 must be turned off after head positioning or writing to the disk is impossible.'

[24] Levy misspelled it as "Spiradisk," however, which is incorrect according to the protection code's own banner message [40], a fact that I confirmed on a Spiradisc-protected *Frogger* image.

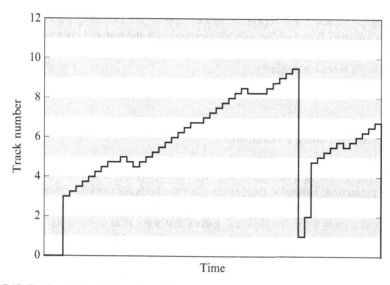

Fig. 7.17 Track read plot of *Maze Craze Construction Set* boot

Access to high-end disk duplication equipment allowed other protection methods involving cross-talk between written track data. Electronic Arts, for example, created disks containing what was variously called track imaging [30], wide tracks [68], or fat tracks [22, 51]. A band of adjacent fractional tracks would contain *exactly* the same data, an effect which was simply not possible to create with commodity drives. The protection code would then compare the data on that band at half-track intervals to ensure that it was error-free [22, 30].[25]

A related family of protections relied on having the data on adjacent tracks positioned relative to each other in certain ways. Commodity disk drives would not have easily performed these feats of inter-track synchronization when copying disks.

Example 7.16 (Video Vegas, 1985). The protection on this game is initially deceiving: the disk is copyable using standard copy programs, but the resulting copy won't boot.[26] The reason is that the copy protection required that the first eight tracks be aligned in a particular way. Starting at track 0, sector 0, the protection code would step to track 1 and compare the first sector number it found with the "correct" value,

---

[25] This check is apparent on the disk read traces for failed boots that I've gathered for some Electronic Arts games, like *Archon* (1983), *Pinball Construction Set* (1983), and *Skyfox* (1984). For extra verification, I was able to boot all three non-booting game images in-emulator by copying the track data samples verbatim from one track in the band to all fractional tracks in the band.

[26] Information for this example is based on [1, 63]. I hand-aligned the track data on a non-booting image track by track until the image booted in-emulator, then verified that it was only reading the sector's address field and that the sector numbers matched the protection code.

then step to track 2 and repeat the process, up to and including track 7. All of the sector numbers found had to match exactly to pass the test and boot the game. This sort of protection could be created using standard disk drives, but duplication would need more precise machinery.

7.4 Sidestepping Protection

Attempting to copy a retrogame directly was equivalent to a frontal assault on the copy protection. However, there were other methods for working around protection to produce a serviceable – or outright cracked – copy of the software.

Some games were "single-load" games that were read completely into memory, passing any copy protection checks in the process, and never accessing the storage media again. This would be an appealing design for slow-loading cassette-based games, but was encountered in floppy-based games too. Unfortunately this meant that the game code and data were sitting unprotected in the computer's memory, if only there were a way to get at it. Typical game protection would guard against typical ways to wrest control from a running program; for example, pressing the RESET key might reboot the machine rather than return the user to a command prompt they could examine memory from. More elaborate hardware devices and modifications presented challenges, though.

Example 7.17 (Wildcard Plus). The Wildcard Plus for the Apple II was representative of a variety of hardware add-on devices for copying, also referred to as "NMI cards" or "freeze cartridges" depending on platform. It was an expansion card that plugged into the Apple II with a button at the end of a cable that snaked out of the Apple II's case. Pushing the button generated a non-maskable interrupt (NMI) that resulted in the victim program being suspended. Control was transferred to the Wildcard's menu, where the contents of memory could be saved to disk such that it could later be restored and the victim program resumed where it left off.[27]

From a more technical point of view, the NMI could not be ignored by the CPU, and the CPU would fetch the interrupt handler address from $fffa...$fffb, normally in the Apple II's ROM. The Wildcard could inhibit those ROMs and respond using its own, effectively forcing a bank switch and thus taking control of execution.

At first glance, these hardware-based copying devices would seem to present an insurmountable obstacle for copy protection. What could software possibly do to protect itself from hardware? One hint exists in an advertisement for another Apple II NMI-based device, the Senior PROM.

The Senior PROM arguably demanded considerably higher technical skills of its users than the Wildcard. Installation required the Apple IIe's ROM chips to be removed from the motherboard and replaced with the Senior PROM board, and a

---

[27] Memory of Wildcard Plus jogged by [13], with additional material from [54, 55].

'Micro-Probe' to be attached 'to pin 6 of the 6502 Microprocessor chip' [11, p. 6] without it touching any surrounding pins – this is the CPU's NMI pin [54]. Installation aside, the Senior PROM offered comparable capabilities to the Wildcard Plus, but one of its selling features was 'Undetectable by any software or hardware' [10].

The reason why this was an important feature was that, without it, copy protection code could look for signatures in memory, i.e., particular checksums or byte sequences. One approach was to look for known copy devices this way; if the copy protection code found such a device, it could scramble the game's memory to thwart successful capture.[28] Alternately, copy protection code could look for known-good configurations. In addition to (or instead of) hardware copying devices, software crackers would use replacement ROMs with additional capabilities, like allowing an aspiring cracker to break into a machine language monitor whilst preserving volatile memory values [34]. As a blanket defense, copy protection code could look for a signature of one of the Apple II's stock ROMs, and refuse to proceed unless the signature matched, a technique which is unfortunately not future-proof. *Choplifter*'s ROM checks, for instance, refused to let the game run on the later Apple IIc.[29]

Other copy protection tricks used against hardware copying devices targeted how they operated. One method was to preemptively disable the motherboard ROMs [11] to prevent the NMI ROM swap from succeeding. Another method was where the copy protection code triggered, but did not acknowledge, its own NMI.[30] Because one NMI could not interrupt another [37], a later NMI from a copying device would have no effect.

Another key method of sidestepping copy protection is boot tracing.[31] As mentioned in passing several times, a platform obviously needed to know how to load in a retrogame's code from storage media and where to start its execution. Boot code tracing involved monitoring this loading process and studying a retrogame's loading/protection code along the way.

Example 7.18 (Apple II floppy disk). The Apple II's floppy disks were plugged into a disk controller card, that in turn was plugged into an expansion slot on the Apple's motherboard. Each expansion slot was allocated a small chunk of the memory address space, and in the disk controller's case that 256 bytes held ROM code to boot from the floppy disk. At minimum, the controller's boot code would: recalibrate the disk's read/write head to a known location[32]; find and read in 256 bytes from track 0, sector 0 to RAM at location $800; jump to address $801. This newly-loaded second-stage boot code could then reuse the primary boot code from the

---

[28] The Freeload loader source contains a signature check for the Expert cartridge on the Commodore 64 along with countermeasures. Other signatures were included in different versions of Freeload [25].

[29] Sather mentions the use of ROM checksums for copy protection [54, p. 5-31]. The *Choplifter* issue on the Apple IIc is noted by [69] and backed up by a disassembly that also reveals the signature method to be byte sequences [49].

[30] Mentioned in [25, 26], and present in Freeload source.

[31] This is described in many sources. The "KRAKOWICZ'S KRACKING KORNER" series of articles, starting with [34], is an excellent reference.

[32] By repeatedly stepping the head out until it beat mercilessly against the outside of the drive, creating the distinctive floppy booting sound the Apple II made.

disk controller to load more sectors from the disk, leading in multiple stages to a disk operating system and/or game being loaded and run.[33]

To begin boot tracing a floppy, it was a simple matter to copy the disk controller's code to RAM and patch it to enter the machine language monitor instead of jumping to $801. Running this patched code would result in the second-stage boot code sitting in RAM, vulnerable to inspection.

While boot tracing is possible, copy protection code did not have to make it easy. There *is* a certain amount of intellectual gratification to boot tracing protected programs, like solving a puzzle where the puzzle pieces can move and transmute themselves. More practically speaking, there were two end goals in mind. First, tracing might be done to understand how and where the data was stored (particularly on disk), with an eye to making a working copy with a disk copying program. Second, and more likely, tracing would be done to remove copy protection and produce a cracked and easy-to-copy version of the game.

For a single-load game, key questions to answer through tracing were where the game was loaded in memory, and what its start address was. That would allow just those portions of memory to be saved in a cracked version; with excess fat trimmed, multiple cracked single-load games could easily be distributed on one disk. Games that required repeated media access required more surgery, but were not impossible to trace and crack. More insidious copy protection could also detect shenanigans, but lie dormant. *Prince of Persia*, for example, had multiple delayed effects up to and including the final scene [14]; one of them, appropriately, is controlled in the source code by a variable called timebomb.[34]

Viewing software protection as computer security authentication allows schemes past, present, and future to be classified and understood. Software copying is still a concern, and some of these methods used for retrogame protection are still with us in some form, like software license keys and dongles.

A modern analogue to sidestepping protection is the side-channel attack, that gleans sensitive information by watching subtle physical side effects of a computation, like timing [73] or power consumption [33]. While plugging a copy card into a computer may be out of vogue, identifying an emulated or otherwise hostile environment is a technique used by malicious software to evade detection, and signature detection is one tool used by anti-malware software [3] (the known-good signature is really a type of "whitelisting").

One lingering question, for protection that relies on secret knowledge, is how those secrets are protected; the answer lies in obfuscation, one of the topics of the next chapter.

---

[33] An excellent description of the DOS boot process is in [71], with hardware details from [54].

[34] As seen in the source code, in case it wasn't apparent. This is for the delayed Level 7 effect Ferrie refers to [14].

References

1. 4am: Video Vegas (4am crack) (12 June 2014). Number 70
2. Apple Computer, Inc.: Apple II Reference Manual. Apple Computer, Cupertino (1978)
3. Aycock, J.: Computer Viruses and Malware. Springer, New York/London (2006)
4. Barton, M., Loguidice, B.: A history of gaming platforms: Mattel Intellivision. Gamasutra. http://www.gamasutra.com/view/feature/132054/a_history_of_gaming_platforms_.php (2008)
5. Brotby, W.K.: Method and apparatus for frustrating the unauthorized copying of recorded data. United States Patent #4,785,361 (15 Nov 1988)
6. Catchings, B., Van Name, M.L.: SideShow. Amiga World 6(5), 66–68 (1990)
7. Central Point Software: Copy II PC option board (advertisement). PC Mag. 5(13), 277 (1986)
8. Commodore Computer: Commodore 64 Programmer's Reference Guide. Commodore Business Machines, Wayne/Howard W. Sams & Co., Indianapolis (1982)
9. Cook, R.: Deadline. PC Mag. 1(7), 110 (1982)
10. Cutting Edge Enterprises: Graduate... to the Senior PROM! (advertisement). Computist (40) (1987)
11. Cutting Edge Enterprises: Senior PROM //e, //c Version 3.0 Documentation (1987)
12. Defendisk Inc.: $10,000 REWARD (classified advertisement). InfoWorld 6(19), 150 (1984)
13. Elite Software Company: Wildcard Plus User Manual (1983)
14. Ferrie, P.: Prince of PoC; or, a 16-sector version of Prince of Persia for the Apple][. POC || GTFO 0x04, 12–15 (2014)
15. Goodwin, S.: The plastic policeman. CRASH Mag. (24), 152–154 (1985)
16. Green, A.: pop-codereview-rw18. https://github.com/adamgreen/Prince-of-Persia-Apple-II/blob/build/Notes/pop-codereview-rw18.creole (2 May 2013)
17. Green, A.: Disassembly of 18 Sector Read/Write Routine. https://github.com/adamgreen/Prince-of-Persia-Apple-II/blob/build/Other/RW18525.S (29 July 2013)
18. Grynberg, A., Klein, H.: Technique for preventing unauthorized copying of information recorded on a recording medium and a protected recording medium. United States Patent #4,734,796 (29 Mar 1988)
19. Guglielmino, P.: Copyprotecting system for software protection. United States Patent #4,584,641 (22 Apr 1986)
20. Gustafsson, R.: Email Communications (10–11 Jan 2015)
21. Gustafsson, R.: Email Communication (12 Jan 2015)
22. Henrikson, K.: Electronic Arts C64 Fat Track Loader. http://c64preservation.com/files/EaLoader.txt (Undated)
23. Hicken, W.: Email Communication (11 Feb 2015)
24. Hughes, P.: Email Communication (24 Apr 2015)
25. Hughes, P.: Email Communication (8 Apr 2015)
26. Hughes, P.: Freeload. http://www.pauliehughes.com/page3/page3.html (Undated)
27. Hull, S.: Jet vs. F/A-18 Interceptor: clash of the Titans. Amaz. Comput. 3(8), 8–9 (1988)
28. Immers, R., Neufeld, G.G.: Inside Commodore DOS. Datamost, Northridge (1984)
29. Intellivision Productions, Inc.: Intellivision II Development History. http://www.intellivisionlives.com/bluesky/hardware/intelli2_tech.html (Undated)
30. Jones, B.W.: Demystifying the quarter track. Hardcore Computist (21), 12–14 (1985)
31. Jones, B.W.: Spiradisk [sic] info. Hardcore Computist (25), 4 (1985). Letter to the editor
32. Kent, S.L.: The Ultimate History of Video Games. Three Rivers Press, New York (2001)
33. Kocher, P., Jaffe, J., Jun, B.: Differential power analysis. In: 19th Annual International Cryptology Conference, Santa Barbara, pp. 388–397 (1999)
34. Krakowicz: Krakowicz's Kracking Korner: The Basics of Kracking I (Undated, probably early- to mid-1980s)
35. Lake, M.: Email Communication (9 Apr 2015)
36. Level 9 Computing: The Price of Magik Instructions (Commodore 64 Version) (1986)

37. Leventhal, L.A.: 6502 Assembly Language Programming, 2nd edn. Osborne McGraw-Hill, Berkeley (1986)
38. Levy, S.: Hackers: Heroes of the Computer Revolution. Dell, New York (1984)
39. Linzmayer, O.: Review of Intellivision II. Creat. Comput. Video Arcade Games 1(2), 82–84 (1983)
40. McFadden, M.M.: Antique softkey for Frogger. Computist (41), 28–29 (1987)
41. Moore, M.: The Parameter Guide. Moore's Microware (Undated, probably pre-1985)
42. Morrison, G.: Atari Software Protection Techniques. Alpha Systems, Stow (1983)
43. Nagashima, T.: Method for executing software program and circuit for implementing the method. United States Patent #5,796,940 (18 Aug 1998)
44. Nakagawa, K.: System for determining authenticity of an external memory used in an information processing apparatus. United States Patent #4,799,635 (24 Jan 1989)
45. Nakagawa, K., Yukawa, M.: Memory cartridge and information processor unit using such cartridge. United States Patent #4,865,321 (12 Sept 1989)
46. O'Donnell, C.: Production protection to copy(right) protection: from the 10NES to DVDs. IEEE Ann. Hist. Comput. 31, 54–63 (2009)
47. Patchett, C., Sherer, R.: Master Memory Map for the Atari. Reston Pub. Co., Reston (1984)
48. Pfleeger, C.P., Pfleeger, S.L.: Security in Computing, 3rd edn. Prentice Hall, Upper Saddle River (2003)
49. qkumba: Choplifter (Brøderbund, 1982). http://www.hackzapple.com/phpBB2/viewtopic.php?t=621 (29 Jan 2012)
50. Reekie, J.: Letter to the editor. CRASH Mag. (26), 45 (1986)
51. Rittwage, P.: Copy protection methods. Floppy Disk Preservation Project web site. http://diskpreservation.com/protection (Undated)
52. Rothstein, E.: Reading and writing; participatory novels. New York Times (8 May 1983)
53. Sanglard, F.: Prince of Persia Code Review: Part 2 (bootloader). http://fabiensanglard.net/prince_of_persia/pop_boot.php (14 June 2013)
54. Sather, J.: Understanding the Apple II. Quality Software, Chatsworth (1983)
55. Schäfer, P.: Apple][Wildcard (19 Mar 1994). Schematic, reverse-engineered from Taiwanese board
56. Simstad, T.N.: Program Protection Manual for the C-64, vol. II. CSM Software, Inc., Crown Point (1985)
57. Sinclair User staff: The lens: 20/20 vision or mirage? Sinclair User (46), 5 (1986)
58. Smith, J. III.: Video game cartridge recognition and security system. United States Patent #4,462,076 (24 July 1984)
59. Taylor, D.M., Taylor, R.H.: C-64 Software Protection Revealed. Value Soft, Portland (1985)
60. Taylor, J.: Letter to the editor. Sinclair User (48), 16 (1986)
61. Texas Instruments: SN54165, SN54LS165A, SN74165, SN74LS165A parallel-load 8-bit shift registers. Data sheet (1976, revised 2002)
62. Thompson, P., Silver, A., Brown, M.: Copy II Plus Apple Disk Backup System. Central Point Software, Portland (1985). Version 5.0
63. toinet: Video Vegas (Baudville, 1985). http://www.hackzapple.com/phpBB2/viewtopic.php?t=163 (15 June 2007)
64. Trixter: Life Before Demos (or, Hobbyist Programming in the 1980's). http://www.oldskool.org/shrines/lbd (25 Sept 1996)
65. United States Court of Appeals, Ninth Circuit: Sega Enterprises Ltd. v. Accolade, Inc. 977 F.2d 1510 (1992, amended 1993)
66. Various Contributors: Software Protection Dongle. Wikipedia. http://en.wikipedia.org/w/index.php?title=Software_protection_dongle&oldid=641430223
67. Vickers, S., Bradbeer, R.: Sinclair ZX Spectrum Introduction. Sinclair Research Limited, Cambridge (1982)
68. Voelcker, J., Wallich, P.: How disks are 'padlocked'. IEEE Spectr. 23(6), 32–40 (1986)
69. Wilson, T.G.: Softkey for Choplifter. Hardcore Computist (23), 10–12 (1985)
70. Wood, J.: Re: copy a CRT image to be used on a real Commodore 64. comp.sys.cbm, comp.emulators.cbm, alt.c64 Usenet newsgroups (20 Sept 2004)

71. Worth, D., Lechner, P.: Beneath Apple DOS. Quality Software, Reseda (1981)
72. Worth, D., Lechner, P.: Beneath Apple ProDOS. Quality Software, Chatsworth (1984)
73. Yarom, Y., Falkner, K.: Flush+reload: a high resolution, low noise, L3 cache side-channel attack. In: Proceedings of the 23rd USENIX Security Symposium, San Diego, pp. 719–732 (2014)
74. Yukawa, M.: Cartridge for game machine. United States Design Patent #294,020 (2 Feb 1988)

Chapter 8
Obfuscation and Optimization

Techniques used for retrogame protection and for making retrogames possible to run at all can be deeply intertwined. There are two topics here. First is obfuscation, efforts to make code and data more difficult to understand. The topic of manual code optimization is second; these can be optimizations done for space (a continuation of an ongoing retrogame theme) but also optimizations for speed. At times the line between this pair of topics is extremely hard to distinguish. For example, is code obfuscated to make it more challenging to crack, or to make it small enough to work?

Example 8.1 (Pac-Land, 1988). Pac-Land for the Commodore 64 was constrained for space even with 64 K of memory to work with. As developer Alan Ogg recalled [5, p. 73], they 'were even using the 6502 stack for running code in [...] Even the tape loader over-wrote its own code at the end of the load.' Furthermore, the tape loading code used run-length encoding to compress data: a bitmap with one bit per target page controlled whether to decompress or whether to copy data literally.[1]

The motivation for *Pac-Land* was space, but these optimizations certainly didn't make boot tracing any easier either. Similar optimization surprises awaited in other retrogames.

Cpus like the 6502 and the Z80 had their official instruction sets, but lurking within them were undocumented instructions too – upon encountering these, the CPU would not register an illegal instruction fault as a modern processor would, but would instead gamely try to execute the "instruction." Results varied. Undocumented instructions could be more bizarre than useful, and there was no guarantee that they would exist from one version of a CPU to the next. Formerly undocumented instructions could be assigned new meanings, too: for instance, the 65C02 added new instructions to the 6502, and any Apple II software that relied on those formerly undocumented opcodes could fail on the Apple IIc and later Apple IIe models that incorporated the 65C02.

---

[1] I verified the claims from the interview quote, and analyzed the compression code, statically and dynamically.

© Springer International Publishing Switzerland 2016
J. Aycock, *Retrogame Archeology*, DOI 10.1007/978-3-319-30004-7_8

Example 8.2 (Jack the Nipper, 1986). Undocumented instructions could enable programmers to perform feats not possible with official CPU instructions. *Jack the Nipper* on the ZX Spectrum was one such case: as the programmer explained in an interview [21, p. 46], 'I had to use illegal Z80 instructions because I ran out of registers.' Specifically, the Z80's index registers were normally only accessible as indivisible 16-bit values, but *Jack the Nipper* used undocumented instructions to directly address the upper eight bits of the *IX* index register.[2]

8.1 Code and Data Obfuscation

Copy protection code is a rich source of deliberate code obfuscation examples. While we will continue to focus on Apple II retrogame protection for consistency, these same techniques were no stranger to other platforms.[3] In fact, a 1985 treatise on undocumented Z80 instructions for the ZX Spectrum notes [40, p. 51] 'you'll find that they're being used more and more in many commercial games [...] these instructions are a very neat way of fooling the hacker.' And obfuscations using undocumented instructions are a good place to begin.

Example 8.3 (Pac-Man, 1984). There were several releases of *Pac-Man* for the Apple II, and the Datasoft version's copy protection condenses a number of obfuscation techniques into the 256-byte boot block of the floppy disk.[4]

0801-	74	**???**
0802-	85 B0	**STA** $B0
0804-	58	**CLI**
0805-	6A	**ROR**
0806-	EA	**NOP**
0807-	73	**???**
0808-	4B	**???**

Fig. 8.1 Datasoft *Pac-Man* initial boot code disassembly

Recall that the Apple II's disk controller code would load a disk's boot block into memory at address $800 and then jump to $801. A would-be cracker disassembling that code from the Apple II monitor would be presented with a rather confusing display, the first part of which is shown in Fig. 8.1. The column in bold normally shows the disassembled 6502 instructions, and the important thing to observe is the question marks indicating the disassembler's failure to translate an opcode into an assembly instruction. In other words, the *very first instruction* executed from the *Pac-Man* disk is a complete mystery.

---

[2] Found and verified in code trace with undocumented Z80 information from [40].

[3] See, for example, [22] regarding self-modifying Atari code, and [28] for use of undocumented opcodes and encryption on the Commodore 64.

[4] Thanks to 4am for the initial tip. I did an independent analysis of the boot code and verified against [1]. Apple IIc boot verified in-emulator.

On the 6502, opcode $74 is an undocumented instruction that acts as a NOP instruction with an (ignored) argument. This is also an instance where an undocumented opcode became documented: on the 65C02, this is interpreted as the instruction M[$85+X] = 0. The change in semantics luckily makes no difference in this case, as the game still boots on an Apple IIc.

```
1   $0801:   nop
2   $0803:   if c = 1 goto $85d
3
4   $085d:   A = $ca
5   $085f:   M[$89d] = A
6   $0862:   if c = 1 goto $895
7
8   $0895:   A = X
9   $0896:   push A
10  $0897:   Y = $98
11  $0899:   A = M[$800+Y]
12  $089c:   A = A XOR $ca
13  $089e:   M[$700+Y] = A
14  $08a1:   Y = Y - 1
15  $08a2:   if Y != 0 goto $899
16           . . .
17  $08b3:   goto $705
```

Fig. 8.2 Datasoft *Pac-Man* initial boot code trace

To understand more of the code and its execution, Fig. 8.2 gives a trace of pseudo-assembly instructions in the boot code as it runs. After the undocumented nop in line 1, there is a conditional branch based on the value of the carry bit at line 2. Normally a conditional branch like this would follow an instruction that sets the state of the carry bit, and thus this can be viewed as an attempt to obfuscate the code's control flow, because it is not immediately obvious that the carry bit is always set by the disk controller's code upon entry to $801.

Lines 4–5 are an example of self-modifying code. Here, this changes the bold value at line 12 from its initial value of $aa. Neither of these two instructions changes the carry bit, and therefore line 6 acts as an unconditional branch to $895.

The next section of note in the trace occurs at lines 10–15. This loop decrypts 152 bytes of the boot code's 256 bytes by exclusive-ORing each byte with the value $ca,[5] and stores the decrypted bytes starting at address $701. The code self-modification from earlier is now seen to be changing the decryption key, an attempt at misdirection that led at least one code analyst temporarily astray [1].

---

[5] This usage of "decrypt" is common in the anti-malware community, and does not necessarily imply strong cryptography.

Fig. 8.3 *Pac-Man* boot code execution, seen as text

Finally, line 17 shows the code jump to the decrypted code at $705. What is interesting about this particular region of memory that the code is decrypted into is that it corresponds to memory-mapped text data. For a brief moment, the user sees a visual representation of the code being executed (Fig. 8.3), just as in *Yar's Revenge* (1981) mentioned earlier. Address $705 is the location immediately following >O:R on the first line of apparent garbage.

Unsurprisingly, self-modification was not only applied to the operands of instructions as in *Pac-Man*. Modifying the actual instructions to confuse humans trying to analyze the code was also fair game.

Example 8.4 (Cannonball Blitz, 1982). Someone trying to boot trace *Cannonball Blitz* would eventually wind up seeing the disassembly shown in Fig. 8.4.[6] Again, the 6502 instruction mnemonics are not important; what is of note is the number of question marks where the disassembler was confused. The only instructions correctly disassembled in this sequence are the first and last ones, in bold, and all this was caused by minor self-modifying changes to only two bytes.

Figure 8.5 shows how the pseudo-assembly version of this code changes as it executes, with *PC* denoting the instruction being executed and the two emboldened instructions from Fig. 8.4 in bold as reference points. The first instruction's execution modifies what becomes the opcode for the next instruction, whose execution

---

[6] Information from [16], partially corroborated by [9]. Verified statically and dynamically in emulator.

```
59E4-    CE E7 59    DEC  $59E7
59E7-    CF          ???
59E8-    EA          NOP
59E9-    59 EF EA    EOR  $EAEF,Y
59EC-    59 AD 51    EOR  $51AD,Y
59EF-    C0 AD       CPY  #$AD
59F1-    54          ???
59F2-    C0 AD       CPY  #$AD
59F4-    57          ???
59F5-    C0 AD       CPY  #$AD
59F7-    52          ???
59F8-    C0 20       CPY  #$20
59FA-    60          RTS
59FB-    5B          ???
59FC-    20 C5 5B    JSR  $5BC5
```

Fig. 8.4 *Cannonball Blitz* obfuscated code disassembly

```
PC →  $59e4:   M[$59e7] = M[$59e7] - 1
      $59e7:   ???
      $59e8:   nop
      $59e9:   A = A XOR M[$eaef+Y]
               . . .
```

⬇

```
      $59e4:   M[$59e7] = M[$59e7] - 1
PC →  $59e7:   M[$59ea] = M[$59ea] - 1
      $59ea:   ???
      $59eb:   nop
               . . .
```

⬇

```
      $59e4:   M[$59e7] = M[$59e7] - 1
      $59e7:   M[$59ea] = M[$59ea] - 1
PC →  $59ea:   M[$59ea] = M[$59ea] + 1
      $59ed:   A = M[$c051]
      $59f0:   A = M[$c054]
      $59f3:   A = M[$c057]
      $59f6:   A = M[$c052]
      $59f9:   call $5b60
      $59fc:   call $5bc5
```

Fig. 8.5 *Cannonball Blitz* execution and deobfuscation

modifies the instruction opcode after it – it is at this point when the correct disassembly for the code is finally visible. This is only temporary, however: when the
instruction at $59ea is executed, the instruction modifies its opcode to be obfuscated
once again.

Presenting a disassembler with invalid or undocumented instructions was one thing, but it was also possible to trick a disassembler into creating a false disassembly. A false disassembly would obfuscate the control flow of the code in a robust, portable way (unlike undocumented instructions) and if carefully constructed could present itself as normal assembly code without the disassembler's telltale question marks.

```
1  $0801:   M[$a]  = X
2  $0803:   M[$a001] = X
3  $0806:   M[$a01a] = X
4  $0809:   if c = 0 goto $883
5  $080b:   if X != 0 goto $80e
6  $080d:   A = M[$9c20]
7  $0810:   push P
```

Fig. 8.6 *Frogger* initial boot code with false disassembly

```
1  $0801:   M[$a]  = X
2  $0803:   M[$a001] = X
3  $0806:   M[$a01a] = X
4  $0809:   if c = 0 goto $883
5  $080b:   if X != 0 goto $80e
6  $080d:   byte $ad
7  $080e:   call $89c
```

Fig. 8.7 *Frogger* initial boot code without false disassembly

Example 8.5 (Frogger, 1982). Spiradisc protected *Frogger*, and false disassembly protected Spiradisc.[7] While there are examples of false disassembly later in *Frogger*'s loading process [20], we do not need to look beyond the code in its boot sector.

Figure 8.6 shows the pseudo-assembly for the beginning of *Frogger*'s boot code. As with *Pac-Man*, some obfuscation derives from knowledge of the CPU state on entry to $801. None of the instructions in lines 1–3 change the carry flag from its entry value of 1, and therefore the conditional branch at line 4 is never taken. The X register's value is always nonzero on entry, the branch at line 5 *is* taken, and this is the false disassembly. Notice that the branch target is $80e, yet there is no instruction in the disassembly that begins at $80e. An additional byte has been added at $80d to cause this false disassembly, and the branch at line 5 neatly jumps over it when executed. The rewritten version of this code in Fig. 8.7 (with changes in bold), while not what the disassembler would produce, more clearly shows what the code does.

---

[7] False disassembly is covered in [16], and I found the example used here in both *Frogger* and *Maze Craze Construction Set* (1983).

The hidden `call $89c` instruction is present the entire time, unlike self-modifying code that would need to be run; the disassembler is simply misguided by the extra $ad byte.

Another method of hiding control flow counterintuitively relies on a frequent method for overtly changing control flow, the `return` instruction. The `return` instruction, on the 6502 and many other processors, retrieves the address to go to from the stack, normally placed there by a corresponding `call` instruction. It is possible to use `return` as a `goto` by priming the stack with the destination address and then, at some later point in the code, executing a `return`. The separation of the stack manipulation and the `return` adds to the obfuscation, as does the fact that the return address the 6502's `call` stores is off by one; the `return` adds 1 to the stored value before transferring it to the program counter.

```
A = $b4
push A
A = $bd
push A
goto $b47a
```

Fig. 8.8 Prelude to a `return` in *Pest Patrol*

Example 8.6 (Pest Patrol, 1982). Pest Patrol sets up the stack for a later `return` fairly blatantly.[8] As the pseudo-assembly in Fig. 8.8 shows, two constant values are pushed on to the stack and followed by an unconditional branch. A `return` executed later would transfer control to $b4b*e*, taking the +1 adjustment into account.

Other examples of control flow obfuscation using `return` were far more subtle.

```
1  $0828:  Y = 0
2  $082c:  A = M[$850+Y]
3          A = A XOR $a5
4          M[$60+Y] = A
5          Y = Y + 1
6          if Y != 0 goto $82c
7          X = $ff
8          SP = X
9          return
```

Fig. 8.9 *Lode Runner* boot code excerpt

[8] This example is drawn from [8]. While it is an excellent, plausible first example of this technique, I have pointedly not verified it for reasons I return to in Chap. 9.

Example 8.7 (Lode Runner, 1983). The boot sector for *Lode Runner* contains a few obfuscations; the important parts are distilled in Fig. 8.9's pseudo-assembly.[9]

Similar to *Pac-Man*, the code at lines 1–6 is a decryption loop, storing decrypted code and data starting at address $60 and continuing into page 1, where the 6502's stack is located. Then lines 7–8 set the stack pointer to $ff, the maximum value possible, which happens to be an area of the stack untouched by the earlier decryption. In that context, the `return` at line 9 is a clever obfuscation. The 6502 increments the stack pointer before fetching the return address, and because the stack pointer already contained the maximum value, it wraps around to fetch the first byte of the return address from the *start* of the stack page (at $100). The decryption loop did place values at that location, surreptitiously setting up the control transfer via `return`.

Exclusive OR has featured in several retrogame examples already, but always in the context of decryption. It could also be used for checksums to guard against unauthorized code modification, possibly in conjunction with other obfuscations that would prevent the checksum from being trivially bypassed.

```
1   $5a91:   A = 0
2            Y = A
3   $5a97:   A = A XOR M[$2700+Y]
4            Y = Y + 1
5            if Y != 0 goto $5a97
6            M[$10] = A
7            A = $20
8   $5aa4:   A = A XOR M[$2700+Y]
9            Y = Y + 1
10           Y = Y + 1
11           if Y != 0 goto $5aa4
12           A = A XOR $b7
13           push A
14           A = M[$10]
15           A = A XOR $11
16           push A
17           if A != 0 goto $5ab8
18           (false disassembly)
19  $5ab8:   return
```

Fig. 8.10 *Cannonball Blitz* checksum-based obfuscation

Example 8.8 (Cannonball Blitz). Figure 8.10 shows pseudo-assembly for a checksum sequence in *Cannonball Blitz*, with some extraneous instructions and obfuscations removed for clarity.[10]

---

[9] Information from static and dynamic analysis, verified in part against [19, 33].

[10] Example from [16], verified statically and dynamically. The presentation here differs from Krakowicz: among other things, it retains the original memory addresses and corrects an error.

This code performs a double checksum on the page of code at $2700. Lines 1–5 compute the first checksum, exclusive-ORing each byte together starting from the value 0; the result is saved in memory at line 6. Lines 7–11 calculate another checksum over that same region starting from the value $20, exclusive-ORing every second byte.

A simple comparison of the computed checksums to the correct values could be easily sidestepped, and instead the checksum is combined with a return-based obfuscation. Lines 12–16 push both checksums on the stack, exclusive-ORing each with a different constant value first. Presented this way, a return instruction is the likely conclusion, but a final misdirection at lines 17–18 sows some doubt. Because the branch is based on a checksum result and the false disassembly byte (not shown) is the opcode for a goto instruction, it is easy to be misled to the goto's destination rather than the return hidden inside the goto instruction.

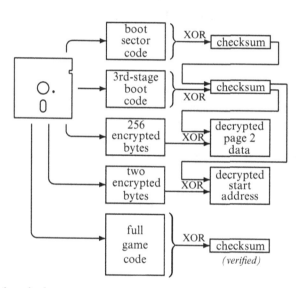

Fig. 8.11 *Sneakers* checksums

Example 8.9 (Sneakers, 1981). *Cannonball Blitz* used checksums, but *Sneakers* embodied them on a completely different level.[11] The easiest way to understand all the activity taking place is in a diagram: see Fig. 8.11.

A combined exclusive-OR checksum of the boot sector code (i.e., second-stage boot code, after the disk controller's first-stage boot code) and the third-stage boot code is computed by the code. This, in turn, is used as a decryption key for 256 bytes of low memory data and the game's start address. The intent is clearly to use this

---

[11] Information from [2], verified statically and dynamically in-emulator. This is a slightly simplified view, and there is even more checksumming done by the code.

dependency chain to guard against boot code changes as well as obfuscate the location of the start address. An exclusive-OR checksum of the game code proper is calculated separately and verified.

One last obfuscation technique is, effectively, to change the language that the code is written in. This technique has appeared in earlier chapters, but not for purposes of obfuscation: interpretation. Whereas before, interpreters gave advantages in terms of size and portability, they also transform code into an unfamiliar form for an outsider trying to analyze the program.

Example 8.10 (Hard Hat Mack, 1983). The boot code for *Hard Hat Mack* contained an interpreter for a 12-instruction virtual machine.[12] The interpreted instruction set was fairly minimalist, with most instructions centering around an eight-bit accumulator along with the ability to call 6502 code from the interpreted program. Even the accumulator-based instructions were limited. For example, there was an instruction for subtraction but not addition, and the interpreted code for *Hard Hat Mack* added 1 to the accumulator at one point by subtracting $ff. All operands to the virtual machine instructions were exclusive-ORed with constants to make their values less apparent in memory.

Normally these retrogame obfuscations are seen only through reverse engineering, after the fact. It is interesting, if rare, to see this from the source code side – how would the programmer create these obfuscations?

Sometimes the answer is simply "without ceremony." For instance,[13] the source code for *Fort Apocalypse* (1982) on the Atari 800 has several subroutines to compute checksums, with no comments or documentation apart from the names of the routines themselves, e.g., DO.CHECKSUM2. A failed checksum leads to a line which contains not a mnemonic assembly instruction, but

```
byte $12
```

This is an undocumented 6502 instruction that halts the processor. Or, since it appears without any comments in the source code, it is an undocumented undocumented instruction. Obfuscations in other games could fare the same or better in terms of their explanation.

Example 8.11 (Prince of Persia, 1989). The Apple II source code for *Prince of Persia* contains several obfuscated copy protection routines.[14]

---

[12] Thanks to 4am for the tip about this protection. Information from reverse engineering and writing a disassembler for the virtual machine code. An analysis for the later *Skyfox* (1984) on the Commodore 64, also an Electronic Arts release, reveals a similar virtual machine but with a more complicated instruction set [13].

[13] Example from static analysis of source code. The example is presented here as pseudo-assembly.

[14] Information from static source code analysis. The code here and in later examples has been converted into pseudo-assembly and lightly reformatted, but the human-readable identifiers and comments (and lack thereof) have been retained verbatim.

```
 1    ; Note: first byte of next junk must be $60 (rts)
 2    PURPcode:    byte $60,$38,$60,$18,...,$63,$be,$20
 3
 4    ; Routine to decode code
 5
 6                 byte $20
 7
 8    PURPsub:     M[4] = Y
 9                 M[5] = A
10                 Y = 0
11                 X = PURPlen
12    L0:          X = X - 1
13                 A = M[PURPcode+X]
14                 M[Mw[4] + Y] = A
15                 Y = Y + 1
16                 if Y != 0 goto L0
17                 return
18
19                 byte $2c
20
21    PURPjmp:     goto Mw[4]
```

Fig. 8.12 *Prince of Persia* "purple" protection

The first one, "purple," had a blob of hexadecimal bytes in the source file (Fig. 8.12, line 2), corresponding to the bytes of protected code stored in reverse order. The PURPsub routine was called first, with the destination location for the unprotected code in the A and Y registers, to unreverse the bytes in the blob; then, PURPjmp would be invoked to go to the newly-decoded area. Lines 6 and 19 are never executed, because they are the way that false disassembly has been added to the source code, guarding the entry points for both routines. $20 is the opcode for a call instruction that would swallow up line 8's instruction in the disassembly, and $2c is a bit-test instruction whose disassembly would claim 2/3 of the bytes of line 21's instruction.

A second piece of copy protection code, "yellow," also has a chunk of hexadecimal bytes embedded in its source code, although these are encrypted. Yellow's identically-commented 'Routine to decode code' decrypts the bytes using exclusive OR, with a constant-valued decryption key that is computed at run time rather than stored overtly in the code. Again there is false disassembly inserted, although here the bytes' meaning is illuminated with inline comments:

```
byte $20 ;jsr
...
byte $a9 ;lda #imm
```

Before moving to code optimizations, we note that obfuscation was not restricted to code, and data in retrogames could be obfuscated as an anti-cheating measure.

Sometimes this came for free as a side effect of data representation: Infocom's Z-machine strings, for instance, would appear obfuscated to a casual viewer [37].

Many examples of deliberate data obfuscation involved exclusive OR, the most straightforward application of which would be to exclusive-OR with a constant value. *Elite* (1984) exclusive-ORed string bytes with 35, as mentioned in Chap. 5.[15] In the 1977 PDP-10 version of *Adventure*, a comment in the code states 'WORDS ARE GIVEN A MINIMAL HASH TO MAKE READING THE CORE-IMAGE HARDER' and the minimal hash is an exclusive-OR with the value PHROG (five characters could fit in one 36-bit word on that architecture).

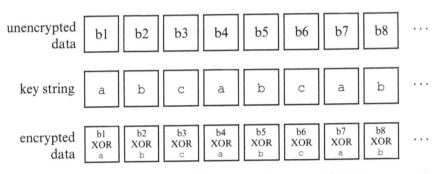

Fig. 8.13 Encryption and decryption data obfuscation with the constant string abc

Instead of constant values, some retrogames would obfuscate data by encrypting it with a constant string. Data bytes would be exclusive-ORed with consecutive bytes of the constant string, which would "wrap around" when all its bytes were exhausted (Fig. 8.13). This method was used, for example, by the 1987 *Trek73*, *Adventure* in 4.2 BSD Unix, and AGI-interpreted games like *King's Quest* (1984). Normally the constant string would look like random gibberish, like *Adventure*'s

```
"Ax3F'tt$8hqer*hnGKrX:!l"
```

but the AGI interpreter used the curious string 'Avis Durgan.' This choice had sentimental rather than technical value: that was the name of AGI programmer Jeff Stephenson's wife [18].

Moving away from constant values and strings, the later 4.4 BSD *Adventure* would checksum data to be saved, and use the checksum to seed a pseudo-random number generator. Each data byte written out was exclusive-ORed with a different random value from the generator (the seed would need to be written out unencrypted to properly re-seed the PRNG and decrypt the data later).

---

[15] *Elite* information from reverse engineering, *Adventure*(s), *Trek73*, and AGI from source code.

8.2 Manual Code Optimizations

"Optimization" has several meanings in computer science. In some circles it is a precise technical term, an assertion that something is optimal and cannot be improved upon. Here, the word is taken in the more colloquial sense: optimization is done to make improvements that make a program better in some way, but there is no guarantee that the result is perfectly optimal.

In the context of retrogames and their platforms, two general types of optimizations were of interest. First, optimization for space, where the goal would be to make a game smaller to fit and work in a constrained amount of memory or secondary storage. Second, optimization for time; here the idea would be to make a game run at a playable speed. At times the two optimization types are complementary, such as smaller code happening to run faster, but often there is a tradeoff to be made – more speed with a solution that requires more memory consumption, or a smaller memory footprint with more code overhead.

We have seen these tradeoffs in earlier chapters. Compression and interpreted code both optimize for space, but impose a cost in terms of speed because decompression and interpretation become necessary. Here, we look at even finer-grained optimizations, some of which serve double duty as unintentional obfuscations to the uninitiated observer.

8.2.1 Space Optimizations

We begin with space optimizations for code that were machine-independent in the respect that they would be usable across different platforms, although the exact details would vary.

```
(3 bytes)   call foo           goto foo   (3 bytes)
(1 byte)    return

            goto GETMODE       ;GETMODE IS A SUBR
          ; return
```

Fig. 8.14 Tail call optimization and use in *Dig Dug*

- Tail call optimization. When a subroutine ends in a subroutine call followed by a return, a space savings can be achieved by replacing the call–return pair with a goto [39, 12:44]. Formally, this is referred to as tail call optimization [23], and yields savings from the instruction change, with additional space savings in stack usage. Figure 8.14 shows the general form of this optimization, and how it appears in the source code for *Dig Dug* (1987): the inline comment,

occasionally retaining the commented-out `return`, served as a reminder to the
programmer that this optimization had been performed.[16]

```
TT68:   call TT27
        A = ':'                 TT68:   call TT27
        call TT27                       A = ':'
        return          ⟹      TT27:   X = A
        ...                             ...
TT27:   X = A
        ...
```

Fig. 8.15 Reusing common code in *Elite*

- Reusing common code. Related to tail call optimization, this space optimization
  relied on code placement combined with the ability in assembly code for one
  subroutine to fall through into another. For example, Fig. 8.15 shows this technique being used in the *Elite* code. The left side shows how this excerpt *could* be
  coded, but wasn't, in favor of the space-optimized code on the right side.[17]
- "Conditional" branches. With obfuscations, there were examples of conditional
  branches used to express control flow in hard-to-analyze ways, where the branching conditions had been set much earlier in the execution. Just as those conditional branches acted unconditionally for obfuscation, conditional branches were
  used the same way for optimization. For example, the *Elite* source code in one
  spot has the sequence

```
A = 119
if A != 0 goto TT27
```

In this setting, the technique is not an obfuscation: the value of *A* is clearly set
just the line prior. A `goto` instruction would occupy three bytes on the 6502,
however, whereas the conditional branch instruction used only two, making it a
space optimization.[18]

Other space optimizations could depend more heavily on particular CPU instructions, and were thus less portable. The 6502's `brk` instruction was one of these.[19]

As an instruction, `brk` was both long and short. It took a long time – at seven
cycles it was one of the slowest 6502 instructions – but only occupied one byte.
Executing a `brk` caused a software interrupt, pushing the status register *P* on the

---

[16] From Atari 7800 source code. The "*X* IS A SUBR" appeared a number of times beside `goto`
instructions, although the commented-out `return` was usually absent.

[17] From *Elite* source. A similar trick was used in the Motorola 6800 code of *Meteor* (1979) to
implement two variants of the same interpreted instruction in a space-efficient manner.

[18] From *Elite* source code. The 65C02 finally introduced a two-byte unconditional branch [17] that
rendered this optimization moot.

[19] `brk` information from [30]. Its use in *Lord of the Rings* was mentioned in [29], credited to M.
Lesser and T. Jentzch; I verified that in-emulator and found the *Winter Games* use.

stack along with the return address, then jumping to an interrupt handler. While 6502 documentation stated 'the most typical use for the break instruction is during program debugging' [30, p. 144], the fact that it saved a return address on the stack meant that `brk` could be pressed into service as a one-byte `call` instruction. The interrupt handler would add additional code space overhead, but with frequent enough use of the `brk`-as-`call` mechanism, the cost would eventually be recouped.

Example 8.12 (Winter Games, 1987, and Lord of the Rings prototype, 1983). Both of these Atari 2600 games used the `brk` as a `call`, although in slightly different ways. *Winter Games'* code passed the number of the subroutine to invoke in the *Y* register and an argument to that subroutine in the *X* register. For instance, the sequence

```
X = $17
Y = $7
brk
```

would print "Winter" onscreen, and setting *X* to $18 would instead print "Games."

The *Lord of the Rings* prototype, by contrast, passes a one-byte argument inline following the `brk` instruction, so the above example might be expressed as:

```
brk
byte $17
```

Only one routine is ever invoked via `brk` in this game, so there is no need to specify the subroutine number. Arguably this is a better match with the semantics of the 6502's `brk`, because the return address it saves on the stack is actually *PC*+2, meaning that by default it skips the `brk` instruction plus the byte following it.

The inline argument of *Lord of the Rings* mixes code and data together, but each is a separate entity. Going one step further leads to space optimizations that overlap code with data, data with data, and code with code. As simple examples, *River Raid* (1982) overlapped a data table with the low byte of the reset vector, and the last byte of a color table was actually the first byte of an instruction, the opcode of which happened to correspond to a dark blue color on the Atari 2600.[20]

Dig Dug's source code left little doubt that space optimization was intended.[21] A ten-line-high file header comment announced 'PUT RANDOM ARRAYS HERE SO THEY CAN BE OVERLAPPED TO SAVE ROOM.' What would also not be known without the source code is the way the optimizations were documented, leaving an audit trail and a visual cue behind so that a later programmer (or the same programmer at a later date!) didn't inadvertently make changes to the code that would introduce bugs. In this excerpt, the overlapped byte's value is commented out but retained in the code, and both arrays are flagged with comments indicating that this optimization has been performed:

---

[20] Carol Shaw mentioned one overlap in an interview [10]; both verified in-emulator.

[21] From Atari 7800 source code. The most interesting overlap was one that was reconsidered and commented out, that had a `return` instruction overlapped with a data array, and *that* array overlapped with the array following it.

```
TLISTSIZ:   byte   5,5,5,5,5,5,5,5,5,5,13,5,5,33,33,5
;           byte   5                        ;OVERLAPS
NUMBYTES:   byte   5,1,1,0,0,1,2,0          ;OVERLAPS
```

Space-saving code-code overlaps can be viewed as an extreme form of reusing
common code. Figure 8.16 shows part of the Freeload tape loader source for *Rainbow Islands* (1990) on the Commodore 64. On the left is an unoptimized version
of the code, two routines that set a flag to either 1 or 0. On the right lies the space-
optimized version that appeared in the code. The two common instructions are commented out, leaving an audit trail, and replaced with the one-byte skw instruction.
Even seasoned 6502 programmers may not recognize this instruction, because it is
undocumented, and can be interpreted as offering a nop that takes a two-byte argument and ignores it.[22] At the beginning of the source code, skw was clearly defined
using an assembler macro to be the value $0c along with the comment 'Skip Word
instruction.' The net result is that SCROLL_ON loads *A* with 1, the skw swallows
up the two bytes of the A=0 instruction, and execution falls through onto the two
common instructions.

```
                                        SCROLL_ON:
                                         A = 1
 SCROLL_ON:                             ; M[SCROLL_TRIGGER] = A
  A = 1                                 ; return
  M[SCROLL_TRIGGER] = A
  return                    =>
                                         skw
 SCROLL_OFF:
  A = 0                                 SCROLL_OFF:
  M[SCROLL_TRIGGER] = A                  A = 0
  return                                 M[SCROLL_TRIGGER] = A
                                         return
```

Fig. 8.16 Overlapping code with code in the *Rainbow Islands* loader

Dragonfire (1982)'s 6502 source code contains a sequence of seven bytes that
is a brilliant example of overlapping code. The bytes were implementing a delay:
depending on where the code jumped in to the sequence, a different number of
cycles would be consumed. What is astounding is that the bytes could be entered
at any point, and they *all* corresponded to legal, overlapping 6502 code that would
carry out the different delays. Figure 8.17 shows the seven bytes along with the code
overlaps and delays.[23]

---

[22] Some sources indicate that the two bytes are taken as an absolute address and fetched [36]; this
might cause problems if the two bytes happened to coincide with the address of some memory-
mapped soft switch. Further illustrating the dangers of undocumented instructions, $0c became
defined on the 65C02 [17]. Example from Freeload source.

[23] From *Dragonfire* source code, verified with instruction timing information from [17]. This code
sequence was well-commented, but a visual representation seems more apropos here.

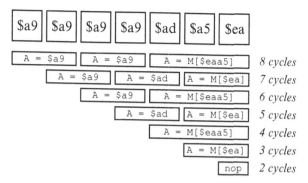

Fig. 8.17 *Dragonfire*'s magical seven bytes of code-code overlap

Despite instances of code overlapping data and other code, all the optimization techniques to this point have treated the code as inviolate. Certainly code in ROM would have been immutable, but code located in RAM would be subject to another optimization that also appeared as an obfuscation, self-modification.

```
X = OPACITY                        L80:
A = M[OPCODE+X]                        A = A AND M[Mw[BASE]+Y]
M[L80] = A                             M[Mw[BASE]+Y] = A

        +
                               =   L80:
OPCODE:                                A = A OR M[Mw[BASE]+Y]
    byte $31 ;and (oper),Y             M[Mw[BASE]+Y] = A
    byte $11 ;ora
    byte $91 ;sta

        +
                                   L80:
L80:                                   M[Mw[BASE]+Y] = A
    ??? M[Mw[BASE]+Y]                  M[Mw[BASE]+Y] = A
    M[Mw[BASE]+Y] = A
```

Fig. 8.18 Self-modifying code in *Prince of Persia*

Example 8.13 (Prince of Persia). Self-modifying graphics code may be found in *Prince of Persia*. An image byte in the *A* register could be combined with a byte of existing screen image data in several different ways, which the code referred to as 'opacity.'[24] The combination methods reduced to three cases: ANDing *A* with the

---

[24] The *Prince of Persia* source actually had more combination methods, but I'm only using the three 'general' methods for simplicity.

existing data; ORing A with the data; replacing the existing data with A. Regardless, the screen data would need to be updated with the new A value in the end.

One way to implement this would be to have one separate piece of code for each combination method, but this would require code duplication and unnecessary space usage. Self-modifying code to the rescue: the mechanism on the left-hand side of Fig. 8.18 creates one of the three different variants of the byte-combination code shown on the right side of the figure. The OPACITY type is used as an index into the OPCODE table to extract the appropriate instruction opcode value, which is written to the first byte at L80 to transmute the instruction there. That first instruction becomes an AND, OR, or store instruction through the self-modification, and it is followed by an (unmodified) store to write the updated value to the screen data. Note that one type of opacity results in an extra, but harmless, store to the same memory location to maintain consistency.

This *Prince of Persia* code example can also be seen as an optimization called run-time code specialization, because the operation becomes hardcoded and customized through self-modification, eliminating the need to check the type of operation each time through a loop. From this perspective, self-modifying code is not only a space optimization; it can also be used to improve performance.

8.2.2 Time Optimizations

Continuing the exploration of self-modifying code, Fig. 8.19 compares some Apple II graphics code that was self-modified in *Prince of Persia* and *Pinball Construction Set* (1983); the modified bytes are in bold. This comparative view gives some insight into the conventions programmers would employ in their code to indicate that self-modifying code was being used: *Prince of Persia* source uses the label s[elf-]mod[ifying] in several places, for instance.[25] Areas of self-modifying code in *Pinball Construction Set* could be located in part through the $ffff address placeholders, but a better indicator was a definition like the one shown for UNWND1, which defined a label pointing to the byte where self-modification occurred. (The code in Fig. 8.19 notwithstanding, many of these labels in *Pinball Construction Set* incorporated the string MOD.)

Returning to what the code *does*, both excerpts are located in loops, where time tends to be a consideration. On the left, for instance, the *Prince of Persia* code belongs to a routine that clears the hi-res graphics screen. It is possible to perform this same task without self-modifying code, or using only one store instruction, or both. The version without self-modifying code would have to use a different addressing mode, however, making that instruction take one more CPU cycle to

---

[25] The information regarding these two games is from the source code, naturally. *Habitat* (1986) used a similar convention, with labels suffixed by _selfmod.

Prince of Persia

Pinball Construction Set

```
loop:                      UNWND1 = ZAPBW + 1
    M[$2000+Y] = A         ZAPBW:
smod:                          M[$ffff+X] = A
    M[$3000+Y] = A             M[$ffff+X] = A
    Y = Y + 1                  M[$ffff+X] = A
    ...                        M[$ffff+X] = A
                               M[$ffff+X] = A
                               M[$ffff+X] = A
                               X = X + 1
                               ...
```

Fig. 8.19 Self-modifying code, a comparison

execute. Having two store instructions rather than one consumes extra space, but the loop only needs to iterate half as many times, saving time on loop overhead. Both of these are thus time optimizations.

The latter optimization with the duplicated store instruction is a simple example of an optimization called loop unrolling, where the main body of a loop's code is repeated multiple times to reduce loop overhead [23]. The *Pinball Construction Set* excerpt unrolls its loop more, hinting at the technique with the label UNW[i]ND1.

```
$1400:   Y = $27
         A = 0
$1404:   M[$2328+Y] = A
         M[$2728+Y] = A
         M[$2b28+Y] = A
         M[$2f28+Y] = A
         ... 60 more omitted ...
         Y = Y - 1
         if Y < 0 goto $14ca
         goto $1404
$14ca:   return
```

Fig. 8.20 A heavily-unrolled loop in *Horizon V*

Loop unrolling can be used even without self-modifying code. *Horizon V* (1982) on the Apple II had a speed-critical loop to clear a portion of the hi-res graphics screen, shown in Fig. 8.20 in all its unrolled glory.[26] The odd jump-over-jump at the end is used because the loop was unrolled so much that a conditional branch had insufficient range to goto the top of the loop.

---

[26] And there was *another* one just like it to clear out the same portion of the second hi-res graphics screen. The game used double buffering, and had a scrolling horizon that needed continual erasing and redrawing. From static and dynamic analysis.

All these manual optimization examples might seem to imply that Apple II graphics presented some hurdles, and this is not an incorrect impression. One problem was how the memory-mapped graphics addresses corresponded to locations on screen. As Sather put it, 'If the Apple isn't famous for the encrypted nature of its screen memory addressing, it should be' [27, p. 5–7].

A hint of this was given in Fig. 8.3 (p. 176). There, even though the *Pac-Man* boot code was decrypted into consecutive addresses in the text screen's memory, the lines of text did not appear consecutively. Hi-res graphics had the same issue. To save a chip, the Apple II design spaced out consecutive lines in memory [27]; the code in Fig. 8.20 is actually clearing adjacent hi-res lines, despite the addresses being 1024 bytes apart.

While the correct base address for each hi-res line *could* be computed when needed, retrogames would trade space for time, and contain a lookup table that mapped the logical hi-res line number into the base address in memory for that line. Indexing into the table to retrieve the address values was a much faster process than performing the arithmetic to calculate the values, at a space cost of 384 bytes. *Prince of Persia* contained its hi-res lookup table hardcoded in the source code, whereas *Pinball Construction Set* computed its table (once) at run-time;[27] these different approaches also suggest that the space being traded for speed may or may not have included space on secondary storage.

More generally, these lookup tables are an example of using precomputation for time optimization. Precomputation was also used to circumvent CPU limitations in a time-efficient way, and a lookup table could compensate for processors like the 6502 that had no multiplication and division instructions. As examples, *Dig Dug* precomputed a "division by 3" table, and *Pinball Construction Set* precomputed the quotients and remainders of numbers divided by 7. The Commodore 64 *Elite* contained logarithm tables, allowing multiplications to be performed using addition instead [7, 26:06]. In terms of the process for hardcoding precomputed tables in the game, as opposed to calculating them at the start of the game, an Atari 800 retrogame programmer recalled 'The general method was often to write BASIC programs to generate the lookup tables which you dumped into the [. . .] assembler' [12].

Retrogame programmers did know their platforms intimately, and it would not do them justice to focus solely on optimizations that were generic enough to use anywhere, or even across one widely-used processor like the 6502. We conclude this look at time optimizations with a closer look at two examples of highly platform-dependent techniques.

Example 8.14 (Parsec, 1982). Parsec had very ornate scrolling ground features (Fig. 8.21) that included a great deal of variety and scrolled at different rates depending on the speed of the player spaceship.

---

[27] All the precomputation examples from *Dig Dug*, *Pinball Construction Set*, and *Prince of Persia* are from the source code.

Fig. 8.21 *Parsec* on the TI-99/4A (Image courtesy Texas Instruments)

At the core of the TI-99/4A was a 16-bit processor with a 16-bit address bus and a 16-bit data bus whose instructions could access 16 general-purpose registers – it even had multiply and divide instructions.[28] Being able to access 16 registers and having 16 registers are not the same thing, however, and the general-purpose registers were not on-chip, but located in 256 bytes of 'scratchpad' RAM. This RAM was small but relatively fast; it had access to the full 16-bit data bus. Any other memory references (such as to a game cartridge ROM) had to be decomposed into two 8-bit accesses. 16 K of video RAM existed, but could only be accessed via the video display unit, and then only through a single one-byte memory address. In other words, the scratchpad RAM was the only quickly-accessible memory resource for a retrogame on the TI-99/4A.

Parsec made the ground scroll measurably faster by exploiting the scratchpad RAM: code for two loops was copied into RAM and run from there. The first loop, which overlapped with four general-purpose registers, read in a vertical strip of 30 bytes from the video RAM into scratchpad RAM (30 bytes was the height of the scrolling ground). The strip's bytes occupied consecutive addresses in video memory to take advantage of the video display unit's ability to automatically increment the address of the byte being fetched. Two adjacent strips' worth of bytes resided in scratchpad RAM at once, 60 bytes in total. The second loop shifted those bytes to

---

[28] CPU and platform information from [31, 32], with game information from static and dynamic analysis, a visualization I built, and help from [35]. Strictly speaking, there was some system ROM on the 16-bit data bus too, but it isn't relevant in this context.

create the scrolling, taking advantage of the TI-99/4A CPU's ability to shift up to 16 bits in a single instruction, and wrote the bytes back out to the video memory. In total, slightly over $\frac{1}{3}$ of the scratchpad was used for the scrolling ground.

TI-99/4A programmers were not alone in making good use of a precious RAM resource. *Dark Chambers* (1988) on the Atari 2600, for instance, dynamically generated code into the zero page RAM because it 'HAD TO TURN ON AND OFF THE PF [playfield] COLOR, LOAD SIX LOCATIONS AND STORE THEM AT THE APPROPRIATE TIMES. IT IS MADE TO BE SELF MODIFYING AND IT IS THE ONLY WAY IT WOULD WORK.'[29] The key phrase there is 'appropriate times,' and some ingenious methods were used to make the 6502 achieve seemingly impossible timings on the 2600.

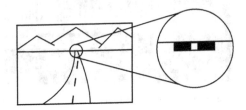

Fig. 8.22 A road receding into the distance

Example 8.15 (Pole Position, 1983). In *Pole Position*, the player drives on a racetrack that recedes into the distance, shown conceptually in Fig. 8.22.[30]

On the 6502, the fastest instruction takes two CPU cycles, and for every CPU cycle, three clocks occur for the video display; in other words, one CPU cycle corresponds to three pixels onscreen, and no instruction can be performed in one CPU cycle anyway – the CPU was at a considerable disadvantage when racing the beam. The CPU did not have to set a screen line's pixels one by one, but instead Atari 2600 games created the contents of each line using five movable objects. These five objects, although named 'player' (two objects), 'missile' (two objects), and 'ball,' could be repurposed to represent any object on a line. It would be entirely too easy to program a game if the horizontal position of these five objects could be assigned directly, however. Instead, each object has an associated soft switch, or 'strobe.' When a strobe is accessed, the horizontal position of the corresponding object is set to wherever the screen's electron beam happens to be in the line. Taken together, all this is summarized by the Atari 2600 programming guide in restrictive terms [38]:

---

[29] Apologia from the source code. Zero-page execution and self-modifying code verified in-emulator.

[30] And if you want to play a game of 'Guess Which Screenshot I Couldn't Get Permission to Use,' go right ahead. The objects don't quite appear evenly spaced by the time they're rendered due to other effects like applying horizontal movement to the objects.

Since there are 3 color clocks per machine cycle, and it can take up to 5 machine cycles to write to a register, the programmer is confined to positioning the objects at 15 color clock intervals across the screen.

Pole Position uses three objects to create the racetrack. The ball and one missile are the edges of the road, and the other missile is the center line. To get the objects impossibly close at the road's vanishing point, the 6502's stack pointer is set to $14 (recall that the Atari 2600 maps the usual 6502 stack page into zero page), and at a precise horizontal location in the middle of screen line 127, a brk instruction is executed. There is no change in control flow, because the game's brk vector is set to point to the next instruction after the brk. As the 6502 attempts to push the status register and return address on the stack, it does so in three consecutive machine cycles to three consecutive bytes: $14, $13, and $12, which are the locations of the strobes for the ball and the two missiles. This trick positions the three objects at horizontal screen positions three apart from one another, something that no normal 6502 instruction sequence would allow.[31]

8.2.3 Anti-optimizations

It may seem that faster and smaller programs would always be laudable goals for a retrogame programmer, but there were instances where it was inappropriate to optimize. These practices were clearly engrained into programmers of the time to the point where obvious cues would need to be left to prevent optimizations from being performed. In the *Habitat* (1986) source code,[32] for instance, a call immediately followed by return seems the perfect set-up for tail call optimization, were it not for the jarring all-uppercase comment accompanying the lowercase assembly code: 'DO NOT PUT A JMP HERE ARIC.'

The Atari 2600's paltry RAM size and challenging display requirements would hardly be the place to find an anti-optimization. Or would it? *River Raid* has bytes in RAM that are always zero,[33] and whose zero values are loaded into registers at various points in the game code. There is no space advantage, as the 6502 instruction to load a register with the constant 0 takes two bytes, as does the instruction to load a value from zero page memory. However, the memory-based version takes one extra CPU cycle.

Precise timing was paramount on the 2600 to get the screen display correct, and it is not unusual in Atari 2600 game source code to see time-critical areas adorned with inline comments keeping track of the aggregate number of cycles each instruction

---

[31] 6502 information from [17, 30], Atari information from [38]. Initial *Pole Position* tip from [29], credited to E. Strolberg, and verified with additional details gathered in-emulator.

[32] From Commodore 64 client source code.

[33] An observation made in [14], verified in-emulator.

took. Without access to *River Raid*'s source code, however, it is difficult to know whether the intent was timing-related. Indeed, anti-optimizations could be made explicit in source code through comments: the code for the Atari 2600 *Dragonfire* (1982) has a load of *A* from a zero page location followed immediately by another load of *A*, making the first one redundant; the first instruction sports the comment 'WASTE 3 MC,' i.e., waste three machine cycles.[34]

Anti-optimizations could have unintended side effects, too. In Chap. 1, the unusual practice of some retrogame programmers using mini-assemblers was mentioned. Because a mini-assembler gives limited support – none, really – for moving and relocating code, programmers would need to plan ahead for the growth of their subroutines. Just as BASIC programmers would leave gaps in line numbering to accommodate later line numbers being inserted in between, programmers using a mini-assembler could leave excess unused bytes in between subroutines for later use if needed [6]. This practice flies in the face of space optimization, obviously, and the gaps turned out later to be useful to third parties.

Creating a cracked version of *Firebird* (1981) on the Apple II required adding some routines to the game code, and the cracker observes 'Throughout much of this code, you will find small gaps of blank memory between routines which can be used for other short routines. There are so many places our routines can be stored' [34]. *Firebird*'s byline credits none other than 'Nasir,' or Nasir Gebelli, one of the programmers known to use a mini-assembler for game development [4, 26]. Analysis of the game code confirms this: many routines were followed by a gap, leaving subsequent code to start at 16-byte boundaries where the low nibble of the hexadecimal address was zero.[35] Adopting this mini-assembler programming practice actually facilitated cracking the game.

8.3 The Story of Mel

It seems fitting to conclude a discussion of obfuscation and optimization in retrogames with the story of Mel, an anecdotal account of the artful and extreme optimization in an old computer blackjack game.[36]

---

[34] The *Dragonfire* information is from the source code, which also contains cycle-counting comments and the overlapping-code space optimization (whose delays can now be seen as a speed anti-optimization).

[35] Information from analyzing the *Firebird* disassembly. The practice can be seen more clearly in Gebelli's *Gorgon* (1981) and *Horizon V*.

[36] As told by the late Ed Nather in 1983 and included in the (public domain) Jargon File [24].

A recent article devoted to the *macho* side of programming
made the bald and unvarnished statement:

Real Programmers write in FORTRAN.

Maybe they do now,
in this decadent era of
Lite beer, hand calculators, and "user-friendly" software
but back in the Good Old Days,
when the term "software" sounded funny
and Real Computers were made out of drums and vacuum tubes,
Real Programmers wrote in machine code.
Not FORTRAN. Not RATFOR. Not, even, assembly language.
Machine Code.
Raw, unadorned, inscrutable hexadecimal numbers.
Directly.

Lest a whole new generation of programmers
grow up in ignorance of this glorious past,
I feel duty-bound to describe,
as best I can through the generation gap,
how a Real Programmer wrote code.
I'll call him Mel,
because that was his name.

I first met Mel when I went to work for Royal McBee Computer Corp.,
a now-defunct subsidiary of the typewriter company.
The firm manufactured the LGP-30,
a small, cheap (by the standards of the day)
drum-memory computer,
and had just started to manufacture
the RPC-4000, a much-improved,
bigger, better, faster – drum-memory computer.
Cores cost too much,
and weren't here to stay, anyway.
(That's why you haven't heard of the company,
or the computer.)

I had been hired to write a FORTRAN compiler
for this new marvel and Mel was my guide to its wonders.
Mel didn't approve of compilers.

"If a program can't rewrite its own code,"
he asked, "what good is it?"

Mel had written,
in hexadecimal,
the most popular computer program the company owned.
It ran on the LGP-30
and played blackjack with potential customers
at computer shows.
Its effect was always dramatic.
The LGP-30 booth was packed at every show,
and the IBM salesmen stood around

talking to each other.
Whether or not this actually sold computers
was a question we never discussed.

Mel's job was to re-write
the blackjack program for the RPC-4000.
(Port? What does that mean?)
The new computer had a one-plus-one
addressing scheme,
in which each machine instruction,
in addition to the operation code
and the address of the needed operand,
had a second address that indicated where, on the revolving drum,
the next instruction was located.

In modern parlance,
every single instruction was followed by a GO TO!
Put *that* in Pascal's pipe and smoke it.

Mel loved the RPC-4000
because he could optimize his code:
that is, locate instructions on the drum
so that just as one finished its job,
the next would be just arriving at the "read head"
and available for immediate execution.
There was a program to do that job,
an "optimizing assembler,"
but Mel refused to use it.

"You never know where it's going to put things,"
he explained, "so you'd have to use separate constants."

It was a long time before I understood that remark.
Since Mel knew the numerical value
of every operation code,
and assigned his own drum addresses,
every instruction he wrote could also be considered
a numerical constant.
He could pick up an earlier "add" instruction, say,
and multiply by it,
if it had the right numeric value.
His code was not easy for someone else to modify.

I compared Mel's hand-optimized programs
with the same code massaged by the optimizing assembler program,
and Mel's always ran faster.
That was because the "top-down" method of program design
hadn't been invented yet,
and Mel wouldn't have used it anyway.
He wrote the innermost parts of his program loops first,
so they would get first choice
of the optimum address locations on the drum.
The optimizing assembler wasn't smart enough to do it that way.

Mel never wrote time-delay loops, either,
even when the balky Flexowriter
required a delay between output characters to work right.
He just located instructions on the drum
so each successive one was just *past* the read head
when it was needed;
the drum had to execute another complete revolution
to find the next instruction.
He coined an unforgettable term for this procedure.
Although "optimum" is an absolute term,
like "unique," it became common verbal practice
to make it relative:
"not quite optimum" or "less optimum"
or "not very optimum."
Mel called the maximum time-delay locations
the "most pessimum."

After he finished the blackjack program
and got it to run
("Even the initializer is optimized,"
he said proudly),
he got a Change Request from the sales department.
The program used an elegant (optimized)
random number generator
to shuffle the "cards" and deal from the "deck,"
and some of the salesmen felt it was too fair,
since sometimes the customers lost.
They wanted Mel to modify the program
so, at the setting of a sense switch on the console,
they could change the odds and let the customer win.

Mel balked.
He felt this was patently dishonest,
which it was,
and that it impinged on his personal integrity as a programmer,
which it did,
so he refused to do it.
The Head Salesman talked to Mel,
as did the Big Boss and, at the boss's urging,
a few Fellow Programmers.
Mel finally gave in and wrote the code,
but he got the test backwards,
and, when the sense switch was turned on,
the program would cheat, winning every time.
Mel was delighted with this,
claiming his subconscious was uncontrollably ethical,
and adamantly refused to fix it.

After Mel had left the company for greener pa$ture$,
the Big Boss asked me to look at the code
and see if I could find the test and reverse it.
Somewhat reluctantly, I agreed to look.
Tracking Mel's code was a real adventure.

I have often felt that programming is an art form,
whose real value can only be appreciated
by another versed in the same arcane art;
there are lovely gems and brilliant coups
hidden from human view and admiration, sometimes forever,
by the very nature of the process.
You can learn a lot about an individual
just by reading through his code,
even in hexadecimal.
Mel was, I think, an unsung genius.

Perhaps my greatest shock came
when I found an innocent loop that had no test in it.
No test. *None*.
Common sense said it had to be a closed loop,
where the program would circle, forever, endlessly.
Program control passed right through it, however,
and safely out the other side.
It took me two weeks to figure it out.

The RPC-4000 computer had a really modern facility
called an index register.
It allowed the programmer to write a program loop
that used an indexed instruction inside;
each time through,
the number in the index register
was added to the address of that instruction,
so it would refer
to the next datum in a series.
He had only to increment the index register
each time through.
Mel never used it.

Instead, he would pull the instruction into a machine register,
add one to its address,
and store it back.
He would then execute the modified instruction
right from the register.
The loop was written so this additional execution time
was taken into account –
just as this instruction finished,
the next one was right under the drum's read head,
ready to go.
But the loop had no test in it.

The vital clue came when I noticed
the index register bit,
the bit that lay between the address
and the operation code in the instruction word,
was turned on –
yet Mel never used the index register,
leaving it zero all the time.
When the light went on it nearly blinded me.

He had located the data he was working on
near the top of memory –
the largest locations the instructions could address –
so, after the last datum was handled,
incrementing the instruction address
would make it overflow.
The carry would add one to the
operation code, changing it to the next one in the instruction set:
a jump instruction.
Sure enough, the next program instruction was
in address location zero,
and the program went happily on its way.

I haven't kept in touch with Mel,
so I don't know if he ever gave in to the flood of
change that has washed over programming techniques
since those long-gone days.
I like to think he didn't.
In any event,
I was impressed enough that I quit looking for the
offending test,
telling the Big Boss I couldn't find it.
He didn't seem surprised.

When I left the company,
the blackjack program would still cheat
if you turned on the right sense switch,
and I think that's how it should be.
I didn't feel comfortable
hacking up the code of a Real Programmer.

The need for modern programmers to perform micro-optimizations on their code is now rare, not to mention that it is extremely difficult to gauge their efficacy on modern systems performing parallel, concurrent, and speculative execution. Many sophisticated optimizations are performed by modern compilers, and just-in-time compilers perform run-time code generation. This does not obviate the need for programmers to know about these optimizations, however; compilers err on the side of correctness, and part of the programmer's job can be providing unambiguous signs that certain optimizations are possible and safe. Especially for modern dynamically-typed languages, there may be limits on what compiler tools can discover about a program, leaving the onus on the programmer to perform optimization still. Higher-level optimization concepts, like time/space tradeoffs, are part of the very fabric of computer science and were, are, and will continue to be important.

202 8 Obfuscation and Optimization

Obfuscation is still used to deter (or more pragmatically, slow down) reverse engineering for intellectual property protection. Obfuscation is interesting, though, because it is a "dual use" technology; it can be used for legitimate or illegitimate purposes. Malicious software uses obfuscation in an attempt to avoid detection – ironically, making itself more obvious by some measures – and also to make its analysis more difficult. Ultimately the problem with reliance on obfuscation is that the code eventually must run and thus can be analyzed. Or can it? The underlying assumption with most software is that it should run on all compatible platforms, but malicious software can be targeted. Parts of code can be encrypted with strong cryptography [11, 25] or produced at run time using cryptographic hash functions [3], based on keys that are externally supplied or derived from the target environment. This leverages cryptographic guarantees: code protected this way cannot be run or seen except under the conditions an attacker intended, barring incredible good fortune. This technique is not widespread, but has been used by malicious software [15].

References

1. 4am: Pac-Man (4am crack) (10 Mar 2015)
2. 4am: Sneakers (4am crack) (27 Feb 2014)
3. Aycock, J., deGraaf, R., Jacobson, M., Jr.: Anti-disassembly using cryptographic hash functions. J. Comput. Virol. 2(1), 79–85 (2006)
4. Barton, M.: Honoring the Code: Conversations with Great Game Designers. CRC Press, Boca Raton (2013)
5. Bevan, M.: Ultimate guide: Pac-Land. Retro Gamer (127), 68–73 (2014)
6. Blackford, J.: Jimmy Huey: The programmer behind *Galactic Blitz*, *Sidewinder*, and *Swarm!* Compute!'s Gazette 1(1), 49–50 (1983)
7. Braben, D.: Classic game postmortem: Elite. Game Developer's Conference 2011. http://www.gdcvault.com/play/1014628/Classic-Game-Postmortem (2011)
8. Colt, D.: Boot code tracing Pest Patrol. Hardcore Computist (4), 20–23 (1983)
9. Colt, D.: Softkey for Cannonball Blitz. Hardcore Computist (26), 10–11 (1985)
10. Edwards, B.: VC&G interview: Carol Shaw, the first female video game developer. Vintage Computing and Gaming (12 Oct 2011). http://www.vintagecomputing.com/index.php/archives/800
11. Filiol, E.: Strong cryptography armoured computer viruses forbidding code analysis: the Bradley virus. In: Proceedings of the 14th Annual EICAR Conference, Malta, pp. 216–227 (2005)
12. Hague, J.: Adam Billyard. In: Halcyon Days: Interviews with Classic Computer and Video Game Programmers. http://www.dadgum.com/halcyon/ (2002)
13. Henrikson, K.: Electronic Arts C64 fat track loader. http://c64preservation.com/files/EaLoader.txt (Undated)
14. Jentzsch, T.: River Raid annotated disassembly, v0.9 (2001)
15. Kaspersky Lab Global Research and Analysis Team: Gauss: Abnormal distribution. http://securelist.com/analysis/publications/36620/gauss-abnormal-distribution/ (2012)

16. Krakowicz: Krakowicz's Kracking Korner: The Basics of Kracking II (Undated, probably early- to mid-1980s)
17. Leventhal, L.A.: 6502 Assembly Language Programming, 2nd edn. Osborne McGraw-Hill, Berkeley (1986)
18. Lowe, A.: Email Communication (28 Sept 2013)
19. Marvin, S.: Revisiting Lode Runner. Computist (28), 26–27 (1986)
20. McFadden, M.M.: Antique softkey for Frogger. Computist (41), 28–29 (1987)
21. Milne, R.: Jack the Nipper. Retro Gamer (127), 44–47 (2014)
22. Morrison, G.: Atari Software Protection Techniques. Alpha Systems, Stow (1983)
23. Muchnick, S.S.: Advanced Compiler Design & Implementation. Morgan Kaufmann, San Francisco (1997)
24. Raymond, E.S. (ed.): The Jargon File, Version 4.4.7 (2003)
25. Riordan, J., Schneier, B.: Environmental key generation towards clueless agents. In: Mobile Agents and Security. LNCS, vol. 1419, pp. 15–24. Springer, Berlin/New York (1998)
26. Romero, J.: Nasir Gebelli at Apple II Reunion. https://www.youtube.com/watch?v=4Me1ycLxDlw (8 Aug 1998)
27. Sather, J.: Understanding the Apple II. Quality Software, Chatsworth (1983)
28. Simstad, T.N.: Program Protection Manual for the C-64, vol. II. CSM Software, Inc., Crown Point (1985)
29. Slocum, P. (ed.): Atari 2600 Advanced Programming Guide (2004 or 2005). http://www.qotile.net/minidig/docs/2600_advanced_prog_guide.txt
30. Synertek Incorporated: SY6500/MCS6500 Microcomputer Family Programming Manual (1976)
31. Texas Instruments: TMS 9900 Microprocessor Data Manual (1976)
32. Texas Instruments: TI-99/4A Console and Peripheral Expansion System Technical Data (1983)
33. toinet: Lode Runner (Brøderbund, 1983). http://www.hackzapple.com/phpBB2/viewtopic.php?t=191 (15 June 2007)
34. Unknown: Softkey for Firebird. Computist (82), 11 (1990)
35. Urbanus, P.: Email Communications (27 and 29 Dec 2013)
36. Vardy, A.: Extra Instructions of the 65XX Series CPU. http://www.ffd2.com/fridge/docs/6502-NMOS.extra.opcodes (1996)
37. Various Contributors: The Z-Machine Standards Document (1997)
38. Wright, S.: 2600 (STELLA) Programmer's Guide (3 Dec 1979). Updated by D. May, 1988
39. Wright, W.: Classic Game Postmortem: Raid on Bungeling Bay. Game Developer's Conference 2011. http://www.gdcvault.com/play/1014635/Classic-Game-Postmortem-RAID-ON (2011)
40. Your Spectrum Staff: Hidden extras. Your Spectr. (18), 51–52 (1985)

Chapter 9
Endgame

Nothing exists in isolation, and retrogame archeology is no exception. There are existing areas of inquiry that consider games and historical games in whole or part, and it is useful to position retrogame archeology with respect to them. This is not to disparage these other areas, but simply to point out the differences that exist – in fact, retrogame archeology is complementary to these other disciplines and they can collectively inform one another.

Game studies, for one, is a field that draws heavily on the humanities. It is telling that the 2013 book *Understanding Video Games*, which 'provides a comprehensive introduction to the growing field of game studies' takes games as "black boxes" and does not consider their internals at all. Implementation of any kind does not figure in the 'main perspectives' or 'major type of analysis' they list [8, pp. 9–10]. Fernández-Vara's *Introduction to Game Analysis* is not quite as exclusionary, citing the 'technological context' as one of eight contextual elements that may be used in a game analysis [9]. Specifically, she points to platform studies, an area which is more technically-oriented but with a dose of the humanities. As platform studies proponents Bogost and Montfort put it [3], 'Platform studies connects technical details to culture.' Finally there are software studies and critical code studies. The former positions itself, in the series foreword of *10 PRINT*, as branching out into nontechnical ways of thinking about software [23]; the latter 'applies critical hermeneutics to the interpretation of computer code, program architecture, and documentation within a socio-historical context' [21]. If they were to be placed on a technical spectrum, game studies would fall at one end, retrogame archeology – and its all-technical approach – on the other, with platform studies, software studies, and critical code studies falling somewhere in the middle.

There is a clear overlap between retrogame archeology and computer history. The journal *IEEE Annals of the History of Computing*, for example, contains the occasional article related to retrogames: the history of *Pong* [19]; the story of a very early Danish computer game [13]; the previously-cited copy protection work [27]. It may seem as though retrogame archeology should be a proper subset of computer history rather than just having an overlap, but there is a danger of it being dismissed

© Springer International Publishing Switzerland 2016
J. Aycock, *Retrogame Archeology*, DOI 10.1007/978-3-319-30004-7_9

as 'excessively technical, and lacking in breadth of vision' [4, p. 41]. While this opinion is a matter of some debate in the history of computing [11], the technical details are of vital importance to retrogame archeology.

In the preface, with a nod to Bogost [2], I mentioned the search for 'tiny treasures' in games as the job of a retrogame archeologist. That is naturally a rather vague description: after all, one person's treasure is another person's trash. I would define retrogame archeology more precisely in terms of three "T"s. The goal of retrogame archeology is to understand the tools, techniques, and technology used in old games' implementation.

Left at that point, it would be easy to construe retrogame archeology as a backwards-looking historical exercise, and that would not be altogether a bad thing. History is important, computers and software are important to our society, computer games are culturally important. But there is more to this exercise than knowing where the current generation of games has come from. Retrogame archeology is pragmatic, and is not just about understanding and documenting the three Ts, but connecting these ideas and placing them in a broader, modern technical context. In other words, where are these old ideas useful or in use today?

Previous chapters made these connections, with particular emphasis on the fact that there are current application areas outside the scope of games. That is an important point: old implementation techniques and ways of solving problems in highly constrained circumstances are generally useful tools for programmers to have in their toolbox.

And constrained retrogame programmers were. To recap: limited memory, miniscule secondary storage, slow incompatible I/O, slow processors, soft real-time constraints, restricted development environments, the need to forge their own development tools. That retrogame programmers got so much working, regardless of how we judge these games' quality in hindsight, is truly a testament to their skills.

9.1 Act Casual

Having taken pains to pick apart original examples of retrogame implementation, it is hard not to feel some sense of loss, that this foundational period of creativity is behind us. Certainly its influence lives on, and it would be hard to identify a modern game genre that could not trace its origins to the retrogame era. An alternate viewpoint is that retrogames have not left at all, but have evolved into something different. Just like the idea that dinosaurs evolved into birds, perhaps retrogames have evolved and live on, in modern casual games. Or maybe some retrogames always were casual – Loguidice and Barton state 'For most modern gamers, *Pac-Man* is a casual game' [18, p. 184], and furthermore that '*Tetris* later led to the rise of what is now called "casual gaming."' [18, p. 291].

Jesper Juul's *A Casual Revolution* identifies five characteristics of a casual game, paraphrased from [14, p. 50]:

1. Fiction. Casual games have a pleasant, appealing environment.
2. Usability. A casual game is easy to start playing.

3. Interruptibility. A long playing time commitment is not required.
4. Punishment. Player missteps are not punished harshly.
5. "Juiciness." Casual games supply (overly) encouraging feedback.

Ultimately trying to delineate casual games is probably not possible: given the multiplicity of games, it is easy to identify counterexamples to many of the above points. One can also argue that 'casual' and 'hardcore' labels are not meaningful or helpful [28]. However, Juul's framework does give us some concrete areas in which we can examine the connections between retrogames and modern games, and an extensive set of areas at that, as other definitions of casual games [9] exclude fiction and juiciness.

Juiciness is added almost as an afterthought by Juul, who says it 'was not predicted by the description of casual players' [14, p. 50]. It could be equally stated that juiciness is not an essential characteristic so much as a part of the casual game business model, to retain players in a crowded market – some games sound more desperate than encouraging – and garner more in-app purchases. Regardless, a retrogame comparison would fare well against this metric. Reflecting on my own experience, the novelty of computers in the early retrogame days was such that *any* interaction with and feedback from them was exciting. Modern juiciness could be the natural inflation of this effect over time, just as modern movie explosions are bigger and the alien threats to Earth are larger than they once were.

Usability and interruptibility are really both about the window of time a player has to devote to a game, both in terms of learning it and playing it. Playing time can extend beyond the boundary of the game itself: one could argue that retrogames have become more casual in their resource demands over the years, despite running the same code and using the same data, because it is faster and simpler to start an emulator (or, more recently, run an in-browser emulator) than to boot an old console or computer. Even punishment can be viewed through the lens of time, although the opposite way that Juul intended; a game that ruthlessly kills off the player can be very quick to play.

A brief amount of playing time was of course ideal for retrogames in the arcade, where 'coin drop' was a business concern.[1] A game that a player could play for a long time was not a game constantly being fed quarters. For game design, retrogame developer Alan McNeil distilled the appropriate length of play into a formula, where the ratio of playing cost to gameplay time should equate to that of an established form of entertainment, movies [7].

Usability and ease of learning a game were almost a necessity for a public unaccustomed to computer games, and early game joysticks and paddles were not all bristling with buttons in the way that controllers are now. Creating a complex interface with the Atari 2600's single joystick button and limited resources would have been challenging.

The fiction characteristic, being subjective, is maybe best considered relative to individual players. It could be that casual games simply provide a greater range of

---

[1] Mentioned by retrogame developer Ed Rotberg in an interview [15, p. 149], and also [2]. The latter mentions complexity with respect to early arcade games too.

environments to choose from for potential players. If the only books published for years were romance novels, and then Western novels arrived, we would doubtlessly speak of a Western revolution as an underserved reading population suddenly appeared in bookstores.

What is interesting about Juul's examples of casual games is the descriptions of them using words like 'abstract' and 'cartoony.' Perhaps the broad audience appeal of casual games is not about a positive, upbeat fiction, but because it is easier for a person to imagine themselves in that fiction. Scott McCloud points out in *Understanding Comics* [22] that abstraction makes images more universal: 'The more cartoony a face is [...] the more people it could be said to describe' (p. 31) and that 'when you enter the world of the cartoon – you see yourself' (p. 36). Retrogames were naturally abstract due to their graphical constraints, making every player character an everyman.

9.2 Use Protection

Speaking of activities done casually for enjoyment brings us to the topic of protection. Specifically, I want to single out retrogame copy protection, since it has proven to be a singularly irritating thorn in my side during this research. Ironically, not because preserved retrogames have copy protection, but because they don't.

It is hardly a surprise that it's possible to acquire playable copies of nearly any retrogame ever made. However, where copy protection guarded the original games, it is often the cracked copies that have survived. On the one hand, it is good to have the games available in some way – there *are* retrogame publishers that still exist and distributors who endeavor to make games available from days of yore, and these efforts are commendable and worth supporting, especially when retrogames can be purchased for a mere fraction of their original cost. Not all retrogames are available, though, and having a game available does not necessarily mean it is available in a form suitable for studying its original implementation. On the other hand, cracked games invariably lose fidelity. An original introductory sequence is discarded; a screen with cracking credits is added; cheat codes are added in; copy protection is removed. Not only can the game playing experience change, but implementation elements have vanished.

This poses challenges for studying retrogames, their implementation, and their copy protection. Sometimes there is no substitute for the original: I was able to verify parts of *Cannonball Blitz'* protective obfuscations in Chap. 8 only because I lurked on eBay long enough to spot and purchase an original copy of the game, and capture an image on original Apple hardware to study in an emulator. For *Pest Patrol* I have not been as lucky, and in all likelihood when it does appear for sale, its scarcity will ensure that verifying the copy protection will not come cheap.

Where original disks do exist, there are ongoing efforts to record disk images at a low enough level to capture copy protected retrogames in their natural state. It is fair to characterize these efforts as both valuable and as producing mixed results, at least for now. Some images need repeated recordings or time-consuming manual intervention to become usable, like *Video Vegas* in Chap. 7. With others, it can be a matter of trial and error to find an emulator that the image works on.

In other cases, preservation formats have excluded copy protection. Many tape images of Commodore 64 retrogames are available and playable, for instance, but since the Commodore cassette player converted the analog signal to digital form internally, it is sufficient from a playability standpoint to record the converted signal for preservation. This comes at the expense of losing the audio from the original tapes that was reputed to include anti-duplication measures [12].

Hopefully these complaints are transient preservation problems, because retrogame media and the equipment to read it are in a race with time that they will ultimately lose.

9.3 Sources Sighted

It is probably apparent in the source code examples from previous chapters that the same smallish pool of games has been drawn on repeatedly. There is a reason for that.

One worrisome thing I have found while doing the research for this book is how little original source code is available for study. With few exceptions, retrogames had many copies (legitimate and otherwise) widely available; source code had few copies and wasn't distributed at all.[2] A lot can be gleaned from disassembly, but it loses information about coding practices, and it loses comments that reveal the intent and thought processes of the programmer. Even when retrogame authors can be contacted now, it would be unreasonable to expect them to remember – and remember correctly – the minutia of decades-old code. The comments in code can capture that forgotten moment in time like an old photograph.

It *is* heartening that code discoveries are still being made. In the course of researching and writing this book, several retrogames' code has been unearthed and made available. Most of these have been already woven into past chapters, where appropriate, but two examples in particular highlight the sort of treasures that might yet be uncovered.

Example 9.1 (Wander, 1974). In April 2015 came the news that 'a lost mainframe game is found' [1, 6], spurring many people to search around and dig up early source code for *Wander*. *Wander* was not a text adventure game so much as a general text game-building system; the manual page describes it as 'a tool for writing non-deterministic fantasy "stories".'[3] Its games were described in files written in a domain-specific language and the range of rediscovered examples spans from a binary number tutorial to *Adventure*-like games.

---

[2] This fact doesn't make preservation of retrogames any easier, or even the decision of exactly what to preserve and how to do it, subjects explored at length by other authors [10, 20, 26].

[3] This quote is from the c. 1980 source, and I wrote example "stories" using a resurrected version of *Wander* whose source appears to date from 1978–1985; a code comment mentioning 'V6' (i.e., Version 6 Unix) also places it in the mid- to late-1970s.

```
 1    : .misc file, containing location-independent code
 2
 3    "Behold... THE PHONE BOOTH GAME!"
 4
 5            words (objects)
 6    phone           0 1
 7    telephone       1
 8    "rotary phone"  2
 9
10            pre action
11            "look phone"  o?phone  m=\
12    "The phone is a robust contraption with a rotary dial."
13
14    : .wrld file, containing location-dependent code
15
16    #1      Telephone Booth
17    You are in a telephone booth.
18            exit    2
19
20    #2      Outside Telephone Booth
21    You are not in a telephone booth.
22            enter   1
```

Fig. 9.1 Extended phone booth game code in *Wander*

It is here where the historical record gets interesting. *Adventure* would have first come about in 1976, but the C version of *Wander* dates back to 1974, and that was a conversion – earlier versions were written in HP BASIC, and 'From the start the idea was for it to be table-driven' [16], i.e., using a domain-specific language. Unfortunately, what seems to be lost (at least so far) is the BASIC code and early C versions; even a chunk of the 1980 version exists only as PDP-11 binaries. *Wander* does seem to be an *Adventure* before *Adventure*, though.

Figure 9.1 shows the *Wander* code for an extended variant of the phone booth game from Chap. 3 (the basic phone booth game was trivially easy to describe in *Wander*). This code would be in two separate files: lines 1–12 in a '.misc' file with location-independent code, and lines 14–22 describing the game locations in a '.wrld' file. Line 3 is a banner message printed once at the start of the game, and lines 6–8 define the phone object and two synonyms for it; the first number after the object name controls whether it is the primary name (0) or a synonym (non-zero), and the second number places the object initially in that location. The section from lines 10–12 defines what happens when the player looks at the phone which, in this case, prints a message (m=) but only if the phone is present (o?phone).

In the '.wrld' file, there are two locations similarly defined. The first one, for instance, gives the location number and short description (line 16), followed by the long description (line 17), and location-specific actions (line 18). Here, if the player issues the exit command from location 1, they end up in location 2.

The early date and general-purpose nature of *Wander* make it very intriguing as an example, both for the retrogames as well as it being used to make games years before more well-known game creation systems like *Pinball Construction Set* (1983).

```
foo_bar::
            cmp #42
            if (lt) {
                cpy #123
                if (!equal) {
                    jmp baz
                }
            } else {
                ldx #0
                do {
                    inc x[buffer]
baz:                inx
                } while (!zero)
                clearb flag
            }
            rts
```

Fig. 9.2 Structured assembly code

Example 9.2 (Habitat, 1986). Habitat was an early graphical multi-user client-server game, where the client ran on the Commodore 64 and communicated via modem (at speeds as low as 300 baud) with a centralized server [25]. During the lead-up to writing this book, the source code was made available, and the Commodore 64 code is nothing short of astounding: easily the nicest-looking, easiest to read assembly of all the examples in this book.

The key was the use of a "structured" assembly code that allowed assembly code to be expressed using high-level language structures like if/then statements and do/while loops.[4] An assembler was developed in-house to handle the structured input.[5]

Figure 9.2 gives a flavor of what the assembly code of *Habitat* looked like.[6] Regular 6502 assembly instructions could be mixed with structured constructs, which in turn could be nested. The conditions for if/else and do/while correspond to mnemonic interpretations of the 6502's status register bits and, as the jump into the middle of a do/while loop shows, structured assembly did not preclude the use of unstructured techniques. The `clearb` is not a 6502 instruction but a programmer-defined assembler macro that would expand into 6502 code.

The important thing to stress is that *none* of this would be visible in the disassembly of the *Habitat* code. It is a powerful example of the things that might never be seen without access to retrogames' source code.

----

[4] Historically, the idea of high-level low-level languages can be traced back to the 1960s, with PL360 being a prominent ancestor [29]. A survey and taxonomy of these languages may be found in [5].

[5] This was actually the second in-house assembler at Lucasfilm Games [24]. The first toolset was described in [17], and that Lisp-based cross-assembler supported high-level constructs but was slow, taking 'about 45 min to assemble a 16K ROM cartridge' [24].

[6] I created this example using the *Habitat* source for syntax guidance. Unfortunately the macro assembler was not available in either source or binary form to check the example's veracity.

9.4 Pleas and Thank You

If you are one of the people who developed games that have aged into retrogames, thank you. Whether they were iconic masterpieces or games forgotten over the years, many people entertained and frustrated themselves for hours with them. Technically, even the most disparaged games may have required substantial programming wizardry to create.

I do want to return to the topic of source code, at the risk of repeating myself. While I won't name names, I have contacted programmers whose code is lost, or resides on disks in some now hard-to-read format. A few game companies from that era are still extant and have archives, but the author retained some rights and there is no business case to be made for trying to sort it out legally. Unfortunately, some retrogame authors have passed away, and any knowledge of the code is gone, or heirs mistakenly think that the code still has value. It may be odd to consider that code written in the span of a lifetime is now an archival document that scholars want to study, but it is. If you have the source code for your games and retain the rights to it, please, *please* consider making it publicly available, warts and all. Even if all that remains are development notes or reference manuals for internally-used languages and tools, please consider making them publicly available. All these things have value when trying to study the past.

This is just the beginning of the retrogame archeology expedition; thank you for joining me for the start of the journey. There are still many implementation gems hiding away in retrogames, waiting to be found. As Calvin said in Bill Watterson's final *Calvin and Hobbes* strip... let's go exploring!

References

1. Ant: Wander (1974) – A Lost Mainframe Game Is Found! Retroactive Fiction Blog. https://ahopeful.wordpress.com/2015/04/22/wander-1974-a-lost- mainframe-game-is-found/ (22 Apr 2015)
2. Bogost, I.: How To Do Things with Videogames. University of Minnesota Press, Minneapolis (2011)
3. Bogost, I., Montfort, N.: Platform studies: frequently questioned answers. In: Proceedings of the Digital Arts and Culture Conference, Irvine (2009)
4. Campbell-Kelly, M.: The history of the history of software. IEEE Ann. Hist. Comput. **29**(4), 40–51 (2007)
5. Crespi-Reghizzi, S., Corti, P., Dapra', A.: A survey of microprocessor languages. IEEE Comput. **13**(1), 48–66 (1980)
6. Dyer, J.: Wander (1974) Release, and Questions Answered. Renga in Blue: Interactive Fiction and Puzzles (blog). https://bluerenga.wordpress.com/2015/04/23/wander-1974-release-and-questions-answered/ (23 April 2015)
7. Edge staff: The making of... Berzerk. Edge Mag. (225), 112–115 (2011)
8. Egenfeldt-Nielsen, S., Smith, J.H., Tosca, S.P.: Studying video games. In: Understanding Video Games: The Essential Introduction, 2nd edn., chap. 1, pp. 7–13. Routledge, New York (2013)

9. Fernández-Vara, C.: Introduction to Game Analysis. Routledge, New York (2015)
10. Guins, R.: Game After: A Cultural Study of Video Game Afterlife. MIT, Cambridge (2014)
11. Haigh, T.: The tears of Donald Knuth. Commun. ACM **58**(1), 40–44 (2015)
12. Hughes, P.: Freeload (Undated). http://www.pauliehughes.com/page3/page3.html
13. Jorgensen, A.H.: Context and driving forces in the development of the early computer game Nimbi. IEEE Ann. Hist. Comput. **31**(3), 44–53 (2009)
14. Juul, J.: A Casual Revolution: Reinventing Video Games and Their Players. MIT, Cambridge (2010)
15. Kent, S.L.: The Ultimate History of Video Games. Three Rivers Press, New York (2001)
16. Langston, P.: Email Communication (23 June 2015)
17. Langston, P.S.: The influence of the UNIX operating system on the development of two video games. In: Spring 1985 European Unix User's Group Meeting (1985)
18. Loguidice, B., Barton, M.: Vintage Games: An Insider Look at the History of *Grand Theft Auto, Super Mario*, and the Most Influential Games of All Time. Focal Press (Elsevier), Burlington (2009)
19. Lowood, H.: Videogames in computer space: the complex history of Pong. IEEE Ann. Hist. Comput. **31**(3), 5–19 (2009)
20. Lowood, H. (ed.), Monnens, D., Vowell, Z., Ruggill, J.E., McAllister, K.S., Armstrong, A.: Before it's too late: a digital game preservation white paper. Am. J. Play **2**(2), 139–166 (2009)
21. Marino, M.C.: Critical code studies. Electronic Book Review. http://electronicbookreview.com/thread/electropoetics/codology (2006)
22. McCloud, S.: Understanding Comics: The Invisible Art. William Morrow, New York (1993)
23. Montfort, N., Baudoin, P., Bell, J., Bogost, I., Douglass, J., Marino, M.C., Mateas, M., Reas, C., Sample, M., Vawter, N.: 10 PRINT CHR$(205.5+RND(1)); : GOTO 10. MIT, Cambridge (2013)
24. Morningstar, C.: Email Communication (27 Apr 2015)
25. Morningstar, C., Farmer, F.R.: The lessons of Lucasfilm's Habitat. In: Benedikt, M. (ed.) Cyberspace: First Steps, chap. 10, pp. 273–301. MIT, Cambridge (1991)
26. Newman, J.: Best Before: Videogames, Supersession and Obsolescence. Routledge, Abingdon (2012)
27. O'Donnell, C.: Production protection to copy(right) protection: from the 10NES to DVDs. IEEE Ann. Hist. Comput. **31**, 54–63 (2009)
28. Tassi, P.: 'Call of Duty' demonstrates the completely fictitious line between hardcore and casual gaming. http://www.forbes.com/sites/insertcoin/2013/10/22/ call-of-duty-demonstrates-the-completely-fictitious-line-between-hardcore-and-casual-gaming/ (22 Oct 2013)
29. Wirth, N.: PL360, a programming language for the 360 computers. J. ACM **15**(1), 37–74 (1968)

Appendix A
Legalese

In this fine appendix are licenses related to various images and code used throughout the book. Riveting reading, all. Please enjoy.

A.1 Hangman

The *Hangman* screenshot shown in Fig. 3.5 was taken from a version of the game built from 4.4 BSD Unix source, which bears this notice:

```
Copyright (c) 1983, 1993
    The Regents of the University of California.  All rights reserved.

Redistribution and use in source and binary forms, with or without
modification, are permitted provided that the following conditions
are met:
1. Redistributions of source code must retain the above copyright
   notice, this list of conditions and the following disclaimer.
2. Redistributions in binary form must reproduce the above copyright
   notice, this list of conditions and the following disclaimer in the
   documentation and/or other materials provided with the distribution.
3. All advertising materials mentioning features or use of this software
   must display the following acknowledgement:
      This product includes software developed by the University of
      California, Berkeley and its contributors.
4. Neither the name of the University nor the names of its contributors
   may be used to endorse or promote products derived from this software
   without specific prior written permission.

THIS SOFTWARE IS PROVIDED BY THE REGENTS AND CONTRIBUTORS ''AS IS'' AND
ANY EXPRESS OR IMPLIED WARRANTIES, INCLUDING, BUT NOT LIMITED TO, THE
IMPLIED WARRANTIES OF MERCHANTABILITY AND FITNESS FOR A PARTICULAR PURPOSE
ARE DISCLAIMED.  IN NO EVENT SHALL THE REGENTS OR CONTRIBUTORS BE LIABLE
FOR ANY DIRECT, INDIRECT, INCIDENTAL, SPECIAL, EXEMPLARY, OR CONSEQUENTIAL
DAMAGES (INCLUDING, BUT NOT LIMITED TO, PROCUREMENT OF SUBSTITUTE GOODS
OR SERVICES; LOSS OF USE, DATA, OR PROFITS; OR BUSINESS INTERRUPTION)
HOWEVER CAUSED AND ON ANY THEORY OF LIABILITY, WHETHER IN CONTRACT, STRICT
LIABILITY, OR TORT (INCLUDING NEGLIGENCE OR OTHERWISE) ARISING IN ANY WAY
OUT OF THE USE OF THIS SOFTWARE, EVEN IF ADVISED OF THE POSSIBILITY OF
SUCH DAMAGE.
```

© Springer International Publishing Switzerland 2016
J. Aycock, *Retrogame Archeology*, DOI 10.1007/978-3-319-30004-7

A.2 Lode Runner

The screenshot in Fig. 3.13 is accompanied by this legal copy:

Tozai Games and Lode Runner are trademarks of Tozai, Inc. registered or protected in the US and other countries. Lode Runner is protected under US and international copyright laws ©1983–2015 Tozai, Inc.

A.3 Robots

The *Robots* screenshot shown in Fig. 3.6 was taken from a version of the game built from 4.4 BSD Unix source, which bears this notice:

```
Copyright (c) 1980, 1993
    The Regents of the University of California.  All rights reserved.

Redistribution and use in source and binary forms, with or without
modification, are permitted provided that the following conditions
are met:
1. Redistributions of source code must retain the above copyright
   notice, this list of conditions and the following disclaimer.
2. Redistributions in binary form must reproduce the above copyright
   notice, this list of conditions and the following disclaimer in the
   documentation and/or other materials provided with the distribution.
3. All advertising materials mentioning features or use of this software
   must display the following acknowledgement:
      This product includes software developed by the University of
      California, Berkeley and its contributors.
4. Neither the name of the University nor the names of its contributors
   may be used to endorse or promote products derived from this software
   without specific prior written permission.

THIS SOFTWARE IS PROVIDED BY THE REGENTS AND CONTRIBUTORS ''AS IS'' AND
ANY EXPRESS OR IMPLIED WARRANTIES, INCLUDING, BUT NOT LIMITED TO, THE
IMPLIED WARRANTIES OF MERCHANTABILITY AND FITNESS FOR A PARTICULAR PURPOSE
ARE DISCLAIMED.  IN NO EVENT SHALL THE REGENTS OR CONTRIBUTORS BE LIABLE
FOR ANY DIRECT, INDIRECT, INCIDENTAL, SPECIAL, EXEMPLARY, OR CONSEQUENTIAL
DAMAGES (INCLUDING, BUT NOT LIMITED TO, PROCUREMENT OF SUBSTITUTE GOODS
OR SERVICES; LOSS OF USE, DATA, OR PROFITS; OR BUSINESS INTERRUPTION)
HOWEVER CAUSED AND ON ANY THEORY OF LIABILITY, WHETHER IN CONTRACT, STRICT
LIABILITY, OR TORT (INCLUDING NEGLIGENCE OR OTHERWISE) ARISING IN ANY WAY
OUT OF THE USE OF THIS SOFTWARE, EVEN IF ADVISED OF THE POSSIBILITY OF
SUCH DAMAGE.
```

A.4 Termcap

The two `termcap` entries in Fig. 3.2 were excerpted from the 4.4 BSD Unix source, which bears this notice:

```
Copyright (c) 1980, 1985, 1989, 1993
The Regents of the University of California.  All rights reserved.

Redistribution and use in source and binary forms, with or without
modification, are permitted provided that the following conditions
```

are met:
1. Redistributions of source code must retain the above copyright
   notice, this list of conditions and the following disclaimer.
2. Redistributions in binary form must reproduce the above copyright
   notice, this list of conditions and the following disclaimer in the
   documentation and/or other materials provided with the distribution.
3. All advertising materials mentioning features or use of this software
   must display the following acknowledgement:
      This product includes software developed by the University of
      California, Berkeley and its contributors.
4. Neither the name of the University nor the names of its contributors
   may be used to endorse or promote products derived from this software
   without specific prior written permission.

THIS SOFTWARE IS PROVIDED BY THE REGENTS AND CONTRIBUTORS ``AS IS'' AND
ANY EXPRESS OR IMPLIED WARRANTIES, INCLUDING, BUT NOT LIMITED TO, THE
IMPLIED WARRANTIES OF MERCHANTABILITY AND FITNESS FOR A PARTICULAR PURPOSE
ARE DISCLAIMED. IN NO EVENT SHALL THE REGENTS OR CONTRIBUTORS BE LIABLE
FOR ANY DIRECT, INDIRECT, INCIDENTAL, SPECIAL, EXEMPLARY, OR CONSEQUENTIAL
DAMAGES (INCLUDING, BUT NOT LIMITED TO, PROCUREMENT OF SUBSTITUTE GOODS
OR SERVICES; LOSS OF USE, DATA, OR PROFITS; OR BUSINESS INTERRUPTION)
HOWEVER CAUSED AND ON ANY THEORY OF LIABILITY, WHETHER IN CONTRACT, STRICT
LIABILITY, OR TORT (INCLUDING NEGLIGENCE OR OTHERWISE) ARISING IN ANY WAY
OUT OF THE USE OF THIS SOFTWARE, EVEN IF ADVISED OF THE POSSIBILITY OF
SUCH DAMAGE.

Index

Printed in the United States
By Bookmasters